THE DIVIDING OF CHRISTENDOM

The Dividing of
CHRISTENDOM

CHRISTOPHER DAWSON

IGNATIUS PRESS   SAN FRANCISCO

Originally published by Sheed & Ward, New York, 1965
First English edition published by Sidgwick and Jackson Ltd,
London, 1971

Cover photograph:
Christopher Dawson, Oxford, ca. 1952
Courtesy of the Department of Special Collections,
University of St. Thomas, St. Paul, Minn.

Cover design by Roxanne Mei Lum

Reprinted in 2009 by Ignatius Press, San Francisco

ISBN 978-1-58617-238-1
Library of Congress Control Number 2007938145
Printed in the United States of America ⬭

PUBLISHER'S NOTE

After the death of Christopher Dawson in May 1970 it was felt that some of his works which had never appeared in England before should be published.

The present volume consists of a selection from the lectures the author gave at Harvard during the years 1958 to 1962 when he was the first occupant of the Chair of Roman Catholic Studies, founded by Charles Chauncey Stillman.

The theme of the lectures was CHRISTENDOM and they fell naturally into three groups—The Formation of Christendom, The Dividing of Christendom, The Return to Christian Unity. The present book contains all the lectures of the second group covering the period from the Reformation to the Age of the Enlightenment.

NOTE ON THE IGNATIUS PRESS EDITION

Some minor changes to spelling and punctuation have been made to the text.

To Chauncey Stillman

CONTENTS

FOREWORD TO THE 2009 EDITION

The Dividing of Christendom (1965) and *The Formation of Christendom* (1967) were the last of Christopher Dawson's books to be published in his lifetime. (*The Gods of Revolution* [1972] was published posthumously.)

Raised a devout Anglican, and converting to the Catholic Church only after long study, Dawson (1889–1970) had a deep personal interest in religious divisions. His chief apologia for his conversion was in his 1933 book *The Spirit of the Oxford Movement*, where he confirmed John Henry Newman's judgment that the crucial issue was not Protestantism versus Catholicism but belief versus unbelief. Newman found Protestantism was unable to confront unbelief because of its reliance on private judgment rather than on a magisterium.

Dawson himself found the absence of theological principles to be the very nature of Anglicanism, which used Anglo-Catholic liturgical practices to conceal theological modernism, a state of affairs which required Anglicans who did have principles to convert to Rome.

Despite these severe judgments, Dawson was an early ecumenist, often lamenting the "scandal" of Christian disunity and warning that, because the Church lacked the capacity to "mold and inspire", men would look elsewhere for guidance. This situation demanded efforts towards religious reunion.

However, Dawson could never accept doctrinal compromise as the price of reunion and, to avoid that, consistently argued that "social obstacles" and the "unconscious clash of cultures" had more to do with religious divisions than beliefs did. He contended that most schisms and heresies were rooted in social or national antipathies, and, if theologians had understood that fact, the history of the Church would have been very different. By promoting the virtues of faith, hope, and charity, Christians could perhaps remove these hidden obstacles.

The Jesuit historian James Brodrick once charged that Dawson's approach seemed "Marxist" and asked, "Does theology count for so little?" Dawson replied that it was a "dubious compliment" to theology to hold it responsible for heresy and schism, but he conceded that religious divisions did involve genuine theological problems. The illusion of easy reunion erred in its indifference to theological issues, but the rigidity of theological beliefs on both sides prevented people from seeing what they had in common.

During World War II, Dawson served as vice-president of The Sword of the Spirit, an ecumenical group formed to work for the spiritual revitalization of Great Britain. He edited The Sword's newsletter and defined the group's purpose as "the coordination of spiritual forces", an attempt to "fill the gap between the Church and the secular state" and to create a "framework of international cooperation", a "crusade against totalitarianism on a spiritual rather than a political plane".

Some Catholic theologians objected to Catholics and Protestants even saying the Lord's Prayer together, but Dawson warned that this attitude made it seem that Catholics did not consider Protestants to be Christian. He explained that he employed the phrase "common prayer and sacraments" merely in the sense that similar forms were used by almost all Christian groups. He did not imply equivalency among these forms but merely stated an objective fact.

It was not permissible to assume that Protestant beliefs and practices meant nothing, since they were potential avenues of "return to the supernatural". This return could be achieved first by the "reconversion of heretics and schismatics" and then by the conversion of the whole world. There was a theological foundation for a common faith, although it was not clear what precisely this foundation was. The Holy Spirit and the kingdom of Christ were wider than the Catholic Church, and the Church itself had condemned the exclusivist interpretation of "outside the Church there is no salvation".

After the war, Dawson warned that relations with non-Catholics were even more necessary, that it was necessary to move to the "higher ground of faith and revelation" and to the "mystery of the unity of the church". The era of disunity was coming to an end. Theological controversies were mainly an inheritance from the past and were not relevant to the future, since historically theology had often been a cover for other issues. Unity was not to be achieved by conceding doctrinal points but rather by "acceding to God's will".

Dawson's ecumenism was based on faith in Christ, which precluded his taking an ecumenical stance towards non-Christian religions. He defined his position through his dialogues during the 1950's with an English Benedictine monk, Bede Griffiths, who had moved to India and was deeply sympathetic to Hinduism.

The two men agreed that Hinduism could be a "preparation for Christ", yet they disagreed on Griffiths' theory of "primitive revelation"—the idea that God had communicated knowledge of himself to various peoples even before the Bible and other sacred books had been written. Dawson argued that such was not divine revelation but merely "natural religion", mankind's subjective religious perceptions. Eastern religions lacked theological truth, although they did possess natural theology and natural law, which underlay all primitive cultures.

In *The Dividing of Christendom*, Dawson elaborated his thesis that cultural and social differences might be the ultimate root of apparent religious disagreement. (In order to understand his views fully, the book should be read in conjunction with *The Movement of World Revolution* [1959].)

Teaching at Harvard University on the eve of the Second Vatican Council, he rejoiced that "God is undoing the social consequences of the Reformation" by placing Catholics and Protestants together in the same land.

Reunion was not imminent, but schism was the worst of evils because it thwarted God's plan for unity. Real dialogue was taking place, and there were new trends towards Protestant unity, which, although they were unlikely to bridge the Protestant–Catholic gap, might culminate in two worldwide religious communities—Catholic and Protestant—organized not against each other but against a "godless world".

By attributing religious divisions primarily to non-religious factors, he made it possible to encourage ecumenical co-operation, even though he probably assumed that ecumenism ultimately meant a return to the Catholic Church.

Thus the Lutheran Reformation could be understood partly through Martin Luther's personality. Europe was ripe for an explosion, and Luther lit the match, his effectiveness lying in the force of his emotions. A man of deep faith, he was also violent and passionate, seeing certain things with intense clarity and being completely blind to other things.

Politics also accounted for a lot. The growth of the national state, if not the cause of the Reformation, was at least its occasion, inasmuch as the Catholic Church, as a universal institution, stood as an obstacle to the emergent national monarchies. While Luther may have been motivated by genuine religious concerns, the German princes determined the forms Lutheranism would take.

The dissolution of the monasteries was the most revolutionary change brought about by Protestantism because it gave free rein to the denial of asceticism, valued action over contemplation, subordinated spiritual to temporal authority, and made faith individual and God arbitrary. The love of money was no longer the root of all evil, and the traditional Christian attitude towards the poor was abandoned for a harsher doctrine.

The Catholic Church maintained its strong opposition to acquisitive capitalism, so the real battle was over Christian economic ideals. Old institutions were considered incompatible with new economic realities, and the bourgeois spirit was able to triumph only when the Reformation had destroyed the power of the Church.

Puritanism imposed asceticism on everyone, thereby making Puritanism repulsive, but it was also the spiritual power behind the economic order that transformed Europe, forging a new society of shrewd, hard-working, and godly merchants who were ready to oppose any interference with their religion or their business and to face a grim world with the determination to do their duty. These merchants saw wealth as a sign of divine favor. They did not live for enjoyment.

This acquisitive spirit was contrary to the Gospel spirit of being "open" rather than calculating. Thus in some ways the Catholic–Protestant conflict of the 16th century was between two different cultures, as exemplified by the revolt of the Netherlanders, who possessed the "mechanistic spirit of a clock", against the passionate Spanish, who were economically stagnant. An independent Netherlands was crucial for the rise of sectarianism, religious tolerance, capitalism, and bourgeois control of the state.

The English Reformation was the clearest example of the subordination of religious considerations to political ones. The only major Catholic uprising of Henry VIII's reign, the Pilgrimage of Grace, was a constitutional and orderly protest against royal absolutism.

Although the alliance of the Counter-Reformation with Spain proved disastrous for the Church, bringing it under suspicion of being an instrument of Spanish imperialism, the Counter-Reformation was truly religious and provided an antidote to rationalism and materialism, as well as to the Protestant charge that Catholicism was merely a religion of externals.

Especially under Jesuit leadership, the Church began its greatest period of missionary activity, a phenomenon unmatched in the Protestantism of the time, possibly because of the Protestant denigration of good works. The Church thereby attained a new level of universal awareness, with the early Jesuit missionaries developing a sense of the relativity of particular cultures.

Once again prescinding from theological differences, Dawson saw Baroque art as the most important expression of the Counter-Reformation, a great international phenomenon extending as far as Latin America and Asia and manifesting anew the power of the spiritual; an ecstatic, mystical spirit alien to the sober piety of the North; a union of heart and head that appealed to the masses as well as to the educated.

Baroque culture was decidedly uneconomical, requiring a reckless expenditure of money for the glory of God and the adornment of human life, something that Protestant culture eschewed. In the end this very uneconomical character left the Baroque culture powerless to resist the "new money power" coming from the rise of capitalism, especially in Calvinist lands.

While in some ways the Protestant North was more intellectually vigorous than the Catholic South, the Baroque movement, as the triumph of the imagination, was able to create a culture that was unified even at the popular level. By contrast, Protestant iconoclasm impoverished the imagination, attempting to Christianize culture through exclusively rational means, namely, the Bible and the sermon.

This too was an expression of new social and economic realities. Baroque culture built churches while the Puritans were busy laying the foundations of capitalism. While the Baroque culture aimed at a triumphant moment of creative ecstasy, bourgeois Protestant culture aimed at a "high average standard" of behavior.

Dawson saw the movement of history in large patterns; hence, in this book, his account of the breakup of Christendom extends two centuries beyond the Reformation itself.

Religion never exerted greater influence in Europe than in the period of 1560 to 1660, but religion proved a source of division and strife rather than of unity and was thereby discredited. Progressive exclusion from culture was the price Christianity had to pay for its disunity, as Christianity came to be viewed as the cause of civil strife rather than as the spiritual basis of society.

The idea of tolerance was the only hope for peace, which meant the end of the attempt to base society on religion. Henceforth the purpose of the state would be the protection of property, and, once it was agreed that the heretic could be a good citizen and a good businessman, the social world became the "real" world and religion became a purely private matter.

The secularization of culture was not directly caused by the new science—the 17th century remained an intensely religious age—but the new science failed to unite with the moral life of the time. In the 18th century the negative side of the rationalist program was successfully carried out, and Europe was secularized.

Deism was a mere shadow of Christianity, an abstraction with no life of its own, which reduced the moral law to practical philanthropy, and divine providence to mechanistic natural laws, yielding a rigidly rationalistic view of the universe—according to which, God was merely the Divine Engineer. Never having a life of its own, Deism was created artificially for certain controversial purposes and then discarded.

Dawson respected John Wesley above all other Protestant leaders, possibly because Wesley had not broken with the Catholic Church directly but with the Church of England. He appeared as a prophet releasing hidden spiritual resources. His organizational achievements were comparable even to those of the Jesuits when Wesley started a revivalist movement that combined asceticism and mysticism in ways antithetical to the 18th-century mind.

No man of such stature was ever more out of touch with intellectual life, but Wesley's influence was everywhere.

While Deism might seem to satisfy rational requirements, it could not compete on religious grounds with Wesley's enthusiasm.

The Enlightenment was the last of the great heresies; its appeal to reason and progress was an act of faith not warranted by the evidence. In reaction to this, Jean-Jacques Rousseau became the driving force for a new religion, repudiating Christianity while retaining the religious instinct the Enlightenment had lost.

Radical political and social ideas took root in a France that had been shaped into uniformity by the Counter-Reformation and the Baroque monarchy and could thereby be revolutionized more easily than could democracies. The radicals of the French Revolution were anti-democratic, their aim being not toleration but the replacement of the unity of Catholicism with a new universal orthodoxy, a counter-church—the religion of Nature.

But the effect of the Revolution was "dechristianization" rather than "secularization" in that more people were detached from the old religion than were converted to the new, a failure which brought a realization of how deeply rooted religion actually was. Persecution did much to restore the Church's prestige as Catholics began to manifest an intensity of devotion previously seen only in Methodists and a few other groups.

But even as Dawson was writing this book, expounding the dividing of Christendom in his characteristically magisterial way, events in his own time were moving very rapidly.

As a professor at Harvard Divinity School, he came into direct contact with the Liberal Protestantism that had repelled him in the Anglican Church. He found the Harvard curriculum unsatisfactory; the faculty's theology "hazy"; and the dean of the Divinity School, Douglas Horton, the only professor with whom he found he could carry on substantive discussions. Horton wrote an introduction to the original edition of *The Dividing of Christendom*, predicting that the book "will do much to help heal the divisions of Christendom".

But Dawson queried Samuel Miller, Horton's successor as dean, about remarks attributed to Miller in which he seemed to be urging that "the edifice of Christianity must be replaced" and that the dogmas of the early Church were no longer relevant. This would not serve the cause of ecumenism, Dawson warned, but would divide Christians even further. (Miller responded that he had been misrepresented and that his views were in fact close to Dawson's own.)

A return to theological tradition was the only solution, Dawson urged. While Catholic theology was "dogmatic", Protestant theology was "thoroughly subjective criticism". Although the differences had been softened, Protestants spoke of a "struggle against the church for the sake of the church", whereas for Catholics the struggle was "the prophetic stance of the church against the world", a struggle in which the Puritan divines who founded Harvard had also been engaged.

Largely incapacitated by a stroke, Dawson left Harvard during the Second Vatican Council, but he recorded some of his reactions to the aftermath of the Council. He dismissed the idea of the vernacular liturgy as a "stunt", jeered at "a whole tribe of Mass dialogians", and confessed that "I hate the changes in the Liturgy and regret that the translations are so bad".

He was "astonished" to read "pro-Lutheran statements" in the Catholic press, judging that any movement that produced such things was not "serious". Noting a new interest in biblical studies among Catholics, he feared that this would lead to "[Karl] Barthian or Existentialist ideas" that were unhistorical.

Shockingly, the English branch of Sheed & Ward, Dawson's long-time publisher, declined to publish *The Formation of Christendom* and *The Dividing of Christendom*, although they were published by Sheed & Ward's American branch. *The Dividing of Christendom* was also published in paperback by the prestigious secular house of Doubleday and Co.

Thus, despite the fact that they were the culminating scholarship of one of the world's greatest cultural historians, Dawson's later books did not have an impact proportionate to their importance, simply because the world had changed so rapidly during the half-decade prior to their appearance. Like many great thinkers, Dawson fell into eclipse shortly after his death. His reputation survived, however, because a number of his books remained in print, and interest in him is now undergoing a revival.

Dawson's knowledge of American religion was not extensive. He tended to see it largely in terms of Puritanism, so the present-day ecumenical relationship between Catholics and Evangelicals or Fundamentalists would no doubt surprise and intrigue him, confirming his early judgment that the real issue in modern culture is not primarily between Catholics and Protestants, but between belief and unbelief.

He was, by both temperament and conviction, a pessimist, and he would not have been surprised that the Western world has become ever more secular during the four decades since his death. But that the United States, however fragilely, now manifests the most vigorous Christianity in the Western world would no doubt surprise him more than any other religious development.

James Hitchcock

Professor of History

ST. LOUIS UNIVERSITY

MAY 2009

INTRODUCTION

In the early years of his long life of study Christopher Dawson set himself the task of surveying the history of European civilization in the light of a master-idea: that religion is the dynamic force, the basic constituent and the inspiration of all higher human activity, and that therefore the culture of an era depends upon its religion, and not vice versa. This task was to him a very demanding one, for it presupposed an intimate and detailed knowledge of the history—political, intellectual, social, aesthetic, and economic—of the cultures he undertook to consider. His first major writing, *The Age of the Gods*, was the outcome of many years of research in the religion of primitive man, and the early civilizations of the East. It remained in many ways his greatest single achievement, and it received immediate critical acclaim. Forty years ago, before the immense success of Arnold Toynbee's work, readers of world-history had been given Spengler's sombre picture of the West in decline, and the tendentious outlook of the *History of the World* by H. G. Wells. Dawson's work was very learned, but there was nothing difficult or esoteric about it. He did not impose patterns on events nor did he create a vocabulary to express his ideas. The ideas he used were those common to all human thought. His mind had the clarity of wisdom, not the simplicity of the superficial, and his style was lucid and free.

The second instalment should have covered the civilization of the classical world, and he would have been fully competent to present this, but he left it aside, perhaps because he felt that generations of fine minds had made it familiar, and wrote of what was then a less cultivated field, the twilight of classical civilization and the dawn of medieval Christian culture. He called the book *The Making of Europe*. This was a less attractive theme for many, but it was probably Dawson's most influential book as it filled a gap that had long existed in general historical knowledge, and set out persuasively and convincingly a twofold thesis: that medieval and modern civilization derived a very large part of its human and secular content from Greece and Rome, and that the spirit that gave life and growth to what seemed to be a ruin was the spirit of Catholic Christianity. It told the strange story of the transmission of Christianity to the West, together with the basic ideas of ancient government and thought, by way of the circumference of Christendom and back to Northern Europe. It was a book that opened a new world to many readers, and though in the thirty-odd years that have passed many have explored the archaeology and art of the Dark Ages, no work has completely taken its place.

The books and lectures that followed did not treat any period in a consecutive way; they were re-statements in various keys and tones of the original thesis. The lectures printed here, however, are an outline of the final volume, or at least of its first half. They are valuable as the only presentation, by a mind of Dawson's quality, of the stretch of modern thought and sentiment between Italian humanism and the French Revolution. They set out in terms of history, and are well illustrated by, the television and printed survey of *Civilization* by Kenneth Clark. In the past forty years much has been written of the period in European history between 1300 and 1550. The epoch of open religious conflict that began with the emergence of Luther in 1517 was indeed momentous, but in many ways the revolution in thought and theology had begun two centuries earlier, when Duns Scotus and William of Ockham departed from the tradition of philosophy as a body of accepted reasonings (*philosophia perennis*) and began the construction of personal systems that has continued ever since, while Marsilius of Padua and John Wyclif broke with the traditional views on the government of the church and primitive Christianity. Dawson saw this well, and began in this period with his story of the break-up of Christian thought. In the lectures that followed he described with great economy of words and an excellent sense of proportion the initial movement of European thought away from religious unity, and later its rejection of traditional religion of any kind.

Thoughts and sentiments have changed in spectacular ways in the past fifteen years. Dawson, who saw continuity between the classical civilization of Greece and Rome and the culture of the medieval and modern world, was at one with such thinkers as Jacques Maritain and Etienne Gilson in France in expounding a Christian humanism in terms of a realist philosophy. This is now an unfashionable outlook. The conception of a stream of historical influences, and of a 'realist' universe of which the individual mind is a part, indeed, but one that can within limits comprehend the whole and recognize truth, is currently under attack in favour of an existentialist or phenomenalist outlook, which is true only for the individual, while history is a series of 'cultures' which inform the thought and sentiment of the present generation but which, when past, have no more meaning for those who come after than the culture of the 'Beaker Folk' or the people of La Tène.

To some Christopher Dawson may seem to 'date' but when truly assessed he is dateless. The principles for which he stood, the truth and beauty that he saw, cannot be lost, even if they may for a time be obscured. It may be that the 'silent majority' here as elsewhere, will feel kinship with a great historian who saw the development of Europe 'steadily, and saw it whole'.

David Knowles
Regius Professor Emeritus of Modern History
UNIVERSITY OF CAMBRIDGE
1965

I

THE CULTURAL CONSEQUENCES
OF CHRISTIAN DISUNITY

O F ALL divisions between Christians, that between
Catholics and Protestants is the deepest and the most
pregnant in its historical consequences. It is so deep that we
cannot see any solution to it in the present period and under
existing historical circumstances. But at least it is possible for
us to take the first step by attempting to overcome the enormous gap in mutual understanding which has hitherto rendered any intellectual contact or collaboration impossible.
From this point of view the problem is not to be found so
much in the sphere of theology, strictly speaking, as in that of
culture and historical tradition. For the changes that followed
the Reformation are not only the work of the Churches
and the theologians. They are also the work of the statesmen
and the soldiers. The Catholic and Protestant worlds have
been divided from one another by centuries of war and
power politics, and the result has been that they no longer
share a common social experience. Each has its own version
of history, its own social inheritance, as well as its own religious beliefs and standards of orthodoxy. And nowhere is this
state of things more striking than in America, where the
English Protestant North and the Spanish Catholic South
formed two completely different worlds which had no mental contact with one another.

It was not until the 19th century that this state of cultural
separation came to an end; and the change was especially
sharp in the English-speaking countries when Catholicism
and Protestantism finally came together within the same
societies and cultures. In England this was due to the movement of intellectual rapprochement which is represented by

the Oxford Movement and the personality of Newman, while in America it was the result of external forces—above all the mass immigration of the Irish Catholics to America in the middle of the 19th century, which produced such profound social changes, particularly in New England. Nowhere in the world have Catholicism and Protestantism been brought together more suddenly and closely than in Boston. Throughout the 19th century these two sections of the population remained separate peoples, although they necessarily shared the same national and regional citizenship. It is only in quite recent times that they have come to share a common culture. But this culture is a purely secular one; and one of the reasons that it is so completely secular is that there has been this complete cleavage of spiritual tradition and absence of intellectual contact between Catholics and Protestants.

No doubt there are many other factors in the secularization of modern culture, but this is one for which Christians are directly responsible. The movement of history, which for Christians in some way reflects the action of divine providence, has put an end to the social division of Christendom which followed the religious revolution of the 16th century. Hence it is now our business to see that the inner division in our culture should also be overcome by a progressive movement of intellectual understanding, the reconstitution of a common world of discourse and of a new dialogue between Catholics and Protestants.

In this work of mutual explanation there are two main fields to be covered. First there is the theological field, in which the student has to study the positive developments of Catholic and Protestant doctrine so as to understand the exact nature of the divergence in our beliefs. In the past this field had become a battleground of theological controversy so that it was a source of division and antagonism rather than understanding. Indeed it was the controversial character of theology that did more than anything else to discredit it in the eyes of the world. It is only in recent times that theological studies have taken a new direction and there is a growing tendency to reexamine the whole question in the light of first principles. We see the results of this new theological orientation in the French series published under the title *Unam Sanctam*, and there has been a parallel movement of theological thought in Germany. Indeed it was there that the new approach first originated more than a century ago with the writings of John Adam Moehler. Today there is an international literature on the theology of Christian unity, which is likely to increase as a result of the Ecumenical Council.

But in addition to this theological study we have also to study the historical background and the cultural development of Catholic and Protestant society during the centuries of disunity. It is these historical studies that have been most neglected in the past, owing to the artificial separation between ecclesiastical and political history, which has had the effect of focusing the light of historical research on certain limited aspects of the past and of neglecting others that were intrinsically no less important.

Thus political history has developed as the history of the European State system and the power conflict between the European dynasties and empires, and finally of the political revolutions that have changed the forms of the state.

It is only in modern times that historians have attempted to rectify this one-sided emphasis by opening up the new field of economic history, which today is generally recognized as no less important than political history.

But this is an exception, and there are still important fields of culture which are relatively uncultivated by the historians. The obvious solution would seem to be the expansion of historical science to include the whole of human culture in all its manifestations; but in spite of the efforts of German culture-historians to create a new study of this kind, it has failed to establish itself as a scientific discipline and is still looked on with considerable suspicion by the professional historians. In any case, we have to consider the question of religious history as a field of study which historians ought to take account of, but which they have in fact neglected. No doubt their answer would be that this is the business of the ecclesiastical historians. This is true enough in theory. In practice, however, ecclesiastical history is as highly specialized as political history, which it resembles in certain aspects.

The ecclesiastical historians have dealt exhaustively with the history of heresies and theological controversies, but they have shown little interest in religious culture. Even such a famous book as Ritschl's *History of Pietism* is not a genuinely historical work. It is a polemical work, devoted to the demonstration of a theological thesis rather than to the exposition of a phase of religious history or the explanation of a form of religious experience. In fact it is not to the ecclesiastical historians but to the literary historians that we must look for the main achievements in this field. With all his faults Sainte-Beuve was a real religious historian when he wrote his *Port Royal*; and in our own days I think that the best approach to religious history has been made from the literary side, in respect of Catholicism, by Bremond in his literary study of religious experience in France in the 17th century, and of Protestantism by Professors Perry Miller and Johnston in their study of the New England mind.

When we come to the subject of this work, which is the development of the Catholic and Protestant cultures in modern times, we shall find ourselves in a no man's land, between the political and the ecclesiastical historians. For while the actual schism which destroyed the religious unity of Western Europe has been studied exhaustively by both groups of historians, neither of them has paid much attention to the development of the new forms of religious culture which took the place of the old common culture of medieval Christendom. Yet no one can deny their importance, for they had a considerable effect not only on the development of literature and music and art but also on the structure of social life, as we see in a very striking way in the contrasts in the social development of the two Americas.

And it is the same with the following period. For the political and ecclesiastical historians have both written a great deal on the history of the 18th-century Enlightenment and on the political and religious revolution which followed it, but the religious revival of the 19th century, which transformed and re-created the Christian world that we know and in which we live, has, I believe, never been studied in its cultural aspects. One should perhaps make an exception as far as North America is concerned. For American Catholicism is the creation of this period, and in so far as historians attempt to study American Catholicism, they are bound to focus their attention on the 19th-century development. Even so, it is impossible to study that development without studying the European background from which it emerged and which influenced its development in so many different ways. Yet there has been no study of the European Catholic revival by American historians, so far as I am aware, and very few translations of European works on the subject.

Moreover there is another and more fundamental reason why religious history during the last century or two should be a neglected and difficult field. For this is the age when the secularization of Western culture was triumphant and when religion was consequently pushed out of social life and increasingly treated as a private affair that only concerned the individual conscience. Whereas in the past religion had occupied the center of the stage of world history, so that a monk and a mystic like St. Bernard had moved armies and had become a counsellor of kings, now it had withdrawn into private life and had left the stage of history to the representatives of the new political and economic forces.

This progressive extrusion of Christianity from culture is the price that Christendom has had to pay for its loss of unity—it is part of what Richard Niebuhr has called "the Ethical Failure of the Divided Church". The tragedy of schism is that it is a progressive evil. Schism breeds schism, until every social antagonism is reflected in some new religious division and no common Christian culture is conceivable. In the old world of united Christendom these social antagonisms were as strong as they are today, but they were antagonisms within a common society, and the Church was seen as the ultimate bond of unity. As William Langland writes, "He called that house Unity—which is Holy Church in English." No one was more aware than Langland of the evils of contemporary society—the whole of *Piers Plowman* is an impassioned plea for social and religious reform, so much so that he has sometimes been regarded as a harbinger of the Protestant Reformation. But his emphasis is always on unity: "Call we to all the Commons that they come into Unity" "and there stand and do battle against Belial's children." As I have pointed out elsewhere, the creative age of medieval culture was the result of the alliance between the Papacy and the Northern Reformers, represented by the Cluniacs and the Cistercians, and when this alliance was broken, the vitality of medieval culture declined. The Protestant Reformation of the 16th century represents a final breach between the Papacy and the Northern Reformers—between the principle of authority and the principle of reformation. But both principles were alike essential to the traditions of Western Christendom, and even in the state of division neither part of the Christian world could dispense with them. Therefore the Catholic world developed a new reforming movement, as represented by the Jesuits and the other new religious Orders; while the Protestant world had to create new patterns of authority and theological tradition, such as we see in the ecclesiastical and theological discipline of the Calvinist Churches. But this pattern was never a universal one, and the Protestant world was weakened from the beginning by continuous theological controversies which produced a further series of schisms and permanent divisions between the different Protestant Churches.

It is difficult to exaggerate the harm that was inflicted on Christian culture by the century of religious strife that followed the Reformation. The great controversy between Catholicism and Protestantism rapidly degenerated into a state of religious and civil war which divided Christendom into two armed camps. There could be no question of spiritual reconciliation so long as Catholics and Protestants were cutting one another's throats, and calling in foreign mercenaries to help in the work of mutual destruction, as was the case in France in the 16th century and in Germany in the 17th. Even within the Protestant world religious controversy became the cause of social conflict or its pretext, as we see in the case of the Civil War in England. That war was indeed far less destructive and atrocious than the great religious wars of the Continent, but it demonstrated even more clearly the essential futility and irrationality of religious conflict, in which each military victory led to fresh divisions and further conflicts until no solution was possible save a tired and disillusioned return to the traditional order in Church and State.

It was during this century of sterile and inconclusive religious conflict that the ground was prepared for the secularization of European culture. The convinced secularists were an infinitesimal minority of the European population, but they had no need to be strong since the Christians did their work for them. All they had to do was to point the moral, very cautiously at first, like Montaigne, and then with gradually increasing confidence and vigor, as with Hobbes and Bayle, and the English Deists. It was, however, an Anglican clergyman, a High Churchman to boot, who spoke the final word in *The Tale of a Tub*.

Thus it is not too much to say that the fate of Christian culture and the development of modern civilization have been determined or conditioned by the state of war which existed between Christians from the Reformation to the Revolution—first a century of civil war in the strict sense and then a century or more of cold war and antagonism. And though today Christians are at last emerging from this atmosphere of hatred and suspicion, the modern Christian world is still divided by the religious frontiers established in that age of religious strife. As a volcanic eruption changes the face of nature—overwhelming fertile lands with fields of lava and changing the course of rivers and the shape of islands—this great religious cataclysm has changed the course of history and altered the face of Western culture for ages to come. It is impossible to ignore this dark and tragic side of religious history; for if we do not face it, we cannot understand the inevitable character of the movement of secularization.

On the other hand, it is a still greater mistake to see the dark side only, as the thinkers of the Enlightenment did, and to ignore the spiritual and cultural achievements of the post-Reformation period.

For the energies of divided Christendom were not all absorbed in internecine conflict. On both the Catholic and the Protestant side the Reformation was followed by the development of new forms of religious life and thought. These were of course very different, so that they have sometimes been regarded as opposite to one another. Yet I think it is possible to trace a certain parallelism between them, which was no doubt due to their common historical background and to common cultural influences. In the first place there was on both sides of the religious frontiers a return to moral discipline after the laxity of the early Renaissance period. On the Protestant side this took the form of the Calvinist discipline, which was the main inspiration of English and American Puritanism in the 17th century and the parallel ethos of the Presbyterian Covenanters in Scotland. It is one of the paradoxes of religious history that a theology which centered in the doctrines of predestination and reprobation and denied or minimized the freedom of the human will should have developed an ethos of personal responsibility which expressed itself in moral activism. There can, however, be no doubt that the hallmark of the new Protestant culture is just this spirit of moral activism, which was based on intensive theological training, but which found expression in secular life—in war and business—no less than in the life of the Churches.

On the Catholic side the restoration of moral discipline took the form primarily of a return to the tradition of monastic asceticism. But this tradition was now brought out of the cloister into the world and applied by the new religious orders, above all by the Jesuits, to the contemporary situation, that is to say, to the needs of the Church, to the restoration of ecclesiastical unity and order, to the education of both the clergy and the laity, and to preaching and missionary propaganda.

But in addition to the moral asceticism of the Counter-Reformation there was also on the Catholic side a certain tendency to theological rigorism which is much more akin to the theological tendencies of Puritanism. It produced the Jansenist movement, which caused a serious breach in the unity of Post-Reformation Catholicism, at least in France. The theological feud between the Jansenists and the Jesuits and the controversy about grace and free will bear an extraordinary similarity to that between the Puritans and the Arminians on the same questions.

In the second place the Post-Reformation period is characterized by the interiorization of religion and the intensive cultivation of the spiritual life. In the Catholic world this expressed itself above all in the great mystical movement which began in Spain and Italy in the 16th century and spread to France and England in the following century. But it is also represented by the ascetic spirituality of the Counter-Reformation. Indeed the most influential of all the spiritual works of the age—the *Spiritual Exercises* of St. Ignatius—was, as its name denotes, essentially ascetic, and used the reason and the imagination in order to produce a psychological change in the personality. On the Protestant side, the mystical element is less significant, for the main emphasis was always placed on the experience of conversion and personal conviction of sin and redemption.

The Pietist movement in the Lutheran church (which was later in date than the Catholic spiritual revival) was not devoid of an element of mysticism, while some of the minority sects, like the Quakers, were more definitely mystical and ultimately came to be influenced strongly by the less orthodox representatives of the Catholic mystical tradition. There was in fact an interesting underground movement towards religious unity and spiritual reconciliation which was carried on by representatives of these extremist groups, such as Peter Poiret in the Netherlands, who attempted to create a common eirenic theology based on the *consensus mysticorum*; and Isaac Watts translated Jesuit sacred poetry. Though this movement was an isolated one, which affected an infinitesimal minority of Protestants, it does indicate the existence of Catholicizing tendencies in the Pietist movement as a whole, which explains the hostile reaction to the movement on the part of Protestant historians like Ritschl.

Finally, in the third place, both Catholic and Protestant Europe were deeply influenced by the culture of the Renaissance. On both sides there was a continuous effort to use the new learning for Christian ends and to bring the new culture and art into relation with the Christian tradition. Thus the ideal of a Christian Humanism held a central place in both Catholic and Protestant culture and provided an important link or bridge between them.

It is true that its influence was much stronger in Catholic Europe owing to the fact that Italy was both the home of the Renaissance and the center of Catholic culture. Moreover, Catholicism was able to use the new art and music and architecture of the Renaissance in the service of religion in a way which the aniconic and non-liturgical character of Protestantism made impossible.

Thus the Baroque culture, in which the spirit of Christian Humanism found its full social and artistic expression, was exclusively or predominantly Catholic, and the sharing of this common culture gave the entire Catholic world from

Peru to Poland an international unity which Protestant Europe never possessed. In Northern Europe the influence of humanism was confined to the educated classes and found expression only in literature. But in this field it was triumphant, and throughout the 17th century, in England above all, the spirit of Christian Humanism inspired not only the poetry of Donne and Herbert and Milton and Vaughan but also the thought of the Cambridge Platonists and the Caroline divines, as well as of men of letters like Sir Thomas Browne and Isaac Walton.

Nevertheless all this wealth of literary culture could not prevent an increasing divergence between the social and psychological tendencies of Catholic and Protestant society. The Baroque culture integrated asceticism with mysticism, and humanism with popular culture, through the common media of art and liturgy; but in the Protestant world, the religious culture of the masses, which was derived from the Bible and the sermon, had no access to the imaginative world of the humanist poet and artist. Thus it was on the popular level that the differences between the two cultures are most obvious and their separation is most complete. For what could be sharper than the contrast between the popular culture of Catholic Europe with its pilgrimages and festivals and sacred dramas all centering in the great Baroque churches which were the painted palaces of the Saints, and the austere religious life of the hard-working Protestant artisan and shopkeeper which found its only outward expression in the weekly attendance in a bare meeting house to listen to the long sermons of the Puritan divines and to sing long psalms in metrical but far from poetical versions?

This difference in the form of the religious life found expression in a corresponding difference of psychological types and spiritual personalities. A man like Cotton Mather had no doubt received a good classical education, but no one can call him a Christian Humanist. His character was formed in the same mould as that of his congregation. Whereas on the other side, men like St. Francis de Sales or Fénelon were humanists not only in their classical culture but in their spirituality and their personal relations. This failure of Protestantism to assimilate the Christian Humanist tradition completely caused a certain impoverishment and aridity in English and American cultures and led ultimately to those defects which Matthew Arnold was to criticize so vigorously in the 19th century.

Nevertheless Protestant culture had its own distinctive qualities. The moral energy of the Puritan tradition inspired the new bourgeois culture of the English-speaking world in the later 17th and 18th centuries and gave it the strength which enabled it to overcome its rivals and dominate the world. What I am concerned with at the moment, however, is not to judge the values of these two forms of culture, but to point out their differences and show how their divergence contributed to the disunity of the Christian world. For when the age of religious war was over, Europe was still divided (and America also) by a difference of moral values and psychological antipathies. And these differences are harder to surmount than the theological ones, because they go so deep into the unconscious mind and have become a part of the personality and the national character.

When we come to the 19th century we shall find plenty of cases of men who have lost all conscious connection with religion but who nevertheless retain the social and national prejudices which they have inherited from their Catholic or Protestant backgrounds.

Similarly when the barriers were first broken down it was due not only to the theological converts and apologists, like Newman, but to the cultural converts, like Arnold and Ruskin. Arnold is a particularly significant case, because he admitted his debt to the Oxford Movement, though he did not concern himself with the theological questions which were its *raison d'être*, but concentrated all his attention on the cultural weaknesses of the Protestant tradition and the need for a revision of English cultural values. The same phenomenon is to be found on the Catholic side, though it is less easy to point to a representative figure. But one may mention the attempt of a group of Catholic sociologists in France in the later 19th century to criticize Catholic social ethics by comparison with the moral energy and activism of Anglo-Saxon culture—an attempt which was, I believe, the real source of the Americanist controversy.

Now I do not wish to suggest that we should approach the study of Catholicism and Divided Christendom in the spirit of Matthew Arnold rather than in that of Newman or Moehler. These are theological questions, and the last word must always rest with the theologians.

Yet as an historian I am convinced that the main sources of Christian division and the chief obstacle to Christian unity have been and are cultural rather than theological. Consequently, I believe that it is only by combining the study of the history of Christian culture with the study of theology that we can understand the nature and extent of the problem with which we have to deal.

II

THE DECLINE OF THE UNITY OF
MEDIEVAL CHRISTENDOM

THE breakdown of the medieval synthesis and the loss of the unity of medieval Christendom was a gradual process which covers some two and a half centuries of European history, from 1275 to 1525. This two hundred and fifty years of progressive decline corresponds to the preceding period of unification—the two hundred and fifty years of centripetal movement which ran from the year 1000 to 1250 and which saw the foundation and growth of the papal reform of the Western Church. This second period, of declining unity, is as much a part of medieval culture as the first. Indeed, many of the phenomena which we regard as typically "medieval" belong to this period—for example, the histories of Joinville and Froissart, the poems of Dante and William Langland, the writings of St. Catherine of Siena and the German mystics of the Rhineland, the *Imitation of Christ* and Sir Thomas Malory's *Morte d'Arthur.*

Nevertheless the whole period shows a steady disintegration of the medieval ideal of unity, marked by two main features—negatively by the loss of international unity and the transcendent supra-political authority of the Papacy, and positively by the growth of the modern states and the national political unit.

In the earlier Middle Ages, the State in our sense of the word hardly existed. There were a vast number of political and social units—feudal fiefs, duchies, counties and baronies, loosely held together by their allegiance to king or Emperor. There were Free Cities and Leagues of Cities, like the Lombard Commune or the Hanseatic League. There were ecclesiastical principalities like the German prince-bishoprics, and the great independent abbeys. Finally there were the religious and military Orders—international organizations which lived their own lives and obeyed their own authorities in whatever country of Europe they might happen to be situated.

And all of these groups were inextricably intermingled so that it was difficult to say which of them was the State. For instance, much of Southwest France belonged to the king of England, but not as a part of the English kingdom. It remained a fief of the French crown, to which the English king was bound to do homage for it. Such a situation is inconceivable in the modern political organization of Europe. It was possible then because the whole of Western Europe formed part of a single society—Christendom—not a political society it is true, but much more than anything we understand by a common religion or a common culture. It was rooted in the medieval belief that the whole Christian people formed a single body with a twofold organization—the Regnum and the Sacerdotium, the Empire and the Papacy, and though the former never succeeded in making good its claim to universal authority, the latter gave Western Europe a real international organization, which was far more powerful than the local and partial authority of the secular states.

At the end of the 13th century, however, the sense of the common unity of Christendom was beginning to weaken. The fall of Acre, the last remnant of Christian territory in Palestine, in 1291 marks the decay of the Crusading spirit, and the destruction of the great Order of the Templars by Philip IV of France from 1307 to 1312 was even more symptomatic of the coming of a new spirit. The rise of the national feudal monarchies in the West had already begun to threaten the supremacy of the international Church. Throughout the second half of the 13th century, France had been growing in power and prosperity. She was no longer a loose confederation of feudal principalities. She was a national state, the unity of which was embodied not only in the monarchy, but in the States General, the representative assembly of the Estates of the Realm, which first appears in 1302, seven years after the similar organization of the English Parliament. Moreover, the king no longer governed through the great hereditary officers of state and the bishops. Their place was being taken by a professional class of officials and lawyers, many of them men of humble origin from southern France, who had acquired from their study of the Roman Law the ideals of royal supremacy and absolute sovereign states.

These forces, represented by men like Pierre Flote, Dubois, and above all, Nogaret, the professor of law from Montpellier, came into violent conflict with the papal theocracy in the person of its most uncompromising representative, Boniface VIII, in regard to the right of the secular power to tax the goods of the Church. The French emissary had declared to the Pope: "Your power is in words, that of my master is in deeds," and Nogaret proved the truth of the boast by the brutal outrage of Anagni, which sent a shock of horror through Christendom, as is testified by Dante's famous lines: "I see the flower-de-luce Anagni enter, and Christ in his own Vicar captive made; I see him yet another time derided; I see renewed the vinegar and gall, and between living thieves I see him slain" (*Purgatorio* XX, 86). Two years later, a French pope was elected, and the Papacy was transferred to France. The victory of the French monarchy seemed complete.

Nevertheless, the international position of the Papacy was not immediately affected by the change. In some respects, it actually gained by its close union with the power of France, which was the great creative force in the culture. It was during the Avignon period that the supremacy of the Pope over the Church attained its highest point, especially in ecclesiastical taxation and in the right of provision to vacant benefices. It was its moral power and prestige that were declining. At the time of the struggle of the investitures, the conscience of Europe was on the side of the Papacy against the secularized feudal state; but now the danger of secularization came from within, from the luxury of the court of Avignon and the enormous development of the international system of papal finance. The reforming party began to look to the state as the power that might free the Church from the incubus of material wealth and leave it free to devote all its energies to its spiritual function.

Yet it may be said that in a sense both these problems in the form they assumed during the later Middle Ages were actually due to the achievements of the earlier reforming movement. For the recognition of the Holy See as the effective ruler of the Church and of the Curia as the ultimate court of appeal for the whole of Christendom had involved a highly organized system of ecclesiastical centralization which required an elaborate financial and fiscal system to support it. This international ecclesiastical bureaucracy and financial system came into existence while the medieval state was still organized on a feudal and agrarian basis, so that when the western kingdoms came to develop an efficient administrative and financial system they found themselves face to face with the highly organized pontifical system. As a result the royal chancery and the papal chancery claimed jurisdiction in the same cases and the royal and pontifical exchequers claimed rights of taxation over the same sources of revenue. This conflict was an inevitable one, since there could be no question of a separation of Church and State. No one denied the universality of the Church, yet it was equally impossible to deny that the clergy were an integral part of the Kingdom— an Estate of the Realm.

If the claims of the Papacy, as asserted, for example, by Boniface VIII in the bull *Clericis Laicos*, had been accepted in full, any system of national taxation would have become impossible, and similarly with the papal claim to appoint its own nominees to bishoprics and ecclesiastical dignities at a time when bishops and abbots held high public offices in the national kingdoms. On the other hand, if the regalist position of the Kings' lawyers had been accepted, the central government of the Church would have been deprived of the economic means of existence.

This dilemma was overcome owing to the fact that while each party insisted in theory on their total rights in their laws and public pronouncements, in practice they reached an agreed settlement by negotiation of each point as it arose. But this was an unsatisfactory solution, since it involved a great deal of hard bargaining and subordinated the spiritual interests of the Church to the economic interests of rival bureaucracies. The increasing importance for the Papacy of these financial questions led to a growing criticism of the abuses that seemed inseparable from the system. These criticisms were already frequent in the 14th century when the Papacy resided at Avignon. John XXII (1316–1334) and his successors were not bad popes, but they were primarily lawyers and administrators, and the more efficient was their administration, the richer became the court at Avignon—actually the cardinals had more of this wealth than the pope—and the louder became the protests of its critics.[1]

Consequently it is not surprising that this period saw the final break between the Papacy and the spiritual reformers whose alliance had been the dominant factor in the formation of medieval Christendom. The left wing of the Franciscans had been in revolt since the end of the 13th century, and now in 1328 the head of the Order, Michael of Cesena, supported by its leading philosopher William of Ockham, defied Pope John XXII and appealed from the court of Avignon to the judgment of the universal Church, as represented by a General Council.

This was an event of no small importance, for William of Ockham was the leading mind of his age. He was the initiator—the "venerabilis inceptor"—of the *via moderna* which took the place of the classical scholasticism of the 13th century—the *via antiqua*—as the accepted doctrine of the uni-

---

[1] There is one important exception—Benedict XII (1334–1342), the Cistercian theologian Jacques Fournier.

versities for nearly two centuries, down to the time of Luther. The fact that such a man should have broken with the Avignon Papacy and devoted the last twenty years of his life to supporting the cause of the temporal power against it, both in Germany and in England, and advocating a new theory of the Church and its authority, shows the seriousness of the situation. In his view, which may have been influenced by the even more radical theories of his contemporary and ally, Marsilius of Padua, the ultimate authority lies not in the Pope but in the Church as a whole, and if the Pope fails, as John XXII in his view had done, it was the right and duty of the whole body of the faithful to intervene by means of a General Council.

Meanwhile Europe was entering on a period of economic decline and social disaster. In the previous period—that is, from the 11th to the 13th century—the population and wealth of medieval Christendom had been steadily increasing, owing to the revival of trade and the movement of internal colonization which created new villages in the forests and wastelands. But from the beginnings of the 14th century a movement of decline began which lasted for two hundred years. The origins of this change are difficult to explain, since according to the economic historians, population had already begun to decline at the end of the 13th century. But about the middle of the 14th century the decline is obvious and catastrophic. The Black Death, the greatest of all recorded epidemics, swept over the whole of Europe and destroyed a third of the population in three years, from 1347 to 1350. At the same time the Hundred Years War wrecked the work of Philip IV and his predecessors. The richest land in Europe fell a prey to foreign invasion and the ravages of the Free Companies of mercenary soldiers. The churches and monasteries were destroyed and the open country was reduced to a desert. At the same time in the Southeast the Turks entered Europe, and after establishing their capital at Adrianople in 1366, proceeded to destroy the flourishing Christian kingdoms of the

Balkans, while Christian Russia still remained under the Tartar yoke.

All these disasters had a demoralizing effect on the Church and on Christian culture in general. The effects of the Black Death, for example, on the clergy and the religious orders were serious and far-reaching, since at the same time it reduced the clerical personnel and weakened ecclesiastical discipline. Yet in spite of all this, the 14th century cannot be described as an irreligious age. On the contrary it was the great age of medieval mysticism which produced a series of great saints and spiritual writers all over Europe, such as Tauler and Suso in Germany, Ruysbroeck and Gerard Groote in the Netherlands, Richard Rolle and the author of "The Cloud of Unknowing" in England, St. Catherine of Siena and Bl. John Colombini in Italy, and St. Bridget in Sweden. This movement of spiritual introversion may have been due in some degree to the turning away of the Christian mind from a world which was in revolt against the Church and the Christian order. But this is only partially true, for the great women mystics or prophetesses of the age—St. Bridget of Sweden and St. Catherine of Siena—intervened repeatedly in the external life of the Church and were in part responsible for bringing about the return of the Papacy from Avignon to Rome from 1367 to 1370 and again in 1377.

Yet this proved no remedy for the ills of the Church. On the contrary, the return of the Popes from Avignon to Rome was followed by the violent crisis of the Great Schism during which all the evils of the Avignon period became magnified. Christendom was divided, not as at the Reformation by theological differences, but on the purely juridical question, which of the two rival popes was the legitimate one. Public opinion had protested only too loudly against the abuses of the Avignon regime. It now found itself faced by two identical systems, each claiming to be absolutely exclusive, so that the evils of the previous period were all precisely doubled.

From this impasse there was no outlet by the accepted

principles of canon law, and the time had come when William of Ockham's revolutionary ideas could bear fruit. The leadership of Christendom now passed to the University of Paris, which was the last stronghold of medieval unity and also the great center of Ockhamist thought.

For the next thirty or forty years the doctors of Paris championed the cause of unity against the Popes and Kings and succeeded in achieving a brief triumph through the Conciliar Movement.

The Conciliar Movement represents the final effort of medieval Christendom to assert its unity against the centrifugal tendencies represented by the Great Schism and the national heresies of the Wycliffites and the Hussites. It was the culmination of medieval constitutionalism in its attempts to give constitutional form to the ideal of Christendom as a single religious society, divided politically among a number of national kingdoms. The General Councils which were convoked to end the Schism under the influence of the University of Paris and the French monarchy were unlike the General Councils of the past. They were parliaments of Christendom, which were attended by the whole body of Christian princes with two or three exceptions, and in which the representatives of the universities played a larger part than the bishops.

The Conciliar Movement was prepared by the two national Councils held in Paris in 1395 and 1406. In these the conciliarist policy was worked out—viz., the withdrawal of obedience from the two claimants to the Papacy in order to induce their resignation. But they were unable to coerce the obstinate resistance of the Avignon Pope Benedict XIII. He withstood both the withdrawal of the French obedience and a seven months' siege of the Palace of Avignon; and after his escape from Avignon in 1403 he himself summoned a General Council to meet at Perpignon in 1408 which was almost entirely Spanish in composition.

But at this point the cardinals of both popes united to

withdraw their obedience alike from the Avignon and the Roman popes and summoned a joint Council to meet at Pisa in the spring of 1409 for the election of a new pope. This was in agreement with the policy of the French monarchy, which had declared its neutrality between the two popes and had decided at a national council in Paris to support the forthcoming Ecumenical Council.

This Council, which met at Pisa on March 25, 1409, was an extraordinarily representative body. In addition to bishops and abbots, it included hundreds of deputies from cathedral chapters and from the universities, the generals of the great religious and military Orders, together with the ambassadors of seventeen states representing almost the whole body of Christian princes. In spite of this varied membership this assembly showed a remarkable degree of unanimity in dealing with the crucial issue of the schism.

They summoned both the claimants to the Papacy to appear before them, and on their non-appearance proceeded to try and depose them both, in accordance with the conciliarist thesis of the Universities. Next they proceeded to the election of a new pope of the united Church, chosen by the joint efforts of the cardinals of both obediences. After a short conclave of eleven days these agreed unanimously on the choice of Peter Philarghi, the Greek archbishop of Milan, who took the name of Alexander V. The Council then dissolved after decreeing the convocation of a new General Council to meet in April 1412 to carry out further measures for the reform of the Church.

But the apparent outstanding success of the Council of Pisa was deceptive. The new Pope lived only ten months. His successor, John XXIII (Baldassare Cossa), elected May 17, 1410, lacked the moral authority to make good his claims against the Roman Pope, Gregory XII, or the Avignon claimant, Benedict XIII, who had now withdrawn to his family fortress at Peñiscola in Aragon. Consequently, after the failure of the General Council which John had summoned at Rome in 1412, he was forced to acquiesce in the Emperor Sigismund's plan for a new Council to be held at Constance on November 1, 1414.

The new Council was even more a parliament of Christendom than the Council of Pisa had been, since it was divided into four nations—Italian, German, French and English—in whose deliberations the representatives of the princes and of the universities, as well as the bishops, were entitled to vote. Thus from the beginning the Council of Constance was dominated by the Northern people—the French, the Germans and the English; and the position of the Pope, John XXIII, who relied on the Italian vote, became increasingly difficult, until on March 2, 1415, he was prevailed upon to abdicate. But he soon repented of his action, and on March 20 he escaped from Constance and took refuge with Frederick of Austria.

This, however, led to an explosion of anti-papal feeling, in which the famous Four Decrees were passed. These declared that the Council derived its authority directly from Christ, that the whole world including the Pope himself was subject to this authority, and that the flight of the Pope was an act of contumacy which justified the suspicion that he was joining the schism and had fallen into heresy. This action of the Council met with a wide measure of secular support. The Emperor issued the ban of the Empire against Frederick of Austria, whose lands were overrun by the Swiss and the Bavarians, so that he was obliged to surrender the Pope to the representatives of the Council.

The Council next proceeded to the trial of the Pope, who was condemned and deposed on May 29, 1415, as "unworthy, useless and harmful". The sentence was accepted by John XXIII, who was now a prisoner in the hands of the Council. The Church was now practically without a pope, since Gregory XII, the Roman Pope, abdicated shortly afterwards (July 14, 1415) and Benedict XIII was deprived of his last support, the King of Aragon, by the Treaty of Narbonne at the end of the same year. Meanwhile the Council had asserted its authority by the trial and execution of John Hus (July 6, 1415), who had presented himself at Constance, trusting in the safe conduct of the Emperor. This act precipitated the national revolution of the Czech people against the Emperor and the Church, which was to defy all the crusading efforts of the rest of Christendom for seventeen years.

But the Council, oblivious of the storm which it had aroused, went on to consider the election of a new pope, and to devise a wide program of reform. By the decree *Frequens* (October 5, 1417) it laid down that the General Council was the chief instrument for the cultivation of God's field, the Church, the neglect of which was the chief reason for the disorder of Christendom. It decreed that the next General Council should be convened in five years' time, and thereafter they must be held at intervals of from seven to ten years. It then proceeded to elect Oddo Colonna as Pope Martin V on November 11, 1417. At last the schism was brought to an end.

The Council was now approaching its own end. There only remained the difficult question of reform, which occupied the final sessions—especially the question of Papal Taxation, which was finally settled by the four national Concordats—with Italy, Germany, France and Spain—signed on May 3, 1418. But already the Council had been dissolved after a closing session on April 22. The new Pope, refusing the offer of Avignon or a German city, began his slow progress back to Rome, which he finally entered on September 30, 1420.

From this moment the Papacy separated itself from the Conciliar Movement, which had reached its high water mark at Constance. When the Council of Basel met in 1431, it soon showed itself determined to assert its authority as the infallible representative of the universal Church. Pope Eugenius IV, who had succeeded Martin V early in the same year, ordered his legate, Cardinal Cesarini, to transfer the

Council to Bologna on account of the scanty attendance. It replied by a reassertion of the decree of Constance—that a General Council "derived its power immediately from Christ, and that all men, even the Pope, are bound to obey it in matters pertaining to the Faith, the extirpation of heresy, and the reformation of the Church in head and members".

Thus the open breach between the Pope and the Council threatened a renewal of the schism which had been so painfully ended at Constance. But the fact that the Hussites had accepted the Council and that negotiations with them had been initiated by the Papal Legate Cesarini—who had resigned his presidency of the Council when the Pope ordered its dissolution but did not conceal his sympathy with the Conciliarist position—delayed the final break. Pope Eugenius was induced to recognize the Council, and withdrew his decree of dissolution in September 1433. But the strength of the Council was due to the support it received from the Northern and Western secular powers, the Emperor Frederick III and France and Spain. The Council itself was composed mainly of the delegates from the Northern universities, but the bishops were very few; their numbers sank to only twenty by 1436. It was this minority assembly, dominated by its anti-papal majority, which did all in its power to reduce the authority and the revenues of the Holy See.

The breaking point was brought about by the negotiations for reunion with the East, when both the Pope and the Council sent embassies to Constantinople in 1436–1437, inviting the Greeks to a conference. The Pope's proposal for a meeting in North Italy was naturally preferred to the Council's proposal of Avignon. The Pope accordingly transferred the Council from Basel to Ferrara in September 1437, where the Greeks were received in March 1438. But while the reunion of the Western and Byzantine Churches was being worked out at Ferrara and Florence, the Council of Basel had declared the supremacy of the Council over the Pope as a truth of faith, and went on to depose Eugenius IV as a heretic and destroyer of the rights of the Church (June 25, 1439). Thus at the very moment when the historic schism of the Eastern and Western Churches was being extinguished at Florence, the Council of Basel, now reduced to a mere handful of bishops, created a new schism in the North by the election of Amadeus, the Duke of Savoy, on November 5, 1439, as Pope Felix V. The new anti-Pope met with scanty recognition, except in Germany and Aragon. Even here the diplomacy of the Roman Pope was triumphant. In February 1447, Eugenius IV received the restoration of the obedience of the German envoys at Rome a few days before his death.

His successor, Nicholas V, was a man of exceptional moral stature. He did all in his power to facilitate the abdication of the anti-Pope and the dissolution of the Council in April 1449. Thus the long and bitter controversies of the Conciliar period, which had threatened the subversion of the traditional order of the Church, were ended in an atmosphere of apparent good will and mutual tolerance.

At the same time the age of the Councils saw a further catastrophic decline in the countries in Northern Europe which had been the center of the earlier medieval culture. After an interval which enabled France temporarily to recover its prosperity, the Hundred Years War was resumed in 1415 and complicated by the disastrous civil war between the Burgundians and the Armagnacs which led to the English conquest of France. The years from 1419 to 1444 were perhaps the most disastrous that the French people have ever experienced. The strength of popular religion at this time was shown by the career of St. Joan who came to the help of the people when their leaders had failed them, but the tragic end of her mission also showed how weak and time-serving the French Church had become.

The same failure is to be seen in the rise of the new heresies in England and Bohemia. William Langland's poem, *Piers Plowman*, reveals the depth of the religion of the people in the 14th century. But though he still writes as a faithful

Catholic, he despairs of the state of the Church, and it is not to the Papacy or the religious Orders but to the King and the Commons that he looks for help. At the same time the reforming movement in England first expressed itself in a definitely revolutionary form. The author of the movement, John Wycliffe (c. 1330–1384), was in many respects a typical figure of the late scholastic period at Oxford, where he had been master of Balliol College in 1360. He achieved notoriety as a spokesman of the national grievances against the Papacy.

As the chief clerical spokesman on behalf of John of Gaunt's anti-clerical policy, he was brought into conflict with the bishops and finally with the Papacy, by which his opinions were condemned in 1377. But he continued to enjoy the protection of John of Gaunt thenceforward until his death in 1384, and so was able to continue to propagate his ideas, which became steadily more uncompromising and more unorthodox. By the time of his death he had completely broken with Catholicism and had given his followers, the Poor Preachers, a store of heretical principles that they were to develop still further in the years that followed. He denied the supremacy of the Papacy and the Divine Authority of the hierarchical Church, since the true Church is the assembly of the predestinate and no one can know with certainty who are its members. He held that the only certain rule of faith was to be found in the Scriptures, which everyone must interpret for himself and which should be made available to all men in their own tongue. Wycliffe insisted that the doctrine of Transubstantiation had no ground in Scripture and that the sacrifice of the Mass was not of divine institution. Above all, and this was the starting point of his doctrine, the Church has no right to have possessions, and the temporal power has the right to appropriate them and correct the misdeeds of the clergy.

The propagation of Wycliffe's ideas was suppressed or driven underground in England by the repressive policy of the new Lancastrian dynasty in the early 15th century, but it was destined to have a profound impact on the opposite corner of Europe through the work of John Hus and Jerome of Prague. Bohemia had enjoyed a period of great prosperity in the 14th century under the rule of the House of Luxemburg, and the University of Prague had become the greatest center of studies in central Europe; but the prosperity of the kingdom brought it into close relations with Germany and the rest of Europe, so that the University had become a center for foreign influences. In the course of the century, however, Czech national feeling asserted itself, and the beginnings of the vernacular literature made their appearance. This movement found its focus in the demands for the reform of the Church, which had suffered from the moral and financial corruption of the Avignon period.

This reforming movement found expression in the vernacular preaching and writing of John of Millitz, Thomas of Stitny, and Mathias of Janov. In its beginnings it was entirely orthodox, though there arose some opposition among the clergy, especially those of German origin. But at the beginning of the 15th century, the new leader of the reformers, John Hus, came under Wycliffite influence, and thenceforward the movement of reform became identified with the doctrines of Wycliffe, the personality of Hus, and the cause of Czech nationalism. At first the support of King Wenceslaus permitted Hus to carry on his work, and he was able to make the University of Prague a center of his teaching. But in 1415, in face of the opposition of the bishops, he appealed to the General Council which had just met at Constance and presented himself to defend his own cause. In spite of the safe conduct which had been granted him by the Emperor Sigismund, the Council put him on trial and condemned and executed him as a heretic. Thus the leader of the reforming movement was put to death by the reforming Council.

In Bohemia Hus was regarded as a martyr, and the whole Czech people rallied in defence of his doctrine, led by the

University of Prague from which the Germans had been expelled.[2] And when the Emperor Sigismund succeeded to the crown on the death of his brother, King Wenceslaus, the Czechs rose in arms against the man who had betrayed their national hero. It is true that they were not united, since the Hussite principles of private judgment and the free interpretation of Scripture naturally tended to produce divisions, ranging from the Utraquists, dissident Catholics demanding only the reform of the Church and the right of the laity to receive the chalice in Holy Communion, to the Taborites, who adopted the principles of Wycliffe in their full rigor and attempted to establish the law of the Gospel and the Rule of the Saints by the sword; while outside these two main parties a great variety of sectarian extremism was to be found, as in England under the Commonwealth. Nevertheless they were sufficiently united under the great Taborite leaders, Ziska and Procopius, to repel triumphantly for eleven years the successive crusades that were launched against them by Sigismund and the Church. Thus for the first time the unity of Western Christendom was broken by a movement which was both religious and national, and which foreshadowed the revolt of the German people in the following century. Nevertheless this warning was disregarded by the Western Church, and the closing period of the Middle Ages, from 1440 to 1520, was occupied with very different problems.

For when the restored Papacy, in the person of Martin V, at last returned from Constance to Rome in 1420, it went back to a new world. It left the world of the schoolmen for that of the humanists and the world of the feudal monarchies for that of the city states. It came out of the autumn shadows of the Gothic North into the springtime of the Italian Renaissance.

---

[2] It must be noted that John Hus and the Czech reformers differ from Wycliffe and the Protestants alike in their insistence on the doctrine of the Real Presence and the importance that they attached to the Sacrifice of the Altar.

At the same time, the Papacy was faced with a new set of problems. It had to deal not only with the theoretical ecclesiastical issues which had been raised by the Conciliar Movement, but with the concrete problem of establishing its position amidst the fiercely competitive political life of the Italian States. And while the Council of Constance had been preoccupied by the dangers of the new Hussite heresy that had emerged in Bohemia, the Papacy was faced with the more formidable danger of Turkish conquest which overshadowed the Mediterranean world. This was a matter of life and death for the great Italian maritime republics which lived by their trade with the Eastern Mediterranean and their colonial possessions in the Aegean and on the Black Sea. Greece and the Aegean were now a mosaic of Greek and Italian States with Florentines at Athens, Venetians in Crete, and Genoese at Constantinople and in the Crimea. Conditions had never been so favorable for a reunion of Greek and Latin Christendom, since the Byzantine emperors were no less anxious than the popes to end the schism between the Churches which was the main obstacle to the establishment of a common front against the Turks.

The achievement of this union was the first task of the restored Papacy, and it was brought to a successful issue at the Council of Florence in 1439[3] by the joint efforts of the Byzantine Emperor John VIII, supported by Archbishop Bessarion of Nicaea and Archbishop Isidore of Kiev, on the one side, and the Florentine humanist Ambrogio Traversari. From a political point of view the union of Florence was a failure, since it came too late to avert the Turkish danger; and the efforts of the popes, above all of Calixtus III and Pius II, to organize a last crusade ended in failure and disillusionment. The ecclesiastical union also proved abortive. Though officially it survived until the Turkish conquest of Constantinople (1453), it was vehemently rejected by the great mass

[3] Mark of Ephesus was actually the only Orthodox bishop to refuse his signature.

of Byzantine Christians. They even preferred Turkish rule to union with the Papacy. "Better", said they, "the prophet's turban than the pope's tiara." But from the cultural point of view the temporary reunion was more significant, since it helped to strengthen the Hellenic element in the Renaissance and brought to Italy some of the leaders of late Byzantine culture, like Cardinal Bessarion, a great scholar and a great Churchman who might have been elected pope in 1455 had it not been for the opposition of the French party, voiced, appropriately enough, by the Cardinal of Avignon.

The failure of the union of the Churches and of the movement for the rescue of the Christian East was a great misfortune for the Church, since it was the one issue which might have once more united Christendom under the leadership of the Papacy and given it the power to transcend the petty politics of the Italian principalities. We see this in the career of Pius II (1458–1464), who was a typical representative of the new Renaissance culture, a humanist of the humanists, the first, and perhaps the only, popular novelist to be elected pope and the only pope who has written his autobiography.[4] Yet from the moment he became pope he threw himself heart and soul into the cause of the crusade and devoted all his energies and eloquence to an effort to overcome the divisions of the West and to unite Christendom in a common effort. Nor were his efforts limited to words. He took the cross himself, and although he was a dying man, he travelled to Ancona to launch the crusade in person.

But with the fading of this last hope of uniting the west to save Eastern Christendom, the Papacy became more and more absorbed in the little world of Italian politics. No doubt the Renaissance popes were generous patrons of art and literature, but so were the other Italian princes, and the more successful the Papacy was in establishing its temporal power

---

[4] His romance *Lucretia and Euryalus*, written when he was a diplomat at Vienna in 1444, was extremely popular and was translated into English in the 16th century.

and prestige, the more it came to resemble the other Italian princedoms. The dangers of secularization had never been so great as at the end of the century—when the protest of the Italian reformers was silenced by the execution of Savonarola and Alexander VI and his son Cesare Borgia dominated the scene. It seemed as though the evil times of the 10th century were returning, when the Papacy had been the prey of local factions among the lawless nobles of the Campagna. That situation had been ended by the intervention of the German emperors and by the reformed monasticism of Northern Europe, and now once more northern armies broke into Italy, and the rivalries and ambitions of the Italian principalities became overshadowed and absorbed by the wider conflict of the great European powers. Once again a movement of religious reform arose in the North, but this time it was a movement of religious revolution which subverted the bases of the medieval order and Catholic unity.

III

THE RENAISSANCE

THERE is a tendency of modern historians to minimize the importance of the Renaissance and its effects upon European culture. Many of them hold that it was neither so original nor so influential as has hitherto been believed. There has been, on the one hand, a revaluation of the medieval contribution to science and thought (e.g. as by Lynn Thorndike), and, on the other, a reaction against Burckhardt's concept of the Renaissance as marking the birth of the modern world and the self-discovery of modern man.

Nevertheless the concept of the Renaissance as an epoch-marking change in Western culture is not due to Burckhardt (who wrote in 1860). It is a commonplace of the writers of the Enlightenment and of their predecessors, the writers of the Grand Siècle. It had also been accepted as a part of the Protestant view of history, e.g. in America by the Puritans and earlier in the 16th century in Europe.

> Incredible Darkness was upon the Western parts of *Europe*, two Hundred years ago: *Learning* was wholly swallowed up in *Barbarity*. But when the *Turks* made their Descent so far upon the Greek Churches as to drive all before them, very many Learned Greeks, with their Manuscripts, and Monuments, fled into *Italy*, and other parts of *Europe*. This occasioned the Revival of *Letters* there, which prepared the World for the Reformation of *Religion* too; and the *Advances of the Sciences* ever since.[1]

When a view has obtained such general currency, it cannot easily be dismissed, since it has itself become a part of history.

[1] Perry Miller, *The New England Mind:The 17th Century* (Cambridge, Mass.: Harvard, 1954), p. 97.

Thus I do not think it is possible to deny that educated Europeans were conscious that a great change had passed over European culture in the 15th and 16th centuries—what may be called a cultural *revolution*, and that this was no delusion but an historical fact. Furthermore they were right in thinking that this change had come about in Italy as early as the 14th century and that it had been transmitted to Northern Europe gradually and perhaps slowly, so that its impact on the North tended to coincide with the other great change—that of the Reformation—with the result that the two movements tended in some cases, especially perhaps in Germany, to be confused with one another.

But while the traditional view of the Renaissance as marking an epoch in Western culture is correct, the traditional explanation of the Renaissance as due to the revival of the study of Greek, and of this being occasioned by the capture of Constantinople by the Turks, is not only inadequate but fundamentally erroneous. Here at last modern historical criticism has played an essential part in widening and deepening our understanding of what the Renaissance was and why it had such a revolutionary influence on Western culture.

The Renaissance was not merely a revival of classical studies, as our forefathers believed. It was the coming of a new culture—a new way of life—which had its roots deep in the past and which had been developing for centuries in the Mediterranean world before it achieved its full expression in 15th-century Italy.

I. THE RENAISSANCE IN ITALY

This new culture was the culture of the city, like the traditional culture of the Hellenistic and Roman world, which had never become fully acclimatized in Northern Europe, where the foundations of medieval culture had been laid by the Carolingian culture, which was essentially agrarian, a creation of the territorial Church and the territorial nobility. Even after the 11th century, when the new towns and communes began to spread in the north, this did not alter the predominantly rural character of the northern feudal culture, which was to outlast the Middle Ages themselves. But in Italy the cities had never disappeared. The maritime cities like Venice and Pisa and Amalfi and Genoa had retained their links with the Byzantine world. Their trade stimulated the growth of the communes and the free cities of Lombardy and Tuscany, which became more and more the vital centers of Italian society. Here for the first time in medieval Europe there developed a true urban society, entirely unlike the feudal and territorial hierarchy of the North.

No doubt the nobility still existed, but it was no longer an independent territorial power, as in the North. It had been brought into the city and played its part in the class struggle and party politics of the city republics, as in ancient Greece, until it gradually lost its monopoly of political power and even its social privileges. In fact the city states of Italy in the later Middle Ages resembled the city states of the Hellenic world in the vigor of their internal civic life and in the intensity of their political and economic rivalry. Like the Hellenic cities they extended their colonies and factories throughout the Eastern Mediterranean and the Black Sea, beginning with the ports of the Crusading States in Syria and extending to the partition of the Byzantine Empire itself after the Fourth Crusade. Eventually the Venetians controlled the Ionian Islands, the Aegean and Crete, while the Genoese established themselves at Constantinople (in their colony of Galata) and in the Crimea and at Tana on the Sea of Azof. Even Athens itself became an Italian colony under the Florentine Dukes of Athens in the 14th century.

In this way the path was opened for a new contact between Greek and Italian culture, and as Asia Minor and the Balkans were gradually overrun by the Turks, it was the Italian cities, above all Venice, Florence and Rome, rather than Russia or the other Eastern Orthodox lands, that provided the natural refuge for Byzantine exiles and kept alive the traditions of

Byzantine scholarship and Greek classical literature. To this extent there is a limited justification for the old legend that links the Renaissance with the fall of Constantinople in 1453. But it was a comparatively small factor, and the Renaissance as a whole was essentially the result of a cultural process which had its roots in a specifically Italian environment.

It was in the Italian city, above all in the self-governing republics like Florence, that an opportunity existed for the rise of a new lay educated class which possessed political rights and a sense of citizenship not unlike that which had existed in the classical Hellenic world.

In his important work on *The Crisis of the Early Italian Renaissance* (2 vols., 1955), Hans Baron has shown that these civic ideals first found their full expression when the Florentine Republic was struggling to preserve its liberty against Milan at the end of the 14th century (1390–1402), and it was the great humanist, Lionardo Bruni, afterwards to become the historian of Florence and the Chancellor of the Republic, who gave these ideas their classical expression. This attempt to maintain the freedom of Italy, first by an alliance of the republics and afterwards by a system of balance of power which succeeded in uniting all the Italian States in the "Holy League" of 1454–1455, provided the political basis for the later Renaissance culture, a culture which itself transcended political frontiers and was common to the whole Italian world of republics and principalities, including Papal Rome and the Neapolitan Kingdom.

So long as this system endured, it provided a wonderful opportunity for men of outstanding talent whose services were eagerly sought for in the rival courts and cities and whose freedom of choice was almost unlimited. It was this opportunity for individual freedom, not perhaps for the ordinary citizen, but for the intellectual elite of scholars and artists, which became the distinctive note of Renaissance culture.

In medieval society, as in the modern technocratic state, a

man's position depended on his function. He was a craftsman, or a clerk, or a monk, or a soldier, and he was bound strictly to the order of the guild and the university and the religious Order. But in the new Renaissance society he was an individual who tried to assert the freedom of his personality and to realize every possibility of development. Thus the artist did not remain bound to his guild, but aspired to be a "genius", and so too with the man of letters who was not content with being a professor and the politician who was an artist in statecraft. Now the medieval corporative idea was undoubtedly more Christian in so far as it was consciously inspired by the Pauline ideal of an organic unity in which every function, even the most humble, has its part to play in the service of the whole. But the Renaissance ideology also had a religious aspect, since it was inspired by the Christian ideal of the dignity of human nature and the greatness of every individual soul—ideals which were constantly reiterated by Renaissance thinkers from Pico della Mirandola to Campanella.

At the same time the Renaissance introduced a new set of ideal values (or set an ideal value on human activities) which were not necessarily secular but were essentially natural and belonged to the sphere of free human activity. No doubt Thomism had already prepared the way for this by introducing the Aristotelian ethics and the Aristotelian idea of intellectual contemplation as man's highest good. But in Thomism these values were strictly subordinated to religious and supernatural ends, whereas the humanists regarded them as ends in themselves and gave them an autonomous significance. Thus there arose the ideals of "pure scholarship", "pure art" and "pure science" which were to have such a great importance for the development of modern culture.

But it was above all through education that the new culture found its main channel of diffusion. From the close of the 14th century the Italian cities revived the original Greek ideal of *paideia*—liberal education as the necessary preparation for civic life—and began to study once more the old educational literature, beginning with Cicero and Quintilian and ending with Isocrates and Plato. This humanist revival was of immense importance in the history of Western education. It laid the foundations of modern culture, not only by its classical learning and the recovery of Greek, but still more by the new ideals of life and education which it developed. In the humanist circles of the little Italian courts at Urbino and Mantua and Ferrara, as well as at Florence and Naples and Rome, there grew up a new ideal of culture based on the harmonious development of body and mind in all their activities. Such "universal men", as Leon Battista Alberti, at once athlete and scholar, architect and poet, artist and scientist, were a characteristic product of 15th century Italy, and it was this new type of many-sided excellence which took the place of the medieval ideals of chivalry, as the model of the European gentleman and courtier in the following age. Life was conceived, not in the medieval way as a struggle and a pilgrimage, but as a fine art, in which no opportunity for knowledge and enjoyment is to be neglected. It is essentially an aristocratic ideal, and involved a growth of class differences and a loss of that unity of outlook which united a medieval king like St. Louis with the humblest of his subjects. Nevertheless, in a limited way the Renaissance ideal did tend towards social equality, since the scholar and the artist were now the equals of princes, as had never been the case with the medieval noble and the guild craftsman.

Moreover, it must be emphasized that the goal of humanist education was in no sense a revival of paganism, for all the Renaissance writers on education, from Peter Paul Vergerio's treatise *De Ingenuis Moribus* in 1404 to Cardinal Sadoleto's work *De Liberis Recte Instituendis* in 1531, entirely accept the traditional Christian view of the place of religion in education. Liberal education was the education of a Christian gentleman or citizen and in no way rejected the supremacy of Christian ethics and theology.

The great humanist educators, like Lionardo Bruni, Guarino of Verona, Victorino da Feltre and Vergerio, were themselves devout Christians who wished to unite the intellectual and aesthetic culture of Hellenism with the spiritual ideals of Christianity. A striking expression of their approach to education can be found in the following passage from Lionardo Bruni:

> We know, however, that in certain quarters—where all knowledge and appreciation of Letters is wanting—this whole branch of Literature, marked as it is by something of the Divine, and fit, therefore, for the highest place, is decreed as unworthy of study. But when we remember the value of the best poetry, its charm of form and the variety and interest of its subject-matter, when we consider the ease with which from our childhood up it can be committed to memory, when we recall the peculiar affinity of rhythm and metre to our emotions and our intelligence, we must conclude that Nature herself is against such headlong critics. Have we not often felt the sudden uplifting of the Soul when in the solemn Office of the Church such a passage as the "Primo dierum omnium" bursts upon us? It is not hard for us, then, to understand what the Ancients meant when they said that the Soul is ordered in special relation to the principles of Harmony and Rhythm, and is, therefore, by no other influence so fitly and so surely moved. Hence I hold my conviction to be securely based; namely that Poetry has, by our very constitution, a stronger attraction for us than any other form of expression, and that anyone ignorant of, and indifferent to, so valuable an aid to knowledge and so ennobling a source of pleasure can by no means be entitled to be called educated.[2]

However, this humanist ideal of education did represent a sharp reaction against the exclusively dialectical education of the universities, and this tended to conflict with scholastic philosophy and theology. It was never an exclusively lay

[2] From Lionardo Bruni D'Arezzo, *De Studiis et Literis*, translated by W. H. Woodward.

education, but it led to a dualism between the two systems of education, literary studies and philosophy, and between the humanist and the theologian. And this dualism undoubtedly contributed to the breakdown of the unity of Christendom, though of course it is far from coinciding with the religious dualism between Catholic and Protestant Europe.

On the whole the 14th and 15th centuries were not an irreligious age in Italy. They saw great saints like St. Catherine of Siena, St. Bernardine of Siena, and St. Antonino of Florence, who were not living a purely contemplative life, but took a very active part in the social and political life of the time. Some of the scholars and artists of the 15th century were profoundly religious men, like Bl. Ambrogio Traversari of Florence and Fra Angelico of Fiesole. Indeed, Renaissance art, especially in its pre-Raphaelite form, is the principal channel through which the mainstream of Christian iconography and symbolism has been transmitted to the modern world. Even the more extreme forms of medieval asceticism and devotion, as represented by Savonarola's revival, evidently had a powerful appeal to 15th-century Florence and had a profound influence on some of the foremost representatives of Renaissance culture, like Botticelli, Pico della Mirandola and even Politian.

No doubt, in spite of this, the rise of the new lay culture in Italy was accompanied by the growth of secularism and even anti-clericalism in the Italian city states. But this dates back to the Middle Ages, as we see in the case of Frederick II and his supporters, and the thought of Marsilius of Padua in the early 14th century.

Hitherto we have said little about the art and sculpture and architecture of the Renaissance, and yet it is in the artist even more than in the scholar or courtier that the Italian Renaissance culture finds its most complete expression. There has never been a society, not even that of ancient Greece, which was so essentially a society of artists. The aesthetic point of view was dominant in every department of life. Even a political realist like Machiavelli appraised the career of Cesare Borgia with the aesthetic appreciation of an amateur for a masterpiece of art. The conception of virtue had lost its moral connotations and was applied alike to the excellence of the artist and the statesman.

The art of the Renaissance was not, however, due to the direct influence of antiquity, like the literary culture of the humanists. It had its roots far back in the Middle Ages—in the monumental painting of the school of Giotto and the monumental sculpture of the 13th-century renaissance. The art of the goldsmith craftsmen of Florence, of sculptors like Ghiberti, Donatello and Verocchio, and of painters like Pollaiuolo and Ghirlandaio, was still largely medieval, and in sculpture it owed much to the older French Gothic tradition. The Gothic art of the North had already assumed a strongly realist character, so that it was not only in Italy that men were looking to nature for their models. The progress of art in Italy in the 15th century was due to two factors—the influence of scientific observation, especially in the study of perspective and anatomy, and the revived study of classical art, above all of Roman architecture and Hellenistic sculpture. Hence the naturalism of the Renaissance was not an external reproduction of the impressions of real life, as in the North; it aimed at a deeper knowledge of Nature based on a study of the laws of form and space and the study of the human organism. Alike in art and architecture, there was an attempt to realize the classical ideal of harmony and proportion, the rhythmic union of form and idea, of color and emotion in a living unity.

But there remains a double tradition in Renaissance art. On the one hand there is the classical perfection of Raphael, in which the ideal of harmony and proportion is completely realized. On the other, there is the titanic art of Michelangelo with its restless energy and its passionate emotion, which is the forerunner of the Baroque art of the following age.

But the art of the Renaissance did not merely borrow from

the science of the age. It was itself a great creative force in the world of thought, and the artists were the forerunners of the great scientists and philosophers of the following century.

It was Leonardo da Vinci, the greatest of the "universal men" of the Renaissance, who first realized the full possibility of the application of science to life. "Necessity", he says, "is the eternal law of Nature", and by submission to this law by labor and experiment, "the one interpreter between Man and Nature", everything becomes possible to man.

He was interested above all in the application of mathematics to practical ends in the science of mechanics. "O students," he says, "study mathematics and do not build without a foundation"; and he foreshadowed numerous modern inventions in his models and plans, notably that of the flying machine and the helicopter. He was no less original in his study of the earth and of man. He was the first modern geologist and anatomist, as well as a botanist and an astronomer. In his wide vision of the possibilities of science and his comparatively modest and fragmentary achievement, he was a type of his own age, which was lacking in positive results through the very fertility of its genius—in the words that Vasari applies to Leonardo: the love of knowledge was so great, that the work itself was hindered by desire.

II. THE NORTHERN RENAISSANCE: ERASMUS

Meanwhile in Northern Europe there was no comparable development either in social or intellectual life. It is true that city life developed in the North as well as in Italy, especially in the Netherlands, in Southern Germany and along the Rhine. In the industrial arts and in the new art of printing these towns were often in advance of the Italian development. But in social and intellectual matters this was not the case. The Italian cities dominated the whole of Italian culture. The cities of the North were still islands in a predominantly rural society which was dominated by the nobles and the clergy.

The cultural leadership of Northern Europe in these times was in the hands of the Burgundian state, which was comparable to the duchy of Milan in the wealth and prosperity of its cities and in the brilliance of its artistic development. But this Burgundian culture, which has been so well described by Dr. Huizinga in his *Waning of the Middle Ages*, was very far removed from the new culture of Renaissance Italy. It was a court culture of feudal princes and nobles, which still cultivated the ideals of medieval chivalry, often in exaggerated forms as in the inauguration of the Order of the Golden Fleece and the famous banquet of 1454 when Philip the Good and the knights of the Order repeated for the last time the ceremony of a solemn vow of Crusade. So too the England of Sir Thomas Malory and the Wars of the Roses still looked back to a romanticized medieval world that was already dead. Yet the living tradition of Gothic architecture continued to flourish far into the 16th century, and some of the finest examples of the great English tradition of ecclesiastical architecture belong to the period immediately preceding the Reformation, such as the parish churches of East Anglia and the magnificence of King's College Chapel at Cambridge and St. George's chapel at Windsor. And the same persistence and vitality of the medieval tradition is to be seen in the late flamboyant architecture of France and Burgundy.

Thus the Gothic North had no need to look to Italy for a revival of the arts. Flemish painting was no less advanced than Italian, and the late Gothic architecture of the North was a more living popular tradition than the new classical architecture in Italy. On the other hand, in the field of education the North was becoming conscious of its cultural backwardness and was ready to accept in some degree the guidance of the Italian humanist teachers.

The need was greatest in the education of the laity, for as Aeneas Sylvius, the future Pius II, wrote, after his experiences in Germany (c. 1444), "Literature flourishes in Italy and princes are not ashamed to listen to and themselves to know poetry. But in Germany princes pay more attention to horses and dogs than to poets, and neglecting the arts, they die unremembered like their own beasts." [3]

No doubt there were exceptional cases of cultivated aristocrats, like Humphrey Duke of Gloucester and the Count Palatine Frederick I, who were sufficiently educated to take an interest in Italian culture. But on the whole, education in Northern Europe still remained, as in the Middle Ages, almost a monopoly of the clergy—as the use of the word "clerk" for anyone who could write shows in the case of England. The universities, though steadily increasing in numbers and size, still remained thoroughly medieval in organization and curriculum. They were the great fortress of the old learning and became favorite targets of humanist attacks on account of their barbarous Latinity, their sterile hair-splitting logic and their neglect of classical literature.

In spite of the growing attraction exerted by the new Italian culture on individual scholars and men of letters from Northern Europe, the driving force in Northern culture and education was not a purely literary one. It was still inspired by the religious ideas which had dominated medieval culture ever since the 11th century, though they no longer found their typical expression in the movement of monastic reform which had been so powerful in the age of St. Bernard or St. Francis.

During the later Middle Ages, this movement of religious reform in Northern Europe found a new center in the Netherlands where Gerhard Groote, a disciple of the great mystic Ruysbroeck, founded in 1381 a lay community known as "The Brethren of the Common Life". This institute devoted itself to teaching and the foundation of free schools. But some of the brethren also adopted the religious life in the traditional sense and founded the Augustinian priory at Windesheim, near Zwolle, which became the center of an

---

[3] Quoted from Denys Hays, *The Italian Renaissance* (New York: Cambridge University Press, 1961), p. 191.

active movement of monastic reform. These two related movements united to promote what was known as the *Devotio Moderna*, a form of spirituality which finds its classical expression in the famous *Imitation of Christ*, the work of a member of one of the monasteries of the Windesheim group, Thomas à Kempis. The author was a contemporary of Poggio and the great Italian humanists, but he shows no sympathy with the ideals of the new learning. He still adheres to the tradition of St. Bernard and William of Fécamp, which found its inspiration in evangelical pietism rather than in speculative mysticism. Yet it was equally opposed to the spirit of the old learning—to the intellectualism of the scholastic philosophers and the barren disputations of the later medieval universities.

Thus the New Devotion of the Brethren of the Common Life had something in common with the new learning, and the fact that their work was so largely concerned with education eventually brought them into relation with the humanists. The great precursor of the Renaissance in Northern Europe, Cardinal Nicholas of Cusa (c. 1400–1464), was himself a pupil of the Brothers of the Common Life, though he was too original and many-sided a spirit to be classified as a disciple of any school. He was both a great ecclesiastical reformer and a profound metaphysician, who combined a theological mysticism with the study of mathematics and physics somewhat in the tradition of Robert Grosseteste and the 13th-century Neo-Platonists. But he was also a student of the classics and a collector of ancient manuscripts, and he had a wide influence on the leaders of humanism and Christian reform in Northern Europe, such as Reuchlin in Germany, Lefèvre d'Etaples in France, and the circle of Dutch humanists who met at the priory of Adwerth near Groningen under the prior Henry of Rys (1449–1485). Among the members of this group were Wessel Gansfort, Rudolf Agricola, Rudolf von Langen and Alexander Hegius. It was through these men that the new learning was brought into relation with the educational work of the Brothers of the Common Life, for Alexander Hegius was the headmaster of their great school at Deventer from 1483 to 1498, and he had learned Greek from Rudolf Agricola (1443–1485) and became in turn the teacher of Mutianus Rufus and many other famous scholars, above all the great Erasmus of Rotterdam.

Erasmus, who was born probably in 1466, spent the first thirty years of his life in the schools of the Brethren of the Common Life and in the monastery of Steyn, which was part of the Windesheim congregation, so that he must be regarded as the most distinguished product of this tradition. It is true that he never admitted as much and showed little gratitude to his early teachers. He had no vocation for the monastic life and no sympathy for the medieval elements which still predominated in the schools of the Brethren. For he was essentially a man of letters and an individualist who valued his freedom and leisure above all else. He first found a really congenial atmosphere during his visits to England in 1499, 1505, and from 1509 to 1514, where he became an intimate member of the group of scholars and ecclesiastics, notably John Colet, Thomas More, Bishop John Fisher and Archbishop Warham, who were the patrons and pioneers of the new learning in England.

It was in these circles that the spirit of the Italian Renaissance came closest to the movement of religious reform in Northern Europe. For Colet had just visited Florence where he came into contact with Marsilio Ficino and the Platonic Academy; and the School of St. Paul's which he afterwards founded was an outstanding example of the same spirit which led the Brethren of the Common Life at Deventer to use the new learning in the service of the ideal of Christian education.

It was Colet who first inspired Erasmus with the ideal of devoting his scholarship to biblical and patristic studies, a program which was strengthened by his discovery at Louvain of a manuscript of the great humanist Lorenzo Valla's important *Adnotationes in Novum Testamentum,* and which was to bear fruit in his own epoch-making translation and Greek edition of the New Testament in 1516.

Thus Erasmus, the greatest humanist that Northern Europe had produced, became the exponent of a form of Christian Humanism very different from the contemporary humanism of Italy. This movement, which has been called "Biblical Humanism", sought the reform of religion by a return to the sources, above all to the New Testament in the original Greek, and secondly to the study of the writings of the Fathers of the Church. As the Italian humanists had made Classical Antiquity the pattern of culture and the only standard of literary and artistic merit, so now Erasmus and his friends and disciples set up the ideal of Christian Antiquity as its counterpart in the spiritual realm and made it the standard of moral and religious values.

Moreover they related the two ideals to one another by showing the moral elements in each and treating the one as a preparation for the other; so that the ancient philosophers, especially Plato, should serve as guides and heralds of the Gospel. Similarly in Christian antiquity Erasmus paid little attention to the study of dogma and concentrated his attention on the moral wisdom of the Gospel, what he called the *"philosophia Christi"*. And as the Italian humanists had poured scorn on the bad Latin and bad taste of the Middle Ages, so Erasmus directed his criticism against the Church—not only because it had substituted the metaphysical systems of the scholastics for the *philosophia Christi*, but even more because it had deserted the "golden simplicity" of evangelical teaching for a multiplicity of pious practices, the cult of saints and relics, and the proliferation of all kinds of special devotions, some of which were superstitious and all of which, so Erasmus thought, distracted the mind of Christians to what was nonessential.

Erasmus' teaching on these subjects had a very wide diffusion in the decades before the beginning of the Lutheran

Reformation, and made an impact on very influential circles, both at Rome and even more at the Court of Charles V, where some of Erasmus' most devoted followers were to be found both among the Burgundians and the Spaniards.

But the situation changed abruptly with the coming of the Reformation. Both by his appeal to Scripture and his depreciation of devotions and pious practices and monasticism, Erasmus seemed to have prepared the way for Luther; and many Catholics, above all at the Sorbonne and in the Spanish Inquisition, began to treat him as "the man who laid the egg that Luther hatched", or as a secret heretic, all the more dangerous because he was so plausible and moderate.

But it was soon evident that he was separated from the Reformers, and especially from Luther, by a very wide gap. It is true that Erasmus and Luther both spoke against the contemporary Catholic conception of good works, but this agreement was deceptive. For Erasmus' standpoint was essentially that of a moralist, whereas Luther stood for Faith only, against any kind of moralism. No doubt it is true that there are many currents in the Reformation that derive from Erasmus, especially perhaps those that were furthest from dogmatic orthodoxy, like the Anabaptists and the Socinians. At the same time it became evident that the sympathies of Erasmus were with the Catholics rather than with their opponents, not merely because he was a man of moderation who abhorred violence (and especially the violence of the theologians), but most of all because he was a humanist, even though a Christian humanist, and he was repelled by the anti-humanist element in Protestantism and especially its condemnation of free will and its denial of the possibility of natural virtue.

Nevertheless the influence of Erasmus is to be found everywhere, in both camps and outside them as well. As Professor Denys Hay has remarked, "We should remember that Melanchthon, Calvin and Ignatius Loyola, all prescribed in their schools the educational works of the Erasmus they all disliked and that the community of scholars over Europe as a whole was never stronger than it was between 1550 and 1700."[4] It is not that Erasmus was a profound thinker or a great theologian. His mind was like a broad and shallow river which is fed by many tributaries and fertilizes wide tracts of country on either bank. For he was concerned with a problem or series of problems that was of central importance for Western culture, and he solved it in terms that proved acceptable to men of good will on both sides of the theological frontier. The problem was the reconciliation of the new learning with the old religion, and Erasmus' solution was to develop a new Christian culture which would apply the new philological, historical and critical methods to the study of Christian antiquity. No doubt this was not peculiar to Erasmus. The same thing was being done at the same time or a little earlier by Cardinal Ximenes (1435–1517) at the new humanist university of Alcala. But it was Erasmus who was the great representative and publicist of Christian Humanism.[5] His books and his editions were read by everyone in every part of Europe, and the great renewal of Christian studies that took place in the later 16th and the 17th centuries and culminated in the work of Baronius and Petavius, Tillemont, the Maurists and the Bollandists, owed its inauguration to Erasmus more than any other single individual.

To recapitulate, I emphasize the importance of Erasmus because he seems to represent the meeting of the two great forces which changed Western culture in the 16th century: the revival of learning and the reformation of religion. If the two had developed independently, as for a time they tended to do, and if one movement had been associated with the

---

[4] *The Italian Renaissance*, p. 201.

[5] This was the Christian humanism of the scholars; there was also the Christian humanism of the poets which derived from the tradition of the Italian Renaissance more directly than from the Christian humanism of the North—from Bembo rather than Erasmus.

higher urban culture of Italy and the other with the medieval agrarian culture of Northern Europe, it would have had a disruptive effect on the unity of Western culture. Erasmus and his school drew the two movements together by formulating the ideal of a Christian humanism based on the critical study of the original texts—the Bible and the Fathers.

No doubt there were many other scholars besides Erasmus who contributed to this work. And in some respects Erasmus fails to represent the full scope of the two movements. He was not a poet or an artist, so he did not represent one of the most creative aspects of the Italian Renaissance, and he was not a saint or a mystic, so he did not represent the deepest element in the religious reform. In these respects a man like Giovanni Pico della Mirandola in Italy surpassed him; yet Pico (even if he had lived longer) could not have created the Erasmian synthesis, because he did not possess the latter's breadth of scholarship and power of criticism which alone made the meeting of the two movements possible. Erasmus was also defective from the point of view of the Reformers, because he was a moralist rather than a theologian. But it was in morals rather than theology that the two movements could find common ground. Here he was the source of the humanitarian and liberal tradition which was to play such a great part in the history of modern Europe. No doubt, as the modern world has discovered, humanitarianism and liberalism are no substitute for religion. But a religious culture that takes no account of them, as was too often the case in the 16th century, is also a very imperfect thing. The great blot on Western culture in the 15th and 16th centuries was the cruelty of its laws, and neither the Catholics nor the Protestants (still less the Orthodox in Russia) were fully alive to this great evil. It was the Christian Humanists, especially those of the North and West, like Erasmus and Vives, who first aroused the conscience of the educated classes to these issues.

III. ITALY AND RENAISSANCE SCIENCE

The victorious advance of the Renaissance culture was considerably retarded by the religious revolution represented by Martin Luther. The effect of the German Reformation was to absorb men's thoughts and energies in religious questions and produce a distrust of the human reason. It was in fact, as Troeltsch has said, a return to medieval ways of thinking, which produced a renewed domination of the medieval spirit for two centuries. At the same time, civilization and economic prosperity in Italy suffered a setback owing to the Turkish conquest of the Levant, the change in the trade routes and above all the great wars of the early 16th century, which caused the loss of national independence. The resultant pessimism and disillusion find expression in the thought of Machiavelli. He realized the contradiction between Italy's cultural superiority and her political weakness, and felt that spiritual achievement without a foundation of material power is doomed to failure. To him national unity in the modern sovereign state was the one thing necessary, for the sake of which every moral and religious consideration must be sacrificed, and he therefore abolished the union between ethics and politics, which, at least in theory, had dominated medieval thought.

Other men, however, drew a different moral from his premises. If Force is the only right in the world of politics, it is hopeless to oppose the ideal of national liberty to the fact of Spanish power. A wise man will accept the world as it is, and adapt himself to realities. This was the ordinary solution of Renaissance Italy.

Italian culture thus lost its political independence, but gained in cosmopolitan influence, as the culture of ancient Greece had done after the Macedonian conquest. As in the Hellenistic age, men turned away from civic life to the world of science and thought. It was the age of mathematicians like Tartaglian and Cardan, of botanists like Cesalpino, of physiologists such as Vesalius and Fabricio of Acquapendente, of philosophers like Telesio and Giordano Bruno. It is true that scientific thought was active throughout Europe in the 16th century, as is shown by such men as Copernicus and Paracelsus, Tycho Brahe and Vieta, and later on Bacon, Kepler, Harvey and Gilbert. But all of them owed much to the influence of the Italian culture. Some, like Harvey and Copernicus, studied in Italy, the Belgian Vesalius spending his life there. Even the greatest of them, however, remained medieval in spirit.

It was only in Italy that the modern scientific attitude of mind was in the ascendant in the 16th century, and it was there that the first attempt was made to provide a new scientific theory of the universe in place of the orthodox Aristotelian cosmology. But here no less than in literature and art, the influence of classical antiquity was still paramount. The Renaissance thinkers did not reject Aristotle on the strength of their own discoveries, they invoked the higher authority of Aristotle's predecessors—Plato and Pythagoras—against that of Aristotle himself. The sources of the new movement in science and thought are to be found primarily in the Platonic revival of Marsilio Ficino and the Academy of Florence. To them was due the revival of the Platonic-Pythagorean idea of the world as an orderly mathematical or geometrical harmony, the exteriorization of the intelligible order of the Divine Mind, a belief which Copernicus received from his Italian teacher, Domenico Maria da Novara. Thus the Pythagorean mysticism of Kepler, which appears to the modern mind so incongruous with his positive scientific discoveries, was in reality the intellectual foundation and inspiration of his whole work.

Telesio, "the first of the new men", as Baur calls him, conceived nature in terms of matter and force. Bruno, the most original thinker of the new age, was the first to comprehend the full significance of the discovery of Copernicus. Whereas the latter, in spite of his teaching as to the movement of the earth, still held the old view of a fixed stellar sphere that bounded the universe, Bruno taught that the material universe was infinite and that the fixed stars were the suns of planetary systems like our own, uncountable in number and infinite in extent. He viewed nature as a living unity, whose body was atomic matter and whose soul was God the universal substance. Hence there was no room for human immortality, or divine interposition in nature. All was natural and all was divine. Liberty and necessity were identical.

But in spite of his genius and his brilliant intuitions in astronomy, Bruno was essentially a mystic, not a scientist. The real father of modern science, to a greater extent than Copernicus, and the founder of modern physics and dynamics, was the Florentine Galileo dei Galilei, who was from 1592 to 1610 Professor of Mathematics at Padua, the greatest center of scientific studies in Europe, where Vesalius and Fabricio of Acquapendente also taught, and William Harvey, the discoverer of the circulation of the blood, studied from 1598 to 1602. Galileo was a great experimental scientist, the discoverer of the thermometer and the law of acceleration of falling bodies, the first to utilize the possibilities of the telescope. His popular fame rests on his work as practical astronomer and his condemnation by the Inquisition in 1633, but it is as a theorist and as the founder of the great scientific thesis, which is the physical background to all modern thought from the 17th to the 19th centuries, that his importance is greatest. In his four *Dialogues on the Two Systems of the World*, the Aristotelian and the modern cosmologies are at last openly confronted with one another. Without Galileo, the work of Newton is inconceivable, and it was he who accomplished the application of mathematics to physics.

"Philosophy", he says, "is written in the great book of the Universe which lies always open. But we must first understand the language and the characters in which it is written. That language is Mathematics. Its characters are circles, triangles and other geometric figures without which we cannot, humanly speaking, understand the words, and wander aimlessly through a dark labyrinth."

This mathematical view of physics had indeed been taught four centuries earlier by Grosseteste and the Franciscan School at Oxford, Adam Marsh and Roger Bacon, the Dominican Kilwardby, and in Silesia Witelo. These men laid down the principles on which fruitful scientific research must be conducted and thus, in Professor Crombie's words, "created the experimental science of modern times". But although they applied this scientific method in several fields, notably to optics and the study of magnetism, they were, as Professor Crombie points out, far more interested in scientific methodology for its own sake than in its application to concrete problems.[6] It was therefore left to the scientists of the later Renaissance to begin the triumphant advance of scientific knowledge which has gathered momentum ever since and has revolutionized human knowledge and control of nature.

It was only those qualities in nature that are susceptible of mathematical treatment that appeared to Galileo truly real. All those sensible qualities of color, odor and sound, which mean so much to man, have no place in the colorless, soundless world of quantity and motion which for him is the ultimate reality. They are mere names—subjective impressions which vanish, when the observer is removed. Galileo's distinction between the primary and secondary qualities, and the mathematical view of nature on which it was based, were ultimately to lead to an entirely new view of the universe. Man lost his central position as the link between the higher reality of spirit and the lower reality of matter. He became an unimportant adjunct—an external spectator of the closed mechanical order which is the real world. Galileo's successor, Descartes, tried to save the world of human values and of

[6] See A. C. Crombie, *Robert Grosseteste and the Origins of Experimental Science, 1100–1700* (New York: Oxford University Press, 1964); especially Chapter XI.

spiritual reality by his strict philosophical dualism of extended matter and unextended, thinking spirit—*res extensa* and *res cogitans*. But the ultimate effect of the new view of the world was rather to consider the subjective world of the human mind as less real than the objective world of purely quantitative relations and hence to conclude that man himself, both in body and mind, is a by-product of the vast mechanical order, which the new science had revealed. Save for a few exceptional thinkers like Hobbes, it was not until the 18th century that this final step was taken, but it was implicit in the Galilean world view from the beginning.

It is probable that even the Inquisition which condemned Galileo had no inkling of the revolutionary effects of his new theory. Both his opponents and his admirers looked primarily at his positive achievements in astronomy. But though our own age is beginning to realize the limitations of this view, we must remember that it rendered possible the creation of the scientific civilization of modern Europe.

The work of Galileo was hailed by his contemporary, Campanella, as the crowning achievement of Italian culture. "Scrivi nel principio", he writes, "che questa filosofia è d'Italia." For the mind of Campanella himself was dominated by the belief that the new science of nature marked a turning point in the history of mankind. And his strange career—at once friar, philosopher and revolutionary—manifests, even more than that of Galileo, the tragic contrast between the boundless intellectual ambition and the utter practical frustration that marks the later Italian Renaissance. In his wonderful Canone of The Power of Man, Campanella gives unrivalled expression to the central idea of the Renaissance culture— the apotheosis of Humanity. He believed that vast possibilities were on the verge of practical fulfillment. "Men go through greed of wealth to seek new lands, but God intends higher ends." The new heaven and the new earth of Copernicus and Columbus are the prelude to the union of the human race and the renewal of all things. In his "City of the Sun", he sets forth his conception of the new order, a theocracy in which there is neither property nor marriage, where every man works four hours a day and sexual relations are regulated by the state on purely eugenic principles. His wild attempt, like that of Aristonicus of Eunus in the second century B.C., to found his Heliopolis in Calabria, with the aid of the Turks and the dispossessed, led to his betrayal to the Spaniards and his imprisonment under terrible hardships for thirty years. By degrees his sufferings led him to abandon his revolutionary hopes. "Since God is silent and acquiesces," he writes in a terrible line, "be thou silent and acquiesce."

But he never gave up his faith in the coming union of humanity. He devoted the later years of his imprisonment to the construction of a great philosophical synthesis which was to reconcile the new science of nature with Catholic theology. He came to look on the Church and the great Catholic powers, first Spain, and afterwards France, as the destined instruments for the introduction of the new order, and his last work, written at Paris in 1639, just before his own death, is a Messianic Eclogue on the birth of Louis XIV.

But the spirit of the age was hostile to all such visionary hopes. The development of the new science continued, but without entering into any complete union with the mental life of the time, which was dominated by the purely religious currents of the Reformation and the Counter-Reformation.

IV

MARTIN LUTHER
AND THE CALL TO REVOLT

THE Reformation is the name we give to the great religious revolution of the 16th century which destroyed the unity of medieval Christendom and created a new Europe of sovereign States and separated Churches which endured with little change down to the French Revolution. This religious catastrophe was implicit in the later medieval development. It came because the existence of a united international society under the authority and leadership of the Church was inconsistent with the new temporal order as expressed in the States and national monarchies. The inevitable conflict between Church and State could lead only to disorder. In particular, the anomalous position of the bishop as an important functionary in both societies led to the secularization of the Church and to an accumulation of abuses which neither Church nor State was able to remedy, owing to the confusion of persons and jurisdictions.

The hierarchical system of the medieval church had broken down, and no one was strong enough or courageous enough to carry out the drastic reforms that were necessary. Everyone was agreed in theory on the main evils: first, pluralism or the accumulation of ecclesiastical benefices in the hands of one man and the non-residence which was the direct result of this; secondly, simony or the dependence of ecclesiastical appointments and spiritual privileges on money; thirdly, the neglect of the canonical rule for episcopal visitations and diocesan synods; and fourthly, the low standard of clerical education and the religious ignorance of the laity.

In Northern Europe, especially in Germany, the bishops had ceased to be the heads of the local Christian Churches and had become great territorial magnates whose power extended over whole provinces and kingdoms. Since they were sovereign princes, their Sees became prizes that were eagerly sought after by the princely dynasties in Germany, while in England and France they were used by the king as rewards for his ministers and civil servants.

Throughout Northern Europe the bishops were both too few and too rich, too deeply involved in political activities and too neglectful of their spiritual duties. One of the most eminent English bishops of the early 16th century admitted these shortcomings when he spoke of "my cure wherein I have been almost by the space of thirty years so negligent that of four several cathedral churches that I have successively had, there are two—Exeter and Wells—that I never see and innumerable souls whereof I never see the bodies."[1]

These abuses would not have been so serious if the religious Orders of monks and friars had been as active as they had once been. Now, however, the greater abbeys had become primarily great landowning corporations, and the position of abbot, like that of bishop, had become a privilege conferred on the favorites of popes and kings, some of whom, especially in France, were not monks or even clerics. Practically the only Orders that had maintained their primitive ideals were the Carthusians among the monks, and the Observantines, the followers of the Franciscan reform of St. Bernardine, among the friars.

In theory the medieval Church possessed a remedy for all these abuses in its highly developed system of canon law and in the supreme authority of the Papacy which had the power to appoint suitable bishops and to see that they carried out their ministry effectively.

Unfortunately, the Papacy, largely through its own fault, no longer possessed the power or the reforming spirit that had characterized it from Gregory VII to Innocent III. During

---

[1] *Letters of Richard Fox*, ed. Allen, pp. 92ff.

the 15th century it had become profoundly secularized and deeply involved in secular politics, above all in the power politics of the Italian States. Its nominal omnipotence was in practice limited, on the one hand by the need to cooperate with the growing power of the sovereign state which everywhere demanded a large share in the control of ecclesiastical appointments and ecclesiastical revenues, and on the other by the need to conciliate the ecclesiastical oligarchy which controlled the collusion of the episcopal authorities with the secular power.

Finally the canon law had ceased to be an instrument of reform, since the Church courts and canon lawyers had themselves become the organs of vested interests which culminated in the Roman Curia and would prove the most formidable of all the obstacles to the cause of reform.

It was in Germany that these disorders were at their worst, because it possessed no central power and no principle of national unity such as the new monarchies provided in France and England. Germany was a political jungle—a tangled mass of jurisdictions and institutions in which both Church and State were inextricably involved. The medieval Holy Roman Empire still existed—the most venerable political institution of the West—and was surrounded more than any other monarchy by a halo of divine right and sacred authority. It still enjoyed immense prestige and evoked a quasi-religious sentiment of loyalty. But it was bound by the cumbrous archaic institutions of the early Middle Ages and failed to develop into a sovereign state of the new pattern, like France, Spain or England. If the Emperor were left to his own resources, he was little more than the figurehead of an immense disunited body; if he possessed real power, like Charles V, this was due to his non-German possessions, but if he used these external resources to assert his authority in the Empire, he was liable to arouse the national resistance of the German people which was none the less strong for its lack of political organization.

Under the Emperor there were the seven electors—ecclesiastical and lay. Under the electors were the princes—dukes and bishops and prince-abbots. Under the princes were the free cities and knights and counts—all of whom were independent rulers in their own little provinces, which were often no larger than the estates of an English squire. At the bottom of the social pyramid were the peasants, who carried the whole economic burden of the edifice on their shoulders, but who possessed no means of political expression.

Thus more than any country in Europe, Germany was in a potentially revolutionary situation. Peasants, knights and princes were all discontented; yet their discontent could find no outlet because the Empire itself had not the power to make any effective change in the situation, since it was fettered by the elaborate restrictions of its unworkable constitution.

In this confused situation the position of the Church was peculiarly vulnerable. The German people were very conscious of their Christian heritage. They saw the Empire as an essentially Christian society, the very center and heart of Christendom, and consequently they looked to the Church for help and guidance in their spiritual and social needs. Yet it was the Church which was the chief obstacle standing in the way of the creation of a strong and united national state or indeed of any political reform. The princes, who were the strongest and most active element in Germany, were for the most part still too weak or too lacking in economic resources to create independent states after the Western pattern. It is therefore not surprising that they cast their eyes on the neighboring bishoprics and abbeys which were exempt from their authority and yet possessed so large a proportion of the lands and wealth of Germany. But the privileges of the Church were supported by the constitution of the Empire and the authority of the Papacy, and what did the most to arouse the resentment of the secular rulers was the fact that a non-German power was able to use its spiritual prerogatives to draw resources from the German Church.

This national resentment against the Italian Papacy and the desire of the princes to solve their economic and political problems at the expense of the Church were the material motives and forces that brought about the Reformation, not only in Germany where they operated most strongly, but throughout Northern Europe, first in Sweden and Denmark and the Baltic lands, and later in England and Scotland. But the Reformation that they brought about was not a reformation of the Church but rather a reformation of the medieval state at the expense of the Church. The religious reformation had its independent origins, and the two movements were brought together by the ineluctable forces of history on two different planes.

Nevertheless it is impossible to exaggerate the extent to which religion and politics and culture were involved with one another in the German revolution. The religious leaders like Luther may have sought religion and nothing else, but they, even more than the others, were carried away by the stream of history which drew everything together in a revolutionary crisis. This crisis had been preparing from the beginning of the century. Then from the Diet of Worms in 1521 to the Diet of Augsburg in 1530, the tempo was continually increased until it ended in a general collision of forces after 1546.

It must be admitted that *viewed externally* the German Reformation was above all the work of the princes, and a more worthless collection of individuals has never controlled the fate of mankind. Yet the German people were profoundly religious, and there existed a comparatively large educated class which provided the audience for the immense pamphlet literature which was such a characteristic feature of the age. During the later Middle Ages, Western and Central Germany had acquired some fourteen universities. For the princes, for all their barbarism, made it a point of prestige to have each his own university in his territory.

Thus men of almost every class from nobles to peasants

were able to acquire a free education, and though the standard was not very high, it provided at least a knowledge of Latin and a training in scholastic disputation. In addition there was a small but growing class of German humanists, who had acquired some knowledge of the new learning in Italy, and who frequented the courts, especially the imperial court, and the more wealthy cities like Nuremberg and Strasbourg, rather than the universities.

Typical of this new intelligentsia was Ulrich von Hutten, a young noble of the knightly class who had been a wandering scholar at the German universities and a mercenary soldier in Italy, where he had come into relation with the humanists and the friends of Erasmus. He is remarkable as the first spokesman of that extreme romantic German nationalism which exalted the good old German ideals of liberty, courage and honor, and regarded foreign, and especially Italian, influence as the source of every evil. In this, no doubt, he was expressing the ideals of his class, the Imperial Knighthood, which looked back to the united Empire of the past and gloried in its traditions of legalized anarchy and the right of private war. But Hutten was even more deeply affected by the new German humanism. He had taken a leading part in the war of the humanists against the theologians in defence of Reuchlin, as one of the authors of the *Letters of Obscure Men*, the most successful satire against the old learning and the friars, and he had edited Valla's treatise on the forged Donation of Constantine, in the preface to which he attacked the Papacy as the great enemy of German liberty.

But though Ulrich von Hutten was a brilliant writer, he was not destined to play a leading part in German history. His importance is rather as a symptom of the revolutionary situation of the time. He was essentially a revolutionary who saw the Papacy and the Church as the obvious targets of attack. But his motives were political and nationalist, not religious.

Martin Luther, on the other hand, came from a very different world, and it was Martin Luther, not Erasmus the humanist nor Hutten the revolutionary, whose coming marks the beginning of the new world age. Martin Luther was a man of the people and a man of the Middle Ages, who owed little to the new intellectual influences of the Renaissance culture. His development was determined not by humanism, but by his own personal spiritual and psychological conflicts. He was the son of a Thuringian miner of peasant stock, but he was well-educated and had already got his degree at Erfurt University when he entered the order of Augustinian Friars at the age of twenty-one in 1505. Eight years later, when he was almost thirty, he became Professor of Holy Scripture at the recently founded University of Wittenberg, and it was during the next years—from 1513 to 1517—that he developed the new theological ideas which were to be the inspiration of his later career. Like the humanists he reacted violently against the decadent scholasticism in which he had been educated—the tradition of the later Ockhamists and Gabriel Biel—and appealed to a purely scriptural theology—the Pauline theology of the Epistles to the Romans and the Galatians above all, which he interpreted in a new way.

But it was not these ideas, revolutionary though they were, that were the secret of Luther's power; it was the man himself. Luther was undoubtedly a genius, a man of titanic power and energy, who combined to an extraordinary degree the vernacular eloquence of the demagogue with the religious conviction of the prophet. He knew how to speak to "his" Germans in language which the common man could understand, and at the same time he could speak with conviction and profundity of the deepest mysteries of the Christian faith. Yet these great gifts were counterbalanced by equally great defects. His violent and passionate temperament could brook no contradiction, and in every controversy he would overwhelm his opponents with the grossness and obscenity of an infuriated peasant. And secondly, all that is best in his writings springs directly from his subjective personal experience. He recognized no truths except those which he felt and saw directly by an immediate act of psychological intuition. In comparison with this nothing else mattered. The authority of the Church, the witness of tradition, the religious experience of others, the dogmas of the theological schools, counted for nothing or less than nothing when they did not agree with his personal intuitions and convictions. This makes his teaching more subjective and one-sided than that of any other Christian thinker. What he saw, he saw with blinding intensity and certitude. What he did not see did not exist, or was the delusion of Satan. For Satan was very real and close to him, and all his life, in all his conflicts, external and internal, he felt himself to be God's champion against the devil, who in a thousand shapes was plotting his destruction.

The study of Luther is beset with many difficulties. First the amount of his writings; secondly their unsystematic character—all his writings except his Bible and Catechism are occasional and controversial; thirdly, his love of paradox and simplification to drive home his point. (Afterwards, however, he may use extreme subtlety and far-fetched argument to justify the paradox.)

His strength always lay in his subjectivism—the assertion of the rights of conscience, the assurance of the individual's faith, and the right of every man to interpret Scripture for himself. At the beginning the full extent of Luther's alienation from the Church's teaching was not obvious. It was in 1516 that he began to teach clearly his new doctrine of a subjective faith in Christ's redemption without regard to good works. The indulgence controversy in the following year gave him the opportunity to develop and publish his ideas. The two key points of difference between Luther and the Church which came to light in his *Commentary on Romans* in 1516 were (a) the concept of sin and (b) the issue of good works and free will.

For Luther sin is passion, for Catholicism sin is in the will—the act of choice. In Freudian terms Luther's sin is libido, Catholic sin is ego. From this a number of conse-

quences flow. From the Lutheran point of view the conclusion follows that, as nobody is ever entirely passionless (least
of all essentially passionate types like Luther), there can be no
freedom from sin in this world. Man is born and dies in
iniquity. The utmost he can attain is an assurance that this
won't be counted against him—that Christ's redemptive suffering covers all. Hence justice is only *imputed*—the Lutheran
concept which became the center of controversy.

In Catholic teaching, on the other hand, the work of
justification is not limited to the act of faith with which it
begins. It is carried on by the use of the sacraments, the life
of charity and the practice of good works, so that human
nature recovers the spiritual life that was lost by sin and man
becomes a new creature, not by an external act of imputation
but by the appropriation of divine grace—by sanctifying
grace, which is the technical theological term.

Thus there is a difference between Lutheran and Catholic
teaching as regards good works and free will. Luther says that
good works do not make a good man, or evil works a bad
man, but that the good man does good works and the
bad man does evil. This is psychologically true, but it does not
cover the whole ground. The ordinary man is not wholly
good or wholly bad. He is both. He does good acts and bad
acts, and it is psychologically false to argue that his character
is not affected by good or evil practice. Thus it is also true to
say that good habits make a man good and bad habits make
him bad. This second fact was ignored or underestimated by
Luther. It seems that there is a certain confusion in his thought
on these matters. He had become convinced of the worth-
lessness of pious practices—that it is no use fasting or saying
long prayers or making a pilgrimage or a vow. Good works,
however, are not merely pious practices, they are simply what
the words denote—doing good—and it is a fallacy to argue
that such action has no value from a religious point of view.
Luther himself argues that whatever is done in faith is good,
even if it is just the course of the day's business, but if the

assurance of faith is absent, the work is bad however good it may be objectively. Thus there is a tendency to antinomianism in Luther's teaching which, after his controversies with the Anabaptists, he attempted to guard against, but not altogether successfully.

Luther had chosen his ground well by his denunciation of the Indulgence preached by John Tetzel in 1517. His original view of indulgences, as shown in a sermon that he published in 1516, was completely orthodox; and what aroused him to indignation, in common with many faithful Catholics, was the shameless way in which this particular Indulgence was being misused by the Curia and the Archbishop of Mainz to satisfy their financial needs. But when he was once launched on the controversy he was unable to restrain himself from giving utterance to his revolutionary ideas. And the opposition that he encountered at Rome and in Germany led him on, even before his condemnation at Rome, to the final break with the Papacy and the whole tradition of medieval Catholicism which is expressed in the great pamphlets of 1520, "The Appeal to the Christian Nobility of the German Nation", "The Babylonian Captivity of the Church", and "The Freedom of a Christian Man".

Even before the appearance of these famous writings, he had already, in his replies to Alveldt and Prierias "On the Papacy at Rome", taken up his final position against the Papacy. He had asserted that the true Church is a purely spiritual kingdom that has nothing to do with the hierarchy or the Roman Papacy—which was, on the contrary, "The Anti-Christ of whom the whole Scripture speaks and the Roman Curia nothing but the Synagogue of Satan". Yet only two months before this, in his letter to the Pope (which was never sent), he was writing in most effusive terms of his efforts for the honor of the Apostolic See and his conviction that "there is nothing in Heaven or Earth to be preferred to her excepting our own Lord Jesus Christ".

Thus Luther's final break with Rome was very sudden

and was not fully recognized until the publication of the three great Reformation writings in the autumn of 1520. The first of these—"The Appeal to the Christian Nobility of the German Nation"—was perhaps the most effective of all his polemical writings. For it appeals with burning eloquence to the two revolutionary forces that were so strong in Germany at the moment—to the longstanding grievances of Germany against Rome and the anti-clerical feelings of the nobility against the clergy. These feelings had found expression, while he was writing, in the Knights' War, the leaders of which, Franz von Sickingen and Ulrich von Hutten, were among his warmest supporters.

There is, I believe, no doubt that, even if Luther had not come forward, there would have been a Reformation. But it might have had a very different character. It might have centered in Switerland and been Zwinglian in type, or it might have been Anabaptist. It was owing to Luther that it had its center in the far north of Saxony (rather on the outskirts of civilization). If it had centered in the West, in the cities of the Rhine and the south, it would have had a different character.

On the other hand, Carlstadt, one of the leading Reformers, came from Wittenberg too, was older than Luther, and adopted similar ideas. His conversion was due to a visit to Rome in 1515, and on his return he began to speak against Free Will and Good Works; and all over Germany, in these years, new preachers arose almost instantaneously. One must conclude, therefore, that the situation was explosive and Luther set a match to it.

In the "Appeal" Luther passes judgment on theological first principles—above all on the doctrine of the priesthood of the laity. He maintained that all Christians are equal. There is no real distinction between the temporal and spiritual orders. Priests and bishops are merely functionaries of the Christian society and possess no inherent power of jurisdiction. All power belongs to the magistrate who is just as much a functionary of the Christian body as the priest. And if the

Church requires reform, it is for the magistrate to use his power for the service of the whole Christian society so that the Word of God may triumph. It is not for the clergy alone to decide what should be done. The Word of God and the Scriptures are the common possession of all faithful Christians. Pope and Cardinals may go astray, but a little man may have a right understanding of the Scriptures, and then it is our duty to follow him.

Finally, in his treatise "On the Freedom of a Christian Man", Luther unveils his fundamental beliefs on the power of faith and the valuelessness of works so that the man of faith is the spiritual lord of all. "For what can harm such a heart or cause it to fear? Should sin or death befall, it simply believes that Christ's righteousness is its own, its sin not its own but Christ's, and then sin disappears before faith in the Righteousness of Christ. With the Apostle it learns to defy death and sin and say, 'O Death, where is thy sting?'"

The consequences of these doctrines are drawn out in two further works—*The Babylonian Captivity of the Church*, which is directed against Catholic sacramental teaching and denies the validity of the sacrament of Orders and the Sacrifice of the Mass; and the *De Votis Monasticis*, which was written a year later and seeks to show that monasticism is irreconcilable with his doctrine of faith and with the liberty of a Christian man, since it binds on him the heavy and insupportable burden of celibacy as well as countless other external works from which faith has set man free.

All these works, except the last, were written before Luther's final break with the Church and found a wide response from one end of Germany to the other, among clerics and scholars, nobles and men of the people. For the first time in history the power of the press made itself manifest, for this was the great age of German printing, and famous printers (like Frobenius at Basel) put their presses at the service of the new doctrine.

On the Catholic side, the resistance was at first extraordinarily weak. The bishops, who had so heavy a responsibility for the state in which the German Church found itself, did scarcely anything to meet the situation. For the most part they seem to have been weak, worldly, well-meaning prelates who did not understand the seriousness of the issues and who were chiefly anxious to safeguard their temporal rights and privileges; they looked to the secular authorities to deal with the new situation. On the secular side, the Emperor Charles, almost alone, knew his own mind and was resolved to do his duty towards the Church. He was a slow, silent, conscientious Burgundian who had little sympathy or understanding for his German subjects. But he spoke his mind clearly at Worms in 1521 and was strong enough to force the Diet to accept the papal bull against Luther and to pass a Sentence of Outlawry against him in spite of the resistance of Luther's supporters. But beyond this he could do nothing. He was preoccupied with the revolt in Spain, the war with France, and the prospect of a political breach with the Papacy. Immediately after the Diet of Worms he retreated to Spain and remained there for the next seven years—during which the progress of Lutheranism in Germany was almost unchecked.

At first the situation was by no means hopeless from the Catholic point of view, for Charles V's tutor, Adrian of Utrecht, a pious and conscientious reformer, was elected pope at the beginning of the next year (1522), and there was every reason to believe that a serious program of ecclesiastical reform would be undertaken by the joint action of Pope and Emperor. If the Council of Trent had met in 1525 instead of 1545, the history of Europe and the church would have been different. Unfortunately Adrian VI died in 1523, and his successor, Clement VII, left Germany to shift for itself while he pursued his course of Italian power politics, a policy which found its disastrous end in 1527 when Rome was sacked by the Lutheran mercenaries of the Catholic Emperor.

Meanwhile Germany was in a state of anarchy—the knights rose against the ecclesiastical princes in 1522, the peasants rose against the nobles in 1524, the Turks conquered Hungary in 1526, and threatened Germany itself until they were turned back at the gates of Vienna in 1529. In all this turmoil there was no question of executing the Edict of Worms; on the contrary, the forces of Protestantism became every year stronger and more self-conscious, especially in the Free Cities of the Empire and the Hanse towns of the Baltic. In the course of these years almost all accepted the new doctrine, abolishing the Mass, secularizing the monasteries, and establishing a new Church polity.

Martin Luther meanwhile had made his appeal to the nation against the Papacy in his *Appeal to the Christian Nobility of the German Nation*. In it he had come very close to the overt revolutionary propaganda which Ulrich von Hutten was pouring forth at the same period, notably in Hutten's *Vadiscus or the Roman Trinity*. Luther's enforced retirement at the Wartburg, under the disguise of Junker Georg, from 1521 to 1522, marks the break between his life as a reforming preacher within the Church and his new career as the founder of the anti-papal and anti-episcopal evangelical Churches. It was at this time that he broke entirely with monasticism and began to advocate the secularization and marriage of monks and nuns; a matter which was not of purely ecclesiastical importance, since it was by Luther's advice that the Grand Master of the Teutonic Knights in Prussia, Albert of Brandenburg, secularized the property of his Order and made himself hereditary Duke of Prussia, thus creating the first Protestant State. Luther had now gone too far to be affected by the coming of Pope Adrian or by the latter's proposals for a reforming council. Indeed, he attacked the new Pope even more bitterly than Leo X.

At the same time he broke with Erasmus, who had been alienated both from him and Ulrich von Hutten since 1520. Erasmus was continually being urged by his Catholic friends and patrons to write against Luther. Yet for a long time he was unwilling to do so. Luther also wished to avoid a direct conflict with Erasmus, whose pen he feared. Yet the letter that he wrote to Erasmus in April 1524, which was at once patronizing and menacing—bidding him keep away from matters which he did not understand if he wished for a peaceful old age—must have offended the old scholar bitterly and made the clash between them inevitable. But Erasmus chose his ground carefully, when he finally entered the lists in the autumn of 1524. He did not deal with Luther's more obviously anti-Catholic ideas, but concentrated his attack on Luther's condemnation of free will, a doctrine which offended the humanists no less than the Catholics.

But the studied moderation of Erasmus' criticism did more than any controversial violence to make Luther reveal the full nature of his convictions on this fundamental theological issue. His *De Servo Arbitrio* ("On the Enslaved Will") is a much larger work than Eramus' pamphlet. It is perhaps the most powerful and closely knit of all his theological writings. Yet nothing did more to break down the bridges between the reformers and the moderates and to give the impression that the Reformation had already given birth to a new dogmatism more inflexible and exclusive than the old.

Yet the controversy—the fundamental issue of human freedom and divine grace—need not have become such a stumbling block in the way of understanding and unity. The Protestants were indeed all Augustinians, but so were most Catholics also. The sovereignty of divine grace was equally admitted by both parties. But the way in which Luther asserted the doctrine amounted to a total denial of any kind of human freedom whatever and antagonized not only the humanists, but also the Catholic Augustinians and even some of his own followers like Melanchthon, who had some sympathy with Eramus. Luther's reply to Erasmus is most characteristic of his controversial style at its best. But it aims at overwhelming rather than convincing his opponent.

"Who, you say, will endeavor to amend his life? I answer, no man! No man can! For your self-amenders without the

Spirit, God regardeth not, they are hypocrites. But the Elect and those that fear God will be amended by the Holy Spirit, the rest shall perish unamended. Who will believe, you say, that he is the loved of God? I answer, No man will believe it. No man can! But the Elect will believe it; the rest shall perish without believing it, filled with indignation and blasphemy as you here describe them." [2]

Yet Erasmus himself had not been arguing for Pelagianism but in favor of moderation in controversy. He wrote, "It is from the collision of such excesses that the lightnings and thunder arise which today violently shake the earth. And if each side continues to defend its exaggerations so bitterly, I foresee such a struggle between them as that between Achilles and Hector, who since they were so equal in savagery could only be separated by death."

In fact, in spite of the strength of Luther's arguments, and their subsequent reinforcement by Calvin, they could not prevail in the long run against Erasmus' appeal to reason and moderation. As the modern English translators[3] of Luther's great treatise remark, "Modern Protestantism is Erasmian, not Lutheran"; and we can trace the continuity of the Erasmian tradition through Arminius, who was an Erasmian, to John Wesley, who gloried in the name of Arminian.

---

[2] *The Bondage of the Will*, trans. J. I. Packer and O. R. Johnston (New York: Revell, 1957).

[3] Ibid.

V

THE REVOLUTION OF THE PRINCES

WHILE Luther was in retirement at the Wartburg, and Charles V was grappling with his manifold difficulties in Spain and Italy, Germany and the German Reformation were left temporarily leaderless, and the centrifugal and revolutionary forces were everywhere dominant. At Wittenberg Luther's place was taken for a time by his old partner Carlstadt, who was now far more radical than Luther himself and welcomed the advent of even more extreme reformers, "the prophets" from Zwickau, who shared the ideas of Thomas Münzer and declared themselves to be inspired directly by the Holy Spirit.

This extremist movement spread rapidly through Saxony and proved to be the forerunner of the great Anabaptist movement which extended from Switerland to Holland and became the source of the main tradition of popular sectarian Protestantism. From the first it combined several different elements. On the one hand it represented the extremists and the enthusiasts who readily allied themselves with the forces of social revolution and who resorted to violence to purge the Church of image worship and monasticism. But on the other hand it appealed to the mystics and spiritual reformers like Denck, Sebastian Frank and Schwenkfeld, who were enemies of violence and had more in common with Erasmus than Luther.

These new tendencies were already manifested while Luther was at the Wartburg, by Münzer and Carlstadt respectively, and in the following years of unrest they spread with extraordinary rapidity throughout the German lands.

In 1523 Luther returned to Wittenberg and used his influence, both with the Elector of Saxony and with the clergy and people at Wittenberg and Erfurt, to restrain the extremists and to reassure the moderates who had been alarmed and shocked by the proceedings of Carlstadt and his followers. He began to write forcibly on the duty of obedience to the constituted authorities and the evil of rebellion, teaching which he was to repeat even more strongly in the following years when the great Peasants' Revolt broke out.

At the time there were many who regarded Luther as the instigator of these disturbances, and it is easy to understand how they came to do so in view of the violence of his language and the threatening way in which he often spoke of the coming of revolution. Thus he wrote to the Elector of Saxony in 1522: "It has been revealed to me lately that not the spiritual power only, but also the temporal rulers, will have to submit to the Gospel either through love or through force, as is clearly proved by all biblical history. And though at first I did not apprehend a national rebellion, but thought only of a revolt against the priesthood, I fear now that the disturbances may begin against the ruling powers and spread like a plague to the priesthood." [1]

Luther's personal position was a very difficult one. Although he was a theological revolutionary, he was socially a conservative, loyal to his emperor and his prince and temperamentally averse to any kind of social revolution. Yet he saw his ideas adopted by all the subversive elements in Germany—knights, peasants, and religious enthusiasts, and his opponents reproached him for having started the conflagration that burnt out in the terrible social upheaval of the War of the Peasants. As he wrote, "How often did my heart faint with fear and reproach me thus: 'You wanted to be wise before all others. Are then all others in these countless multitudes mistaken? Have so many centuries all been in the wrong? Supposing you were mistaken, and owing to your mistake

---

[1] Johannes Janssen, *History of the German People*, Vol. III, p. 268.

you were able to drag down with you to eternal damnation so many human creatures?' " [2]

Thus he was always fighting on two fronts—against the religious extremists, who invoked his own principles, as well as against the papists, whom he regarded as the servants of the Anti-Christ—and the more troubled he was, the stronger was his language. This explains the violence with which he denounced the peasants in 1525 and called down the merciless vengeance of the princes against them. For in the first place he wished to disassociate his cause from that of the social revolutionaries, and secondly he saw behind the peasants the figure of Münzer and the menace of the Anabaptists.

Now the latter, however (whom Luther usually speaks of as the Schwärmer), presented a very difficult problem to him. They were the advance guard of the Reformation, the men who took Luther's ideas and carried them to their extreme conclusions. They, more than anyone, appealed to the Word of God and the internal guidance of the Spirit, against all authority both lay and ecclesiastical, against all external ceremonials, and against all traditions and intellectual precedents. They naturally found much support among the fanatics and the revolutionaries. But this was not the essence of the movement. It is as though under the English Commonwealth in the 17th century the Quakers had enlisted the Fifth Monarchy Men among their supporters (as indeed they did to some extent). For in addition to these extremist elements, the Anabaptists included some of the most deeply spiritual and intellectual elements among the Reformers, men who had a certain sympathy with humanist culture, on the one hand, and with the Catholic mystics on the other, and who desired a deeper spirituality than they found in Luther's doctrine of imputed righteousness.

Nevertheless they were all confounded under the same

---

[2] Preface to tract "On the Abuse of the Mass" (composed in 1521 at the Wartburg). Cf. also his letter to the Augustinians at Wittenberg on November 25 (Janssens, Vol. III, p. 25).

label, and the scandal of the Peasants' War in 1525 and the rule of the millenarist fanatics at Muenster in 1534 combined to discredit the movement as a whole. But even before this they had been frightfully persecuted—Catholics, Lutherans, and Zwinglians united to suppress them. In fact we may say that apart from France, where the chief persecutions were directed against Calvinism, the "martyrs of the Reformation" were everywhere mainly Anabaptists.

But the effect of Anabaptism on Luther and the Protestant Reformation in Germany was conservative. After the Peasants' War, Luther became much more chary of making direct appeals to the guidance of the Spirit and the freedom of the Christian man. He no longer advocated the congregational principle of the autonomous Christian congregation, which had been his original pattern for an evangelical Church (cf. his letter to the community of Leipig), and came to depend more and more on the support of the secular authority, primarily on that of his own prince, the Elector of Saxony, and the support of the other Protestant princes beginning with Philip of Hesse in 1524. In spite of his youth, Philip became more and more the effective leader of the party. Thus the Religious Revolution became identified with the Revolution of the Princes, which was the greatest of the socio-political forces making for the break-up or reshaping of the traditional unity of the Empire.

Luther was a passive rather than an active agent in the formation of this movement. It was Philip of Hesse who was the real architect of the successive leagues, above all the League of Schmalkalden, by which the Protestants became a political factor, first as the opposition party in the German Diets, and then as an independent political power capable of negotiating treaties with foreign states and waging war on its own account.

But even apart from the work of political organization, the progress of the Reformation was naturally favorable to the power of the princes, since, as I have already noted, the elimination of the ecclesiastical estate and the secularization of the wealth of the Church helped the princes to enlarge and consolidate their states; while the establishment of a Lutheran territorial Church under the supervision and control of the prince involved a thoroughgoing reconstruction of society to the benefit of the prince, who thus acquired a patriarchal religious authority that was almost absolute. In comparison, the power of the Emperor became steadily weaker and more remote. Hitherto he had been able to rely on the support of the cities against the princes, but the triumph of the Reformation in all the imperial cities brought them over to the camp of the princes so that they formed an important element of the Protestant forces. Here again Philip of Hesse played an important part.

But the Revolution of the Princes is only half the story of the Reformation, even though, partly through Luther's personal influence, it became identified with the North German and Scandinavian development and determined the historic form of the specifically Lutheran Churches.

There was also the Reformation of the Cities, which was contemporary with the other and was at first very closely linked with the Lutheran movement. But it followed its own line of development and produced its own leaders who proved to be equally independent in theological matters. The most important of these free cities were Strasbourg under Bucer and Capito, Nuremberg, Ulm, but most of all the Swiss cities, Basel, Berne and Zurich under Zwingli.

It was Zwingli who did the most to separate the reformation of the cities from the Lutheran movement and to impress upon the new Churches independent civic forms of ecclesiastical organization which became characteristic of the Swiss Reformation. For Zwingli had none of Luther's passive attitude of almost mystical detachment from politics. He was a humanist, and to some extent a disciple of Erasmus, but, above all, a Swiss patriot who played an active part in the civic life of Zurich, and he was determined to make the Protestant cities take a leading part in the affairs of the Swiss Confederation as well as in Germany.

Circumstances favored him, for the ecclesiastical organization of Switerland was, if possible, even more irrational than that of Germany. The Swiss Confederation was divided between six sees which in no way corresponded with its political divisions. Neither of the two leading cities, Zurich and Berne, was an episcopal see; and Zurich, with the greater part of Switerland, as well as all Southwest Germany, formed part of the enormous, unwieldy German diocese of Constance.

Thus when Zurich under the leadership of Zwingli took the decisive step in 1523–1524 of rejecting the authority of the bishop and introducing radical measures of reform, it was a political as well as a religious event, for the burgomaster and the city council took over the bishop's authority. Here we find for the first time a congregational church organization, in which church membership became identified with the whole citizen body under the rule of the magistrates, from whom Zwingli and the other preachers received their mandate.

This new pattern of civic law reformation gradually spread through Switerland until it won over Berne, the most important of all the Swiss cities. But it was Zwingli's aim to carry it further still, and to make Zurich the center of a great Protestant League of cities which would extend far into South Germany, while at the same time it dominated the Swiss Confederation.

Thus when the Reformation reached Constance and the bishop was driven out, Zwingli induced Zurich in 1527 to create a new federal union—*Das Christliche Bürgerrecht*—although Constance was a German city, whose application for membership in the Swiss Confederation had just been rejected by the Diet. At the same time he sent an envoy to Bucer and Capito to propose the accession of Strasbourg to this league, while its Swiss basis was immensely strengthened by the admission of Berne, St. Gallen, Mühlhausen and Basel.

The Catholic reply to the creation of this "Christian Civic League" was an alliance between the five old Catholic cantons with Ferdinand of Austria, which was known as "The Christian Union". Thus the stage was set for the first of the Wars of Religion which actually broke out in 1529 and ended quietly and bloodlessly in the First Peace of Kappel. It was a triumph for the Zwinglians, since the Catholic cantons were forced to abandon their alliance with Austria. At this point Zwingli becomes one of the leading figures in the whole Reformation movement. He was already in contact with the leader of the Lutheran princes, Philip of Hesse, and for the next two years they worked together, in spite of Luther's fierce opposition, to unite the Princes of the North and the Cities of the South in a united political front.

It was to this end that Philip arranged the meeting between Zwingli and Bucer and the Lutheran theologians at Marburg in October 1529. If it had not been for the resistance of Luther and his friends, they would have succeeded in creating an inclusive pan-Protestant alliance, in which the difference of sacramental doctrine between Lutheran, Zwinglian and Semi-Zwinglian would have been reconciled by a common formula which would provide a basis for common action. The failure of this attempt at the Conference of Marburg in 1529 caused a division between the Lutherans of Northern Germany who adopted Luther's Articles of Schwabach and the Swiss, while the South German cities formulated their principles in the Confessio Tetrapolitana (by Bucer in 1530), as a compromise between Luther and Zwingli.

In spite of this failure the need for a formulation of common Protestant principles was becoming urgent, if Protestantism was to survive; for the victories of Charles V over his French and Italian rivals had set him free to turn to the German situation. At the Diet of Augsburg in 1530 the Emperor made the first of his many efforts to bring about a religious peace in Germany, which was particularly important for him at this moment, owing to the rising tide of Turkish invasion which had now reached the Eastern frontiers of Germany. It was a strange situation, since both sides met in a conciliatory spirit—that is to say, neither party was prepared to yield an inch, while at the same time they wished to make their differences appear as small as possible. It was primarily a meeting of princes and statesmen, and the theologians appeared as advisers and consultants rather than as principals. Melanchthon, who was at once the most humanist and most conciliatory of the reformers, was well fitted to take the lead in this work, and the result of his labors was the famous Confession of Augsburg, the most un-Lutheran of Lutheran formularies, which slurs over some of the most distinctive doctrines of the new faith. It was an attempt to exaggerate the points of disagreement between Lutherans and Zwinglians, in order to minimize the disagreements between Lutherans and Catholics.

He went even further in his letter to the papal legate, Campeggio, in which he declared that "we reverence the authority of the Pope of Rome and the whole hierarchy." He goes so far as to write, "For no other reason are we hated as we are in Germany than because we defend and uphold the dogmas of the Roman Church with so much persistence." It is true that Luther had written in a similar vein in his letter to Leo X, but that was in 1518: since then the great break had occurred and the Roman Church had been denounced by all the leaders of the Reformation as the Seat of Anti-Christ and the Synagogue of Satan. If it had been possible to disavow Luther and return to a policy of Erasmian conciliation, a basis of union was still possible. For the Erasmians stood high in the councils of Charles V, and some of them were prepared to yield on the two points which Melanchthon declared to be the only vital ones—the marriage of the clergy and the giving of communion under two kinds (the granting of the cup to the laity). But all these overtures of conciliation were more apparent than real, and though at Augsburg Melanchthon could speak the language of Erasmus to Cardinal Campeggio and the rest, his heart was with Luther at Coburg, as he showed in the Apologia in September 1530, which was his last word in the discussions.

The failure of the party of conciliation at Augsburg left the field open for Philip of Hesse's political activism. In November 1530 he signed a treaty with Zurich and began to collaborate with Zwingli in far-reaching plans for an anti-Hapsburg alliance which would include France and Venice, as well as Hesse and the Protestant cities of South Germany and Switerland. But all these ambitious plans came to nothing when the second Religious War broke out in 1531. Zwingli himself died in battle, leading the Protestant attack at Kappel on October 11. Zurich was defeated and forced to yield, abandoning the *Christliche Bürgerrecht* and all Zwingli's plans, retaining only her own civic and religious independence which would prove of such value to the English Protestant exiles later. But Philip of Hesse remained and continued to work out his plans for a political and military alliance of all the Protestant states that still remained. In the course of 1531 he joined with the Elector of Saxony and the other Protestant princes and cities to form the Schmalkaldic League through which Protestantism first became an organized political power in and against the Empire, and a standing threat to the power of the Hapsburgs. From this point the coming of civil war was inevitable, and Luther was obliged to modify his earlier attitude of passive obedience to the Emperor as God's earthly representative and to preach the right of resistance for the defence of the Gospel. He expressed his new attitude immediately after the Diet of Augsburg, in his "Warning to His Dear Germans" and in his pamphlets of the following year.

Nevertheless this inevitable war was extremely slow to come. The Emperor and his brother, King Ferdinand, were preoccupied by the Turkish attack on Hungary and Austria, and were ready to make almost any sacrifice to obtain German unity and military assistance; and the Protestant League led by Philip of Hesse and the new Elector of Saxony, John Frederick, who was a strong Protestant, used this opportunity to extract concessions from the Emperor at the Diet of Nuremberg and to extend the Protestant territories.

Finally in 1534 Philip of Hesse, strengthened by a secret understanding with the French king, actually ventured to make war on King Ferdinand's forces in Wurtemburg and to restore the exiled Duke, Ulrich, the friend of Zwingli, who had been deprived of his possessions by the Emperor and the Swabian League fifteen years before.

This was a most serious setback for the Hapsburgs and the German Catholics. As a contemporary, Witzel, says, "The success of this bold man [Philip] did more for the Protestant cause than a thousand of Dr. Luther's books", and from this time forward the unscrupulous *Realpolitik* of the princes became the driving force of the Reformation in Germany.

But in spite of temporary successes, this league of the princes against the Church and the Emperor contained seeds of anarchy and disintegration which led to its own destruction. Thus Maurice of Saxony, the most able of the younger princes, who had inherited the possessions of the Dresden line, fell out with the Elector of Saxony over their competing claim to the lands of the Saxon bishoprics, Magdeburg, Mueissen, Merseburg and Halberstadt, which they both wished to secularize.

Still more serious was the case of Philip of Hesse, who was the architect of the Schmalkaldic League and alone had the organizing ability to create a Protestant political unity. For Philip, like Henry VIII, although a master of the game of politics, was the slave of his own passions, and what he required was not a divorce but a full ecclesiastical sanction for a bigamous marriage.

This he had little difficulty in obtaining from the three religious leaders, Bucer, Melanchthon and Luther himself, on condition that the whole affair was kept secret. But while this apparently satisfied his moral scruples, his political sense warned him that it was of no avail against the public law of the Empire, which treated bigamy as a capital crime and of which his enemies would have gladly availed themselves. In consequence of this grave situation, he decided to sacrifice his anti-Hapsburg policy and do everything he could to gain the Emperor's favor. Accordingly on June 13, 1541, he signed a treaty with Charles V by which he pledged his support and that of his son-in-law, Duke Maurice, against all his enemies and promised to use his position in the Schmalkaldic League to prevent anti-imperial activities, while for his part the Emperor promised to take him under his special protection and to forgive him all past offenses of whatever nature against the laws of the Empire. This weakened the Protestant alliance at its center and caused increasing distrust among the leaders, even in the case of Luther himself, who could not forgive Philip for his frankness in admitting the fact of his bigamous marriage, which Luther himself continued to deny.

Nevertheless the League still survived, and Charles V, who was temporarily occupied with the new French war, still refrained from an open breach with the Protestants. Thanks to his almost superhuman patience, he was able to win over, one by one, a number of the Protestant princes, above all Maurice of Saxony, who hoped to win the lands and the Electoral position of his cousin, John Frederick.

Thus when the long-delayed war broke out in 1546 it found the Protestant forces weakened and divided. But when the moment of decision arrived, Philip of Hesse remained faithful to the Protestant cause, and he was able, with the help of the Elector of Saxony and the South German cities, to gather larger forces than the Emperor, who was forced to rely on a motley collection of his own Spanish troops under the Duke of Alva, an army from the Netherlands under Van Buren, and an Italian army of papal troops, while his brother Ferdinand and Maurice of Saxony operated on the Northeast flank.

After a long campaign of indecisive manoeuvres, Charles

managed to surprise the Protestant army at Mühlberg, April 24, 1547, and to capture the Elector John Frederick himself. It was a rout rather than a battle, and it had tremendous consequences. Philip of Hesse surrendered without fighting two months later. Charles V found himself at last, after twenty-eight years of exasperating frustration and delays, master of Germany and free to proceed with his plans for the restoration of imperial authority and the revival of Catholicism.

This he proceeded to do at the Diet at Augsburg in September, 1547—the famous Armed Diet—at which he put forward his drastic plans for the reorganization of the Imperial Constitution and for religious reunion, as well as for a permanent league of the Peace, with its own organization and military force.

Unfortunately at this crucial moment, the Pope, Paul III, enraged by the assassination of his son, Pier Luigi Farnese, which he attributed to imperialist machinations, broke with the Emperor, and did all in his power to form an alliance of the Italian states with France against Charles. But the Emperor remained inflexible and determined to carry out his plan for reunion even without the Pope's help. This was the object of the famous *Interim* and the *Formula Reformationis* which he issued in the summer of 1548. They were made binding on both Catholics and Protestants, and though they represented an essentially Catholic compromise, they went some way to meet the Protestant point of view on such questions as the marriage of the clergy and the granting of the cup to the laity in communion.

Charles was able to enforce this settlement on the Protestant cities of Southern Germany which he had conquered and garrisoned, so that the leading Reformers like Bucer were forced to leave their churches and take refuge in England. But it was much more difficult to secure its acceptance by the Protestant princes of the North on the one hand, or by the Pope on the other.

The great weakness of Charles' position was his failure to complete the conquest of the remaining Protestant cities and princes in North Germany, owing to his excessive confidence in the loyalty of Maurice of Saxony, to whom he entrusted this essential task of overcoming North German resistance. Maurice was by far the ablest soldier among the German princes, and the Emperor had rewarded his services by the grant of the Electoral dignity and a great part of his cousin John Frederick's lands. But he remained a Protestant, and he resented the imprisonment of his father-in-law, Philip of Hesse, whose surrender he had negotiated and whom he expected to be treated more leniently.

Hence he used his campaign in Northern Germany to come to a private understanding with the Protestant princes, with whom in 1552 he concerted the supreme treachery of an agreement with the King of France against the Emperor. Moreover it was an act of treason against the Empire as well as the Emperor, since the confederates undertook to cede to France the three frontier bishoprics of Met, Toul and Verdun.

Charles V was completely taken by surprise. For he continued to trust in the loyalty of Maurice, until the war with France had actually started in 1552 and he found his way to join his army in the Netherlands blocked by the Protestant army led by Maurice himself and Albert of Brandenburg. He was forced to escape with a few followers over the Alps into Carinthia.

Thus Charles V's ambitious, and for a time successful, attempt to restore the Catholic Empire ended suddenly and ingloriously, and he was obliged to let his brother Ferdinand sign a truce with Maurice at Passau only a few days later.

Ferdinand was obliged to suspend the *Interim* and guarantee the practical independence of the princes and the release of Philip of Hesse, although the final settlement was postponed until the next Diet, to be held at Augsburg.

Meanwhile the war raged more fiercely than ever. But it was no longer a religious war, but a war of all against all. In the West Charles and the Duke of Alva were now allied with the most ruthless Protestant leader, Albert of Brandenburg, in a desperate attempt to recover Metz from the French. In the East Maurice joined King Ferdinand against the Turks and afterwards turned his arms against the other Protestant leader, Albert, whom he defeated in the tremendous battle of Sievershausen, in which he himself received his death wound. Though he was only thirty-two years old at the time, he had done more than any other man to decide the fate of Germany. For the Emperor, in a state of profound discouragement, had left Germany for good and had decided to abdicate his worldwide dominions, while his brother Ferdinand was determined to abide by the agreement he had reached with Maurice at Passau in the summer of 1552. Thus the elimination of the two great protagonists—the Emperor and Maurice—paved the way for a final settlement between the two parties at the Diet of Augsburg in 1555.

The basis of this settlement, known as the Religious Peace of Augsburg, was the recognition of the status quo. The princes were free to choose their own religion and to decide the religion of their subjects. The jurisdiction of the Catholic bishops was abolished within the Protestant territories, and the princes were allowed to keep the lands of the churches and monasteries which had already been secularized by 1552. But Ferdinand and the Catholics made a very important condition—the famous *reservatum ecclesiasticum*—by which any bishop or abbot who became a Protestant should henceforward be deprived of his benefice, which should pass to a Catholic successor. Finally all the provisions of the peace were confined to the Lutherans—all other Protestants, Zwinglians, Calvinists or Anabaptists, being totally excluded.

This marks the conclusion of the great struggle which had opened thirty-five years before with Luther's appeal to the German Nation. It has often been regarded as a triumph for German Protestantism. Actually it was a defeat, no doubt of the traditional Catholic order in Church and State, but no less of Luther's ideals of Christian Reformation. The cause that triumphed was that of the Revolution of the Princes. It left Germany divided, with a pattern of territorial Churches and tiny quasi-sovereign states which were to be the pawns in the game of European power politics for the next three hundred years. It is fortunate for Luther that he died on the very eve of the final struggle in 1546, so that he did not experience the bitterness of seeing the ruin of his own Saxony and the transfer of Wittenberg and the Electorate to the family of his old enemy Duke George.

But there is no reason to think that Luther would have been opposed to the principles of the Peace of Augsburg, though they certainly failed to realize his hopes. He had always tended to take a very pessimistic view of politics, and he had few illusions about the aims and characters of the princes. The world is thoroughly evil, and how can we expect the princes that rule the world to be any better? His view of history is eschatological, not political—not a new settlement of the Church and the Empire, but their end. For he believed the time was very short—the Gospel had been preached; the rule of the Papacy, which was the reign of the Anti-Christ, had ended; the Turks, who were Gog and Magog, foretold by the prophet Ezechiel, had appeared; it was only a question of a few years before the whole earthly drama would be finished and the reign of Christ and his Saints would be inaugurated. In all these questions the views of Luther were very close to those of the Anabaptists, whom in all other respects he abominated.

From the apocalyptical point of view the Peace of Augsburg was not so bad, since it provided an interim in which the Gospel could be freely preached. But the princes viewed the matter in a different light. They enjoyed the world while they had it and made the most of their opportunities. Consequently, though Lutheranism continued to spread for years after the Peace of Augsburg, it became at the same time cramped and confined by the Erastianism of the territorial

Churches and the aridity of a narrow confessionalism. Meanwhile the leadership of the religious revolution passed from Germany to other lands.

VI

THE REFORMATION IN ENGLAND

THE history of the Reformation in England and France is entirely different to that of the Reformation in Germany. It was not the result of a popular social and religious revolution which destroyed an imperial State Church and led to the disintegration of national unity. Both in England and France the sense of national unity was strong and found its center in the national monarchy which was the creator of the modern national state. In these lands the Reformation became an opportunity for the state to assert its strength still further by identifying itself with the national religion, and thus creating a national Church. In England the state identified itself with the Reformation and the national Church was Anglican. In France the religion of the nation remained Catholic and the Church was Gallican. But in either case, whether the Church was Anglican or Gallican, it was the royal power that was supreme, and it was the State rather than the Church that decided which was to be the religion of its subjects.

In England this union between Church and State was peculiarly close owing to the fact that for centuries the bishops had been directly associated with the King in the government of the realm. They were not the rulers of independent principalities, as in Germany, nor were they recruited almost entirely from the nobility, as tended to be the case increasingly in other parts of Christendom. The English Church remained, like the early medieval Church, a classless society, in the sense that promotion was open to everyone and a man of humble origin could attain the highest ecclesiastical office. But he could not do this as a rule by the exercise of his pastoral vocation. The King appointed the bishops and many of the other higher clergy with the almost nominal approval of the Pope, and he used this power to reward his servants. The average English bishop at the end of the Middle Ages was a good servant—a hardworking, reliable man with some talent for administration. Thus the English Church escaped some of the worst abuses which prevailed on the Continent. There was no room for idlers or aristocratic libertines who used the revenues of their sees for their own enjoyment. They realized the importance of education since they usually owed their advancement to it, and it was these statesmen bishops from the time of William of Wyckham and Archbishop Chichele to Bishop Richard Fox and Cardinal Wolsey who were the founders of the colleges and schools which were to educate the clergy and the laity of the Church of England in future generations.

On the other hand we can hardly expect such a system to produce spiritual leaders or men of independent mind. Under the circumstances the English episcopate under the early Tudors contained a high proportion of men of ability and good character, yet they failed with one or two exceptions when it came to making a stand for their principles and the rights of the Church. It must, however, be admitted that they were in an exceptionally difficult situation. They were one and all loyal servants of the King, whom they had always looked upon as a pillar of orthodoxy. When the great religious revolution broke out in Germany, Henry VIII had been the first to make a public defence of Catholic doctrines, and his services had been publicly recognized by the Papacy, which then granted him the title—Defender of the Faith—that is still to be seen on the English coinage. He was the last man in the world that the bishops would fear as a menace to the Church and the Catholic faith, and when the great matter of the King's divorce first arose, it was generally regarded as a routine matter which could be easily settled by canonical procedure. Louis XII had succeeded in getting his marriage with Jeanne de France dissolved in somewhat similar circumstances only a generation earlier.

But the case proved different, and the bishops came to realize that they were faced with no ordinary difficulty. Henry VIII still prided himself on his orthodoxy, and he had a very sensitive conscience, but his reason and his conscience followed his self-will, and when his will and his conscience were set in a particular direction there was no power on earth or in heaven that could stop him.

Thus during the years of negotiations with Rome over the divorce, he was led, step by step, to assert his supremacy over the Church and to destroy one by one the pillars on which the old order of Church and State in England rested. When the final break with the Papacy occurred in 1533, he had already secured the submission of the clergy and their surrender of the independent powers of convocation and their canonical dependence on Rome. Yet he played his game so close and so carefully that he succeeded in inducing Rome to grant the necessary bulls for the institution of Cranmer as Archbishop of Canterbury after his own marriage to Anne Boleyn had already taken place. Moreover Cranmer himself was a crypto-Protestant who had just contracted a secret marriage with the niece of the German Reformer Osiander, and though he swore the normal oath of obedience to the Holy See, he also signed a document declaring that he regarded the oath as an empty form and that he regarded himself as free to work for the reformation of religion and the government of the Church under the Crown.

Thus it is clear that the King's original hostility to Protestantism had already been considerably modified in these years. But the English Lutherans or Protestants were still very few, mainly confined to the little group that met at the White Horse Inn at Cambridge and to the local groups of heretics, known as Lollards, who survived in the Chilterns and in parts of southeast England, but who possessed no education or social influence. Even so, the former group were as much Erasmians as Lutherans, since they had had their minds awakened by Erasmus' teaching at Cambridge and devoted themselves to the propagation of his writings. It is indeed a remarkable fact that men who had been influenced by Erasmus were most prominent on both sides and were the first to shed their blood for diametrically opposite principles—on the one side More and Fisher; on the other Bilney and Tyndale. The King, for his part, did not go very far in his approach to the Lutherans, and if he used Cranmer, it was because Cranmer was an exceptionally supple and adaptable character. But he also used Gardiner, who represented the Catholic majority in the episcopate and was less amenable to the new system, though he also adapted his conscience and convictions to the King's policy.

But the man who above all others influenced the course of the English Reformation and was deepest in the King's secrets was a layman—Thomas Cromwell—a political soldier of fortune who was dedicated to the new philosophy of *Raison d'Etat* and who would shrink from no extreme of treachery and violence to accomplish his purpose. If Cardinal Pole was wrong, as I think he must have been, in saying that Cromwell had admitted his debt to Machiavelli as early as 1529, he was right in principle; indeed Cromwell could have given lessons to Machiavelli's Prince in the art of managing popular assemblies and creating public opinion.

There is no reason to suppose that he possessed any strong religious convictions, or indeed any religious convictions of his own. In so far as he favored the Protestants it was because they were useful allies or instruments in his work. If we wish to find his counterpart, we should look not to any of the continental Reformers, but to the legists like William of Nogaret who engineered the great attack on Boniface VIII and the Order of the Temple in France two centuries before; and it is noteworthy that Cromwell recognized this relationship, since he published the writings of this earlier anticlerical movement, such as the *Dialogue between a Clerk and a Knight*, and the *Defensor Pacis* of Marsilius of Padua in English translations as weapons in his propaganda campaign. But what was now at stake was not the reputation of one Pope or the existence of a single religious Order, but the institution of monasticism and the Papacy itself as the organ of the universal Church.

Cromwell's rise to power was extraordinarily rapid. In 1533 he became the King's secretary, and early in May 1535 he was appointed Vicar General or "Vicegeneral in Things Spiritual" with powers to conduct a general survey of all the churches and monasteries in the kingdom. His was the mind behind the revolutionary legislation of 1534—the Act of Succession, the Act of Supremacy and the Statute of Treasons—above all he was responsible, with the King, for the reign of terror which forced every man to take the oath of succession and the oath of supremacy or undergo the penalties of high treason. By this procedure the religious issue, or the question of conscience, was subordinated to the political issue, or the question of loyalty. Henceforward this was to be the distinguishing character of the religious conflict in England. The decisive question was not, as on the Continent, the issue of orthodoxy and heresy which could be solved by a profession of faith, but the issue of royal supremacy and allegiance which could be solved by an oath. But whatever were the intentions of the government, this did nothing to lessen the spiritual tension. Indeed the issue of the rights of conscience has never been more plainly and nakedly exposed than in the two great treason trials which inaugurated the new regime in 1535.

Accustomed as men were to acts of violence, the execution of a Cardinal and a Lord Chancellor, men who were well known throughout Christendom, for no crime or theological error, save the refusal of the oath, was something unheard-of and terrifying. More had throughout based his defence on the injustice of the new procedure by compulsory oath which forced men's consciences. "I am the King's faithful servant and daily bedesman", he said, in his examination by Cromwell, on April 30th; "I say no harm, I think no harm, but I wish everybody good. And if this is not enough to keep a man alive, in good faith, I have no desire to live." And in his first trial before the Lords, he said, "You say that all good subjects are bound to reply, but I say that a faithful subject is more bound to his conscience and his soul than anything else in all the world beside; namely when his conscience is in such sort as mine is, that is to say when the person giveth no occasion of slander, or tumult or sedition against his prince, as it is with me; for I assure you that I have not hitherto to this hour disclosed and opened my conscience and mind to any person living in all the world."

The execution of Sir Thomas More was the test case of the new policy of identifying the religious and the political issues, for if there was any man in England who could not be suspected of treason in the ordinary sense of the word, it was the ex-Chancellor, who died, as he himself said upon the scaffold, as "The King's good servant, but God's first". But the injustice of the sentence did nothing to lessen its effectiveness; and the leaders of the Catholic party among the bishops, such as Lee and Gardiner and Tunstall, became henceforward entirely subservient to the royal policy. When the Convocation met in 1536 under the presidency of Cromwell, as Vicar General, and his deputy, Dr. Petre, the government had no difficulty in imposing its program of reform, even though this involved a considerable advance towards Lutheran principles in the book of the Ten Articles and a disavowal of the conciliar theory by a resolution that denied the right of General Councils to meet ". . . except with the express consent of all Christian princes". Nor did the bishops object when Cromwell issued in the summer of 1536 a series of injunctions to the clergy, over their heads, laying down in detail the way in which the new reforming principles were to be applied in the parishes.

These injunctions brought the facts of the new order home to the common people throughout the land, and so even more did the dissolution of the lesser monasteries which had been decided by Act of Parliament in the spring of 1536 after Cromwell had carried out a very rapid visitation by his agents, Layton and Leigh, during the preceding winter. But here at last the Cromwellian reformation met with a determined movement of resistance. In October 1536 the whole of the North rose in arms in a sort of popular crusade under the leadership of a Yorkshire lawyer, Robert Aske. The government was taken by surprise, and when the King's army under the Duke of Norfolk reached Doncaster, he found himself faced by a *levée en masse* of the northern counties and was obliged to grant a truce while their deputies presented their demands to the King.

The remarkable thing about "The Pilgrimage of Grace", as it was called, was its orderly and constitutional character. It was no peasant rising, like the later movements in Norfolk and in Devonshire, but an organized movement in which every class of northern society—nobles, gentry, yeomen and peasants—were fully represented. When Henry VIII's answer to their delegates proved to be unsatisfactory, the pilgrims held an assembly first at York and then at Pontefract, which was in fact a parliament of the North, and a more representative one than had ever before been convoked, since every wapentake or rural district in Yorkshire sent its delegates, in addition to the nobility and the clergy. In this assembly all the changes of the last five years were discussed and a comprehensive catalogue of grievances was drawn up. The religious issue was, of course, predominant, and the assembly demanded the restoration of the abbeys, the reestablishment of the spiritual supremacy of the Church, the deposition of heretical bishops, and the punishment of Cromwell, Audley and Rich as "subvertors of the good laws of the realm and supporters of heretics and men who themselves devise heresies". But the political demands were also important. It was objected that the Reformation Parliament was invalid because it was not freely elected, that parliamentary elections must be reformed and made more representative and that a parliament should be held forthwith in the North. The Statute of Treasons should be repealed and the statutes against enclosures enforced. Finally it was stipulated that the Princess Mary should be recognized as legitimate.

This was the free voice of the English people, and Henry VIII was forced to yield for the moment. But he quickly repudiated his concessions and destroyed the leaders of the movement as soon as they had disarmed. But the failure of the movement was not only due to the skill and treachery of the King. It also marked the failure of the Church. The people had risen in defence of the Church and the rights of the Spirituality, but the leaders of the Church had failed to back them up. Cuthbert Tunstall, the friend of Erasmus and More and the most important bishop in the North, was at heart in agreement with the aims of the movement. His people at Durham were among the first to rise under the banner of St. Cuthbert and were, throughout, one of the leading elements in the rising. But all Tunstall did was to escape to a remote castle on the Scots border and remain there in complete inaction till everything was over. And this behavior was typical of the leading prelates—bishops and abbots alike. They had been completely cowed by Cromwell's policy of intimidation and they did nothing to take advantage of the one opportunity they ever had to halt the religious revolution. The result was that Henry was aware he had nothing to fear from such men, and he proceeded to destroy the greater monasteries also and to execute a number of their abbots.

Nevertheless the rising was not without its effect on the King's mind. He realized the unpopularity of Cromwell and the Reformers, and he gradually began to emphasize the conservative and anti-Protestant elements in his policy. In 1539 the Act of Six Articles (which was characteristically entitled "An Act Abolishing Diversity of Opinions") reasserted Catholic doctrines and usages under savage penalties, and in the following year Cromwell himself fell from power and was executed and Dr. Barnes, the agent of Cromwell and the King in their negotiations with the German Lutherans, was burned at the stake as a heretic. The new authoritarian statement of doctrine, known as the King's Book and issued in 1543, was substantially Catholic. When the King made his last speech to Parliament in December 1545 it was an eloquent plea for religious unity based on charity between man and man, which is "the special foundation of our religion" and for lack of which there arise dissensions—"the occasions whereof are opinions only and names devised for the continuation of the same, some being called Papists, some Lutherans, and some Anabaptists". But the effect of this plea for charity was weakened by the burning of Anne Askew and three other Protestants in 1546; and when the King died in 1547 the religious divisions in Court and Church were more bitter than ever before. It may be doubted whether even a strong successor could have maintained Henry VIII's peculiar form of Anglo-Catholicism intact. Actually the new King was a child, and the government fell into the hands of the new oligarchy which had arisen under the shadow of Tudor despotism. Under the Duke of Somerset, who was himself a sincere Protestant, there was an immediate resumption of the regime of religious repression. The Protestant exiles returned, and with them came an influx of Protestant refugees from the Continent, of all nations, including such figures as the German Bucer, the Italians Peter Martyr Vermigli and Bernardino Ochino, the Pole John Laski, and the Spaniard Encinas (known as Dryander).

All these, except Bucer, belonged to the left wing of the Reformation, and their influence strengthened the hands of Cranmer and the English Reformers. But Somerset acted as a moderating influence, and it was not until his fall and the rise to power of Robert Dudley, Earl of Warwick, in 1550, that the more extreme party obtained full control. The pro-Catholic bishops like Gardiner and Tunstall were deposed;

their places being taken by thoroughgoing Protestants like Hooper and Ridley and Coverdale. This time there was no question about the completeness of the change. The Mass was abolished, the altars were removed, and a Book of Common Prayer was imposed which in its second and final form was unequivocally Protestant and Zwinglian or Calvinist. The remaining wealth of the Church and the old corporations was liquidated. Church plate was melted down and the lands which endowed charities, guilds and schools were confiscated.

But these changes were not popular. The introduction of the English Prayer Book produced a determined but short-lived insurrection in Cornwall and Devon, and when Dudley attempted to ensure the continuance of his own power and a Protestant successor by the proclamation of his son's wife, Lady Jane Dudley, as queen, he found no support in the country, and Mary Tudor obtained a bloodless victory and was enthroned amidst universal rejoicing.

With Mary Catholicism at last regained its position in England. But it was not the old religion as it had existed before 1530—there was no question of restoring the monasteries or recovering the old unbroken international Christian unity. The Catholicism which Queen Mary tried to restore was the new reforming Catholicism of Trent, and it had to overcome the resistance not of a few scattered heretics but of an organized ministry which was conscious of its strength and which could rely on the close support of the reformed Churches on the Continent—above all Calvin's Geneva. Moreover the fact that the restored Catholic bishops, above all Gardiner, had been King Henry's bishops and had shared the responsibility for the schism put them at a disadvantage as compared to the Protestant leaders, like Ridley, Latimer and Hooper, who had nothing to disavow.

It is true that the Queen had one great support in her cousin Reginald Pole, who was one of the foremost leaders of the Catholic Reform and who now returned to England as papal legate and Archbishop of Canterbury and proceeded to apply or to anticipate the reforms of Trent in a synod, the Council of London, held in the winter of 1555–1556. Unfortunately the positive value of his work was undone by the effects of the great persecution which did so much to alienate the sympathies of the people. By the execution of the Protestant bishops, Hooper, Ridley and Latimer and finally Cranmer, the unpopular and discredited State Church of Edward renewed its prestige by the heroism of its martyrs. No doubt religious persecution in the 16th century was a commonplace, accepted by all parties, and even in the worst years of the Marian persecution the number of the victims was very small in comparison with France or the Netherlands. There was, however, a growing movement of public opinion against persecution, and the Marian persecution occurred at the psychological moment of this unpopularity and found a lasting echo in Foxe's *Book of Martyrs*, which became the most popular of all the classics of English Protestantism. But the real cause of the failure of the Catholic reaction was its brevity. Mary died after a reign of five years and Pole died a day or two later, only four years after his return to England. By this time it was taken for granted that a change of government would be followed by a change of religion, and Elizabeth, the daughter of Anne Boleyn, was committed from birth to the Protestant cause.

Nevertheless she was far from being a religious fanatic. In fact she was the first of the three later 16th-century rulers who attempted to find a political solution for religious divisions—Elizabeth, William of Orange, and Henry of Navarre. The political situation, at home and abroad, forced her into alliance with the Protestants who returned from exile filled with the latest ideas from Geneva and Zurich. But if it is possible to define her personal position, she may be described as a Protestant Erasmian, with more interest in literature than dogma, and inclining towards the Italian Reformers rather than the Swiss.

Yet in spite of her fundamental lack of interest in theological issues, it was she who was responsible for the distinctive character of the Anglican settlement. Her bishops and ministers at first had no idea of a *via media*. They looked to Geneva or Frankfort or Zurich for their models of what a Church should be and were almost without exception strict Calvinists in theology. But the Queen had no sympathy for Genevan ideas, and she saw from the first that her supremacy could not be maintained without a strict hierarchical discipline among the clergy. It was easy to reach a compromise with the extremists in the matter of externals, for no principle was at stake, and the Swiss Reformers helped the Queen by counsels of moderation addressed to their followers. For they all agreed in regarding kings and queens as "God's lieutenants in ordinary, maintaining the Kingdom of Jesus Christ". But in the matter of discipline and Church order the case was very different. By degrees the Reformers came to realize that the episcopal system was fundamentally irreconcilable with the Genevan discipline, which involved the parity of ministers. This opposition to episcopal government was indeed the essence of the Puritan movement which came to embrace a large and influential section of the Church of England, supported by the House of Commons, but kept in check by the Queen herself, acting through the Court of High Commission which embodied the ecclesiastical authority of the Crown.

On the other hand, Elizabeth still had to deal with the Catholics, who probably represented the majority of the population at the beginning of her reign. But the Catholics themselves were not united. The majority accepted the royal supremacy and would have been satisfied with a return to the Anglo-Catholicism of Henry VIII. This was, however, no longer possible, since the bishops and higher clergy who were formerly their leaders had renounced their allegiance to the royal supremacy when the Queen had accepted Protestantism and denied the Mass. Nevertheless, she was not unsympathetic to this party. Indeed, it would have been difficult for her to maintain her stand against the Puritans unless she had possessed at least their passive support.

But there was also a strong unreconcilable element, which was Catholic in the full sense of the word, and was inspired by the ideals of the Counter-Reformation as represented by the English Catholic exiles on the Continent and by the Jesuit mission. These were the *Recusants*, who refused to take the oath of supremacy and to make the gesture of external conformity to the Anglican rite. After the excommunication of Elizabeth by Pius V in 1570, they were subjected to a long and severe persecution which had cost them more than 180 lives before the end of the reign. It is remarkable, however, that few of these belonged to the old Catholic clergy of pre-Elizabethan days. It has been calculated that of the 123 priests who were executed, only 3 belonged to this category, while of the whole number 54 were converts from Protestantism and no fewer than 9 of them were former ministers of the Church of England.

It is certain therefore that the state of religious opinion down to 1603 was still fluid. Queen Elizabeth's *via media* was different from that of her father, except in so far as it was based on the same fundamental principle of royal supremacy. But it gradually came to acquire its own doctrine and ethos, so that in Elizabeth's later years, men like Lancelot Andrewes and Richard Hooker were laying the foundations of a distinctive Anglican theology.

Up to this time the English Reformation had produced no writers and few personalities who can be compared with those of the Continent. But henceforward for two generations and more, English Protestantism—both in its Anglican and in its Puritan form—acquired a remarkable intellectual and spiritual vitality which had a far-reaching effect on the history of Western culture. The religious wars in which first Germany, then France, and finally Germany again, were plunged, left Continental Protestantism maimed and weakened, whereas

English Protestantism became all the stronger in spite of the civil wars and revolutions in which it was involved. Hence it has been argued by some historians that the English Reformation was one of the most important events in the history of Christendom since the great Schism in the East. For it produced a new form of culture, and indeed a new type of Christianity, which was subsequently diffused all over the world, and especially in North America, so that it became one of the great forces that have shaped the modern world. This is not simply an English Protestant point of view. It has actually been stated most strongly by a French Catholic writer—Professor Janelle, the author of the volume on the Reformation in Fliche and Martin's recent History of the Church—who is a relatively impartial witness.

VII

THE REFORMATION IN FRANCE

BEFORE discussing the Reformation in France something must be said about the Reformation in Switerland which exercised such an important and decisive influence on the French development.

This was the great age of Swiss history—the age when the Confederation was attaining almost its present limits and when it played an important part in European politics, because it was the great source of supply for the mercenary soldiers who formed the backbone of the French, Papal and Milanese armies. It was almost the only republican state in Europe—apart from Venice and the Italian cities—and consequently it provided a very favorable environment for the development of religious or ecclesiastical freedom.

It had grown up outside the regular ecclesiastical organization of the Empire in the little peasant cantons round the Lake of Lucerne and the allied cities of Zurich and Berne, neither of which were episcopal sees. Most of these territories lay within the diocese of Constance, one of the largest dioceses in the Empire. Basel, which had joined the confederation at the beginning of the century, was far less important as a bishopric, and Lausanne and Geneva were as yet outside the confederation altogether.

We have already traced the career of the earliest Swiss Reformer, Zwingli, his close intermingling of political and religious activities. His defeat and death on the battlefield did not destroy the distinctive type of Protestant community he had established.

The republican city-church or church-city of the Zurich type remained the characteristic form of Swiss Protestantism. The political leadership, however, now passed to Berne, which became the most powerful of the Swiss cities and extended its political control and its religious influence into the neighboring territories, especially the French-speaking lands round the Lake of Geneva, where the Catholic bishops of Lausanne and Geneva were allied with the Duke of Savoy. In 1536 Berne conquered these territories from Savoy, driving out the Bishop of Lausanne and introducing Protestantism everywhere. But Geneva still remained independent. It had grown up as a small city state, more after the Italian than the German pattern, under the nominal rule of the bishop, who was himself largely dependent on Savoy. The victory of Berne over Savoy enabled the Genevans to expel their bishop and establish a free republican regime. But though they accepted the Reformation, which was carried through by the French Reformer Farel in 1535, they refused to give up their independence to Berne, and remained in a rather anomalous condition between Switerland, Savoy and France, allied to Berne, but outside the Swiss Confederation. This was the condition in which Calvin found Geneva in 1536, and it was this independent position which enabled it to become, under his leadership, a rallying point for the Reformation in France and indeed for a great part of Europe.

The course of the Reformation in France differed widely from its development in Germany and England. The situation resembled that of England inasmuch as the royal power was the decisive factor in both cases, but in France it was exercised in support of the Church, whereas in England it was used dictatorially to destroy the old order and to impose a new ecclesiastical settlement. Under these circumstances one might have expected the cause of Protestantism in France to be hopeless from the beginning, especially as popular feeling in Paris and elsewhere was fervently Catholic. But this was not the case. For French Protestantism produced the great organizing genius of the Reformation, John Calvin, and though he was forced to carry out his life-work in exile, he gave French Protestantism a cohesion and a power of resistance that enabled it to withstand the power of the royal government and the force of the Catholic reaction. Consequently it was in France that the collision between the opposing religious forces was most severe and long-sustained and the opposition between them most acute. Here there was no room for those efforts of conciliation and comprehension which were so frequent during the struggle in Germany, nor for an official *via media* imposed by the government, as in England. In spite of the imposing unity of the monarchy and the strength of the tradition of national unity, French society was torn asunder by the struggle and a series of bitter and inconclusive religious wars imperilled the very existence of the State.

All this, however, took place in the later part of the 16th century when the development of the German Reformation was complete and that of the English Reformation almost so. It belongs to the same period as the Catholic Counter-Reformation: indeed Calvin was a much younger man than the founder of the Jesuits (by some eighteen years), though he developed earlier. That is to say that the Calvinist Reformation was the second stage of the Reformation, even in France, and that great religious changes had occurred before John Calvin enters on the scene.

In the first place the attitude of the monarchy towards the Church was decided before the religious revolution began by the Signature of the Concordat of 1516 which determined the relations between Church and King for centuries to come and made the preservation of the ecclesiastical settlement a matter of vital interest to the crown. By this agreement the King of France abandoned the independent claims of the Gallican Church, embodied in the Pragmatic Sanction of Bourges of 1438, and received in return the right to appoint his nominees to the 92 bishoprics and archbishoprics and to the 527 greater abbeys and numerous other benefices. In this way the King obtained, by peaceful means, most of the advantages which Henry VIII secured by a religious revolution.

He was able to use the property of the Church as an enormous pension fund for the reward of his ministers and servants, and he used this power to the full without much regard for the interests of the Church and the suitability of the candidates. The King, however, was thus committed not only to the support of the Church against the heretics, but to the support of the abuses of the Church against the reformers. For this system by which the King appointed laymen or secular clergy to abbeys and benefices was itself the greatest of abuses, and remained a permanent source of weakness to the Gallican Church.

In purely intellectual matters the King (Francis I) was not unsympathetic to reform, and he protected the Christian humanists and Erasmus against the persecutions of the Sorbonne, which represented the most uncompromising standards of scholastic orthodoxy. His sister, Marguerite of Angoulème, better known as Marguerite of Navarre, was herself a member of the Christian Humanist group of Lefèvre d'Etaples, a devout Christian Platonist and a patron and protectress of the early reformers, such as the poet Clément Marot, as well as freethinkers like Bonaventure du Periers, the author of the *Cymbalum Mundi*. Although maintaining a minimum of outward conformity, her sympathies were with the Protestants, and she finally evolved a religion of her own, a blend of humanism, mysticism and Protestantism which was characteristic of the unsettled, inquiring, individualistic spirit that prevailed in France during the generation that preceded the rise of Calvinism.

But meanwhile the frontiers were open to the influences that came from the Rhine and beyond. Francis I was the ally of the German Protestants, and relations with the great western centers of Protestantism like Strasbourg and Basel were easy. When the king realized the extent of the Protestant penetration, he reacted violently but spasmodically. It was not until the close of his reign and under that of his successor, Henry II (1547–1551), that a systematic policy of persecution was adopted. But by that time Calvinism had become an organized power.

Calvin was the son of a notary of humble origin at Noyon in Picardy. He was remarkably well educated at the universities of Paris, Bourges and Orleans, where he became a classical scholar, a lawyer and a theologian. In the course of these years from 1523 to 1532 he became a Protestant, but practically nothing is known of the circumstances of his change of belief. In this, as in every way, he is the antithesis of Martin Luther. He seems never to have experienced doubt or fears or psychological crises, but followed one undeviating line with absolute conviction and certitude; an austere, reserved, self-controlled man with a powerful and logical mind and a strong sense of authority and order. Although the following period of his life, from 1533 to 1541, was a very unsettled one in which he travelled continually in France and Germany and Italy and Switerland, his principles remained unchanged, and it was during this period, probably while he was at Basel in the early part of 1535, that he produced the first edition of the great work which was to dominate the Protestant mind for two hundred years and more—*The Institutes of the Christian Religion*—which was first published in the following year, 1536, and which he translated into French in 1541.

But no less important was his institution of the Church of Geneva, where in 1541, after a preliminary trial from 1536 to 1538, he established his model of a Christian society. It became the headquarters of French Protestantism and a pattern of organization for all the Protestant Churches of the West and eventually also of many parts of Eastern Europe.

From a purely doctrinal standpoint the differences between Luther and Calvin are extremely small. Both of them base their systems on the central dogma of justification by faith alone; and both emphasize the all-importance of the doctrine of predestination and the necessity for the believer to possess a consciousness of his justification; both make the Bible the only rule of Faith to the exclusion of all ecclesiastical tradition; both denounce the Papacy as Anti-Christ; and both conceive the true Catholic Church as an invisible society of elected saints. Thus the margin of theological difference is very narrow, and it was easy in theory to entertain the notion of a common Protestantism. Nevertheless the spirit of the two systems differed as widely as the spirit of the two Reformers. The theology of Luther is always Christocentric, whereas that of the *Institutes* is theocentric and centers in the mystery of the Divine Decrees. But, above all, it is in the practical working out of the two systems in the organization and discipline of the Church that the differences are most extreme. Luther's Reformation was, from the beginning, directed against the Church as an embodiment of spiritual power and against the canon law as the expression of this power, with the result that the spiritual power was utterly destroyed and the Church was left under the supremacy of the temporal power. Calvin, on the other hand, was determined to uphold and defend the autonomy of the Church. He had no patience with the confusion of thought, the dogmatic anarchy, and the moral disorder that accompanied the earlier phase of the Reformation, most of all perhaps in France.

In his view the first essential of a reformed Church was to be reformed in discipline and morals. And therefore he brought back the spiritual authority and law of the Church in an even more drastic form than that of the Catholic Church. This was accomplished by the association of the laity with the clergy in a common institution: the consistory, which included the four orders of teacher, pastor, elder and deacon (or at least the last three of these). This authority exercised a most strict control and supervision over the faith and morals of the whole congregation. The consistory, of course, possessed no civil jurisdiction, but it possessed the power of excommunication and the right of admonishing and imposing public penance. Thus membership of the Church and admission to the sacraments was controlled by the consistory with the most minute care.

Every year before Easter every household was visited by a minister and an elder, who inquired as to the fitness of the prospective communicants and who could report any moral disorder or breach of religious practice to the consistory. And this domestic inquisition was far more effective and practical than the papal Inquisition, since it was not hampered by the forms and procedures of ecclesiastical bureaucracy.

Thus after enjoying a generation of almost unrestricted liberty and individualism, Protestantism was brought back to the strictest standards of religious conformity, alike in ideology and behavior. The strain was a severe one, but the inner strength of the Genevan discipline gave the Calvinist Churches the power not merely to withstand hostile pressure but to react successfully by aggression and revolutionary action. Calvin was no political revolutionary. He respected the rights of the civil authority, and it had always been his hope that the King would tolerate the reformed religion or even become its protector. But his disciples who went out from Geneva to organize the reformed Church in the face of bitter persecution were of a more militant temper and were prepared to meet force with force in the spirit of the Old Testament.

The new Churches, which were organized after the Geneva model during the sixth decade of the 16th century— in France, in the Netherlands and in Scotland—almost immediately became a formidable political and military power. Even where their membership was relatively small, it was better organized than the Catholic majority and far more easily mobilized. Thus the Saints became soldiers and the Genevan discipline produced that new type of militant Protestantism which is to be seen in the armies of the Huguenots and the Puritans.

This militant Calvinism first appeared in Scotland in 1557 in the First Covenant, when "the Lords of the Congregation" pledged their lives to defend the Congregation of

Christ against the powers that were threatening it. The moving spirit in this was John Knox (1515–1572), perhaps the greatest of all Calvin's disciples and the man through whom the theology and organization of Geneva became the basis of the Scottish Kirk and eventually of English, Irish and American Presbyterianism.

John Knox had begun to organize the churches in Scotland in 1556 until persecution had forced him to take refuge once more in Geneva. There he issued his Appeal to the Commonalty of Scotland in which he proclaimed the rights of the people as "God's creatures created and formed in His Image" to defend their conscience against persecution and to provide for the welfare of religion. This appeal to natural rights is characteristic of Knox, more so perhaps than of Calvin himself, and it also appears in his instruction that in times of persecution every man was "bishop and king" in his own house, to constitute, as it were, the separate cells of the true Church.

Knox returned to Scotland early in 1559 and put himself, with the Lords of the Congregation, at the head of the revolution which deposed the regent and drove out the French forces with the help of an English army. It was under these circumstances that the Reformation Parliament of 1560 was held. The Confession of Faith which had been prepared by Knox and three other preachers on strict Calvinist lines was approved and ratified by the Estates, and they proceeded to pass three acts—the first abolishing the jurisdiction of the Pope, the second repealing the old ecclesiastical laws, and the third prohibiting the saying or hearing of Mass, publicly or secretly, under pain of confiscation of goods, banishment (on the second offence) and death (on the third), and empowering all sheriffs, bishops and provosts to make inquisition throughout the land for the discovery and arrest of such offenders. Finally Knox's *Book of Discipline* was approved, which applied the Genevan discipline to the Scottish national Kirk.

The religious revolution could not have been more complete, and this was no doubt mainly due to the furious energy and eloquence with which Knox had conducted the campaign. But what made it so significant for the future was its political character. Knox was quite aware that he was playing the game of high politics. The strengthening of the new Protestant monarchy in England and the weakening of the Catholic party that controlled the French government were an integral part of his design. Not only the fate of Scotland, but that of France and the Netherlands too, was at stake. Already the leaders of the French Calvinists, who corresponded to the "Lords of the Congregation", were organizing their forces. Calvin, now in his last years, was still averse to violence, and he wrote a vigorous letter to Coligny in 1559, saying that it was better that they all perished a hundred times over than that the Gospel should be exposed to reproach as a cause of civil war and bloodshed. Nevertheless he did nothing to hinder the alliance of the French Protestants with the political opposition, with the partisans of the Bourbons against the party of the Guises, which was to lead in a very short time to civil and religious war. It was the identification of these political factions with the religious forces that divided the country which made the conflict so bitter and so unappeasable. As I have already said, the Calvinist spirit was essentially militant and drew its inspiration from the most warlike passages in the Old Testament. When war broke out, as it did in 1562, two years before Calvin's death, the Huguenots at once proved their military qualities, and when in 1572 Queen Catherine and the Guises destroyed all the chiefs of the political opposition at one blow, by the Massacre of St. Bartholomew, and left the party leaderless, it was the Churches of La Rochelle and the other Protestant towns who saved the situation by their heroic resistance.

No doubt from the religious point of view the civil wars were a disaster for French Protestantism. Though it survived in the South and the West, all its outlying congregations were destroyed and the possibility of Calvinism becoming the national religion of France was definitely ended. The very success of their armies increased their unpopularity, for their progress was marked by a trail of wrecked churches and burning monasteries, and the iconoclasm which was so marked a feature of Calvinism everywhere did much to arouse the passions of the Catholic majority, who might have been neutral if the wars had been merely a political conflict between Bourbon and Guise.

Throughout the whole course of the wars down to the moment of Henry IV's change of religion, the conflict preserved this double character—of a dynastic family feud allied with a religious crusade. But it was the second element which gave the struggle its European importance, so that it became the center of a wider conflict which was to involve England and Spain and the Netherlands, and to change the whole balance of power in Europe.

When the Religious Wars in France broke out, the Netherlands were also on the verge of a similar crisis which was even more acute because it involved the issue of national independence. Charles V—Charles of Luxembourg—was born and brought up in the Low Countries and his tutors, advisers and companions were Netherlanders or Burgundians, and when he went to Spain to take up the government there, he brought his northern ministers and courtiers with him, so that at first it was Spain and not the Netherlands that was resentful of foreign rule. But when Charles abdicated in favor of his son Philip in 1555, the case was entirely altered. Philip II was a complete Spaniard in temperament and manners. He surrounded himself with Spanish courtiers and put his trust in Spanish troops. It was inevitable that a strong anti-Spanish national movement should develop, devoted to the defence of the constitutional rights of the provinces of the Netherlands, and led by the great nobles, like Count Egmont and the Prince of Orange.

But at the same time there was also, as in France, a strong movement of religious unrest. From the beginning of the Reformation, Protestantism had made considerable progress in the Netherlands, in spite of the fierce persecution to which it was subjected. The chief victims were the Anabaptists, who were numerous in Holland and the northern provinces.[1] But from the middle of the 16th century, Calvinism began to penetrate the Netherlands, alike from France and through the ports like Antwerp. From 1559, congregations and consistories organized by ministers from Geneva and Strasbourg, spread with extraordinary rapidity throughout Hainault, Artois and Flanders. Their numbers were strengthened by numbers of French Calvinist refugees during the first War of Religion (1562–1563), and ministers began to hold great open-air meetings to which the common people flocked in spite of the ferocious laws against heresy.

Thus there were two distinct movements—the aristocratic constitutional opposition which was centered in Brabant and at Brussels, and the popular religious movement which found its most enthusiastic support among the urban proletariat of Flanders and Artois, who were suffering from a serious economic crisis during these years. The constitutional opposition was at first predominantly Catholic, though it was in favor of a relaxation of the heresy laws. But there was a small party among the lesser nobility, led by Nicholas de Hanes, Henry Brederode, and the brothers Philip and John van Marnix, who were Calvinists and in touch with both movements.

In the autumn of 1565 they formed an association, pledged to resist the introduction of the Spanish Inquisition and to obtain some measures of toleration. This association was joined by Louis of Nassau, the Prince of Orange's Protestant brother, and developed into a widespread movement known as the League of the Beggars which aimed at uniting all the

---

[1] It has been calculated that out of the 878 Protestants who were executed for their religion in the Netherlands, 717 were Anabaptists. Of the total, 223 suffered under the reign of Charles V and 655 under Philip II.

elements of political and religious discontent. In Flanders the Calvinists were greatly encouraged by this support, and the English envoy to Antwerp reports that the preachers attracted vast crowds numbering thousands of people to their meetings outside the city.

Suddenly in the summer of 1566 this religious movement assumed a revolutionary character and took the form of a systematic attack on the churches. The movement began on August 10 among the workers in the region of Armentières and Hondschopt and in the course of the next few days, all the great churches of Flanders except those of Bruges had been wrecked. The English envoy, Gresham, writes of the destruction of the Cathedral at Antwerp that he witnessed on August 19—"and coming in Our Lady church it looked like hell where there were above 1000 torches burning and such a noise! As if heaven and earth had gone together with falling images and falling down of costly works." From Flanders the disturbances passed northwards into Holland and Zeeland and south to Tournai and Valenciennes.

The violence and the wide distribution of these outbreaks made the revolutionary character of the new religious movement clear and left no room for the moderate policy of the constitutional opposition who sought to combine Catholicism and loyalty to the crown with liberty and religious toleration. Henceforward it was the Calvinists who became the leaders of the movement of national resistance, and the constitutionalists had to make common cause with the religious extremists if they were to be effective.

The Calvinist insurrection, it is true, in Flanders and Artois, which followed the riots, was easily repressed by the government, and Orange still refrained from supporting them openly. But Philip II put an end to all doubts and hesitations. He was determined to crush the movement of resistance once and for all. He sent the Duke of Alva to the Netherlands with a strong force of Spanish troops with instructions to establish order at all costs and to exterminate heresy without mercy. In this he made no distinction between constitutionalists and revolutionaries or between Catholics and heretics. The leaders of the Catholic opposition, Egmont and Horn, were arrested and executed, and the Prince of Orange would have no doubt shared the same fate if he had not taken refuge in Germany. Here he issued his famous manifesto and proceeded to levy war against the Spaniards with the help of the German Protestants, the French Huguenots and the exiles from the Netherlands who had found refuge in England.

The Duke of Alva with his army of veterans had no difficulty in defeating William of Orange and his German mercenaries and Huguenot allies and in reducing the Netherlands to submission by a systematic reign of terror. But Louis of Nassau took up his quarters at La Rochelle, the Protestant free city which was the center of Huguenot resistance, and here he organized a campaign at sea against the coasts and shipping of the Netherlands. It was a merciless war of piracy and reprisals, not only against the Spaniards but against the Catholic and peaceful inhabitants of the coastal territories. It was carried on by adventurers of many nationalities—Dutch refugees, Huguenots and others—the Sea Beggars—bound together by their thirst for plunder and their hatred of Spaniards and Catholics; but their raids were more effective than the official campaigns of William of Orange, which were uniformly unsuccessful.

At last in April 1572, the Beggars secured a foothold in the island of Walcheren, at Brill and Flushing. They were quickly reinforced by Louis of Nassau with Huguenot troops from La Rochelle and by Queen Elizabeth, who sent a small expedition under Sir Humphrey Gilbert. From this point a revolt spread through the provinces of Zeeland and Holland, and in June a meeting of the Estates of Holland that was held at Dort proclaimed William of Orange Stadtholder of Holland and the other northern provinces. Thus a rallying point was established which was never lost and became the nucleus of the

United Provinces. But elsewhere Protestantism was everywhere defeated. In Brabant, the great effort of Orange and his brother, Louis of Nassau, was crushed and all vestiges of resistance in the southern provinces extinguished. At the same moment in France the Huguenots suffered the crowning disaster of the Massacre of St. Bartholomew. It seemed as though the Protestant cause was lost both in France and the Netherlands. But William of Orange did not despair. He resolved to throw in his lot with the new revolt in the North, and from the autumn of 1572, he made Holland his permanent base of operations.

In fact he had chosen—or rather had been forced to choose—the vital strategic point in the struggle with the world power of Spain. For Holland possessed immense potential strength in its shipping and its seafaring population. From the beginning it represented a serious threat to the Spanish control of the seas, since it was in close relations with England and with La Rochelle. Philip II's dream of a Spanish world empire based on the alliance of Spain, the Empire, and the French Catholics in the service of the Counter-Reformation was broken by the emergence of this new Protestant combination of Holland, England and the French Protestants which came to control the seaways which were the lifeline of the Spanish empire. Fifteen years after Holland had asserted its independence, the Spanish Armada was defeated off Flushing by the joint efforts of the English and the Dutch. And in the following years, the French Huguenots contributed their share to this international revolution by their stubborn resistance and their continual attempts to co-ordinate the Protestant forces. It was the intervention of Philip II against the Huguenots in 1589 and the following year which saved the United Provinces at the moment when they were most hard-pressed by the Spanish armies, which were now diverted to the aid of the French Catholics. Thus a new Protestant state had been created in a single generation which almost immediately became the greatest naval commercial power in Europe and one of the chief centers of the new Protestant culture.

The effects of these changes on religion are very hard to estimate. From the Protestant point of view Calvinism lost rather than gained by being associated for so long with political causes and with leaders who cared little for religion save as a weapon in the war of parties and nations. And from the Catholic point of view, the loss was even greater. The Church, the common mother of the whole Christian people, lay prostrate and helpless, while different factions which called themselves Catholic or Reformed fought over her body. Christendom was divided not merely by the war of words and the conflict of opinions, but by rivers of blood, countless executions and exiles, and a spirit of vendetta which dwelt on the atrocities of the past.

And, as I have pointed out more than once, the religious divisions of this divided Christendom were not determined by purely religious forces—by the winds of doctrine or the tide of opinion—but by war and statecraft and diplomacy. Thus Flanders, which was the cradle of Calvinism in the Low Countries and the great center of popular Protestantism, is today one of the most fervently Catholic regions in Northern Europe, and the change was brought about or rendered possible by Alexander of Parma's campaign of 1583 to 1585. Similarly the Northeast of England, which was the center of the strongest popular resistance to the Reformation in the time of Henry VIII, was to become in later centuries the source of the new Protestant movements which influenced the whole English-speaking world—the country of William Brewster, the father of the Pilgrims, and of John and Charles Wesley, the fathers of Methodism.

This does not mean that religion is the servant of politics or that purely religious forces are powerless to affect the course of history. But it means that the process is a complex one which can only be understood by careful historical study. Thus we see religious toleration emerging out of religious war and persecution. This, however, was not the will of the persecutors or the persecuted, but of a third party whose influence was only felt when the religious factions had become exhausted. If the religious factions had dominated the whole field of culture, Europe would have been divided by a theological Iron Curtain. In this case we should have had two distinct cultures in Western Europe as widely separated from one another as that of the Orthodox East from the Catholic West. But the existence of the third party interfered with this development, so that there still remained a common Western culture, in which Catholics and Protestants could meet in so far as they shared the same discipline of humane letters. But the common people did not share in it. For them the religious Iron Curtain was total, and thus Western Europe was divided for centuries between two worlds—Catholic and Protestant—each possessing its own cultural development, although the final stage of cultural segregation was never reached.

VIII

THE COUNCIL OF TRENT AND
THE RISE OF THE JESUITS

A T LAST we come to the Catholic side of the story. It is a highly controversial subject. For centuries scholars and theologians have debated the causes and effects of the Reformation, and even among Catholics there have been wide differences of opinion. In the past it was the generally accepted view that the Reformation was followed by a reaction, known as the "Counter-Reformation", when the Catholic Church put its house in order again and launched a counteroffensive, led by the Jesuits, which reconquered much of the ground that had been lost. Recent Catholic historians, however, such as Professor Janelle and L. Christiani, have opposed this view on the ground that the Catholic Revival had already begun before the Protestant revolt and was not a reaction against it but an independent movement that had its roots in the past and followed its own path of development.

It is true that the spiritual state of Catholicism was by no means so degenerate as has been generally maintained by the Protestant historians of the period. There were a number of movements of spiritual revival in Italy and Spain, especially at the end of the 15th century and the beginning of the 16th, and saints like St. Catherine of Genoa (1477–1501) had a deep influence on the religious life of the time, and in the North too the Benedictine reformer and mystic Louis de Blois (1506–1566), a compatriot and contemporary of Calvin, continued the highest traditions of medieval spirituality.

But this does not alter the fact that the hierarchy and the government of the Church were in a state of grave disorder and had failed again and again to find a remedy for the worst abuses or to make provision for the most urgent needs of the time. The Papacy had become involved in the complicated game of Italian power politics and was primarily concerned with the creation of an independent principality. The bishops throughout Northern Europe were equally involved in national politics, whether as ministers of the crown in France and England and Burgundy, or as independent secular princes, as in Germany. Everywhere the Church was bowed down by the weight of her possessions, which no longer served spiritual ends but were used by kings and popes to endow their relatives or reward their servants. In consequence, the Church became more and more secularized, both as being involved in secular business and being governed by men with secular aims and ambitions. Everyone recognized the existence of these evils and everyone demanded their reform. But so many vested interests were involved and so many legal precedents, privileges and exemptions existed that every attempt at reform was frustrated again and again.

During the 15th century the idea of reform by General Council had become odious to the Papacy owing to the antipapal attitude of the great councils at Constance and Basel, and consequently Rome had preferred to deal directly with the secular power over the heads of the episcopate by the system of concordats. This, however, by increasing state control of the Church, only increased the tendency to secularization. In fact it was this three-way tension of pope, council and kingdom which produced a kind of deadlock which made the question of reform temporarily insoluble.

This deadlock was broken by the cataclysm of the Reformation, which entirely changed the religious and ecclesiastical situation of the West within the space of a single generation. Although this movement has always been known as the Reformation, it was no reformation, in the sense of the Catholic reformers, but a religious revolution. This can be seen clearly enough in Luther's early writings, especially the *Appeal to the Nobility of the German Nation* and the *Babylonian*

Captivity of the Church, which are a summons to revolt against the whole order and tradition of the Catholic Church as it had existed for centuries. For Luther not only appealed to a council against the Papacy, he appealed to the laity against the clergy and denied the autonomy and independent jurisdiction of the spiritual power. Thus the great issues which underlay the controversies on benefices and the rights of papal and royal taxation were solved at a stroke in the most drastic way. Pope and bishops were eliminated in favor of the secular princes, and wherever the new opinions prevailed the princes and the nobles appropriated the endowments of the churches and abbeys and established new church orders based on the territorial principality or city and deriving their authority from the secular magistrates.

During the ten years of Clement VII's pontificate the situation had deteriorated catastrophically, and his continual delays and excuses for the postponement of a council produced a feeling of despair and disgust among the Catholic reformers in Germany. George of Saxony, the one prince who never wavered in his support of the Church, writes at this time, "If the Roman Church were to lose 10,000 ducats of her revenues, excommunications would be hurled and swords drawn and all Christendom called upon for aid; but if 100,000 souls through the fraud of the devil are brought to ruin, the Chief Shepherd unites himself to the counsels of him who is continually bent on injuring and enslaving Christendom."[1] This refers to the meeting of Clement VII with Francis I in November, 1533, at which the King of France persuaded the Pope against the calling of a council. It was not until the election of Paul III, Alessandro Farnese, in 1534, that the question of a general council could be brought forward with any hope of success.

Paul III was a typical child of the Renaissance whose early career was associated with the scandals that disgraced the

[1] Letter to Vergerio of June 14, 1534, quoted in Ludwig von Pastor, *History of the Popes*, Vol. X, pp. 321-22, Eng. trans. (New York: Herder).

court of Rome at the beginning of the century. But he turned over a new leaf about the time of the Fifth Lateran Council in 1511, and in 1519 he was ordained a priest. It was high time, for he had been the holder of bishoprics for twenty years, and a cardinal for twenty-six! Henceforward, however, he was the chief hope of the reformers among the Italian cardinals, and if he had been elected pope in 1523, as he had hoped, the history of the Church might have been very different.

But when the new Pope decided in favor of a council, he had first to meet the suspicions of Catholics and Protestants alike that his intentions were not serious, and secondly to overcome the formidable opposition of the French King, who did not scruple to ally himself with the German Protestants and Henry VIII to make its convocation impossible. But it is here that Paul III showed his qualities. He was a superb diplomat and united extraordinary gifts of tact and intelligence to a wide experience of men and things. Above all, he succeeded in maintaining an attitude of neutrality between the rival powers, so that the French could not treat him as the ecclesiastical instrument of imperial policy. Later on, at the end of his pontificate, this impartiality became prejudiced by his personal bias against Charles V, but at first it was not so, and for years he struggled indefatigably against every obstacle, in the face of repeated deceptions and disappointments, until at last, after ten years, the Council of Trent became a reality.

Meanwhile the forces of Catholic reform gradually made themselves felt at Rome itself. The Pope, at his first consistory, had declared that the reform of the Curia and the College of Cardinals must begin forthwith, and had appointed a commission to deal with the question. Even more important was his decision to call the outstanding Catholic reformers to Rome to make them cardinals and to entrust them with a commission to report on the whole question of reform. The first of these men was a layman, Gasparo Contarini, a Venetian patrician who had served the Republic as envoy in Germany, England and Spain; but he was a man of learning and a devout Christian who was universally known as a leader of the party of Reform. He became a cardinal in May, 1535, and henceforward was the Pope's most influential adviser on this question. He was the chairman of the select council, appointed in 1536 to report on the subject. The other members—Giovanni Paolo Caraffa, the future Pope Paul IV; Giberti, the saintly bishop of Verona; the great Benedictine reformer, Gregorio Cortese; Sadoleto, the Christian Humanist; Reginald Pole, the cousin and adversary of Henry VIII; and Bishop Fregoso—were all his friends or men of similar ideals; and it was he who persuaded the Pope to add two additional members—Aleander, who was an expert on the German situation, and the Dominican Badia. None of these men except Contarini were cardinals, but Pole, Sadoleto and Caraffa were made so a few weeks later, Alexander in 1538, Fregoso in 1539, and Cortese and Badia in 1542.

These men were the nucleus of the movement of Catholic reform, and the report which they issued in March 1537 went to the very heart of the evil by demanding drastic reforms both as regards the administrative system of the Curia and the use of the Pope's prerogatives in the disposal of benefices. These proposals met with very strong opposition from the conservative element in the Curia, who argued that the Lutherans would treat them as justification for their own attitude. But Contarini answered, "Rest assured that nothing will disarm the calumnies of the Lutherans and intimidate the King of England more effectively than a reform of the Curia and the Clergy. The attempt to justify all the actions of all the Popes would be an arduous, and in fact an endless, undertaking. We cast no stones at your predecessors, but from you the world expects better things."

Actually the fears of the hostile party were partially justified. The report fell into unfriendly hands and was translated into German, and finally Luther himself published it, with some violent abuse of "the desperate rascals who were re-forming the Church with cajolery and lies". But this violence defeated its own ends. If Luther had welcomed the cardinals' move and held out hopes of reconciliation, he would have damaged the cause of the Catholic reformers more than he did by his unbridled denunciation. For the Pope continued to support Contarini and the reformers strongly, in spite of the opposition, and the first practical steps towards reform were taken which were to bear fruit later in the work of the Council itself.

But it must be admitted that the efforts of these Catholic reformers at Rome, important though they were, were in some respects remote from the actual struggle that was being waged in Germany and the North. Luther started off with the great advantage that he was a man of the people and talked to the German people man to man, as we see in his *Table Talk*. Calvin and Zwingli and Bucer and the rest were representative of the lower middle classes, which had hith-erto been voiceless. But these Catholic reformers were essen-tially upper-class types—Venetian and Genoese patricians, Italian princes, and the only Northerner was a man who was in the running for the English crown. However deeply they felt about reform, they could only talk as scholars and gentle-men. They were more at home in the court circles of Urbino or Ferrara than in the theological slanging matches which had become normal in the North. Providentially, however, just at the moment when the cardinals were debating their proposals of reform, there appeared at Rome a little group of Spanish and Savoyard pilgrims, ex-students from Paris, led by an ex-soldier from Navarre, who had come to offer them-selves as volunteers to serve the Church and the Papacy wherever and however it was most necessary. They met with the same opposition as the reforming cardinals, and it was through Cardinal Contarini himself that their proposals for a new society were submitted to the Pope.

This was the origin in 1540 of the Society of Jesus, which

was to become in a very few years the most effective instrument for the reform of the Church. Ignatius Loyola, their founder, was only a few years younger than Martin Luther, and like Luther he had passed through the psychological crisis of religious conversion, in 1522. In every other respect they were complete antitheses: the Basque and the Saxon; the soldier and the friar; the man of iron discipline and self-suppression and the revolutionary whose freedom of expression was at once his great strength and his great weakness. The works of Martin Luther run into thousands and thousands of pages, so that their study has become the work of a lifetime. St. Ignatius was the man of one book—a very small book and hardly a book at all but rather a set of directions for carrying out a course of "spiritual exercises" in the literal sense of the words. These were designed to strip the mind of all distracting entanglements and place it squarely face to face with the ultimate issues of the Christian life as seen in the light of faith and in relation to the life of Christ as recorded in the Gospel. Their aim is strictly practical—to arrive at a decision and the choice of a way of life. Every member of the new society performed these exercises, and so ultimately did almost everyone, cleric or layman, who played an important part in the Catholic Reform. They provided the psychological pattern and the personal motivation on which the ecclesiastical and social work of religious revival was to be based. This book of *Exercises*, that is to say, is in so many ways the fundamental text of the Catholic revival.

These *Exercises* begin with a paragraph entitled "Principle and Foundation" that defines their moral purpose in the simplest and barest terms, which, however, even the strictest Puritans would have accepted.

> Man was created to praise, reverence and serve God, our Lord, and thereby to save his soul. And the other things on the face of the earth were created for man's sake and to help him in the following out of the end for which he was created. Hence it follows that man should make use

of created things so far as they do help him towards his end, and should withdraw from them in so far as they are a hindrance to him in regard to that end. Therefore it is necessary to make ourselves detached in regard of all created things—in all that is left to the liberty of our free will and is not forbidden it—so that we on our part should not wish for health rather than sickness, for riches rather than poverty, for honor rather than dishonor, for a long life rather than a short one, and so in all other matters, solely desiring and choosing those things which may better lead us to the end for which we were created.

From this single bare principle the exercises go on after a week to the contemplation of the Kingdom of Christ which is the second foundation, but here again the appeal is a moral one addressed to the will and emphasizing the need for personal decision, as seen in the Meditation on the Two Standards, and culminating in the exercise for the Election of a State of Life which is the center of the entire book. But whatever the choice may be, the whole tendency of the work is towards personal decision, spiritual exertion and the dedication of all man's powers and resources to the service of one supreme purpose—A.M.D.G., AD MAIOREM DEI GLORIAM. Throughout, there is little theology, and no intellectual discussion. It is a direct appeal to the will, based on one spiritual axiom, and to the imagination stimulated by the contemplation of the life of Christ. But this was sufficient to change men's lives and to bring about far-reaching changes in society and culture.

It was on these principles that the missionary action of the Jesuits was based. When they went to Germany, they were warned not to get involved in theological controversy but to confine themselves to the work of moral reform. One of the first of these Jesuits in Germany, Peter Favre, wrote to Lainez shortly before his death:

> . . . whosoever desires to become useful to the heretics of this age must be solicitous to bear them much charity and

to love them truly, excluding from his mind all thoughts which tend to cool his esteem for them. Secondly, it is necessary to gain their good-will, so that they may love us and keep a place for us in their hearts. This we can achieve by familiar intercourse with them, speaking of the things we have in common and avoiding all contentious argument. . . .

When we meet a man, not only perverse in his opinions but evil in his life, we must set about to persuade him to abandon his vices before speaking to him of his errors in belief. It has happened to myself, for instance, that a man came wanting me to satisfy him about some erroneous views which he held, especially concerning the celibacy of the clergy. I dealt with him in such a way that he unburdened his conscience to me, on which lay the mortal sin of many years' concubinage. I persuaded him to abandon that life, . . . and no sooner had he done so and found himself by God's grace able to live without a woman, than he also renounced his errors, without saying another word about them. . . . Such people have need of admonitions and exhortations on morals, on the fear and love of God, on good works, to counter their frailties, distractions, tepidities and other afflictions, which are not principally or in the first place from the understanding, but from the hands and feet of the body and soul.

Of course this spirit of moral activism was not confined to the Jesuits. It is to be found among all the new orders which were concerned in the Catholic revival of the 16th century— such as the Theatines and the Capuchins. Indeed, it is to a Theatine writer, Loreno Scupoli, that the most popular of all the ascetic works of the period—*The Spiritual Combat*—is usually attributed.

What is more remarkable—the same tendency manifests itself in the following century among the English Puritans in spite of their Calvinistic principles which rejected free will and human cooperation with divine grace. For nevertheless there was undoubtedly a Puritan asceticism which expressed itself in similar literary forms, as in the "Spiritual Warfare" of John Downham, and later in the famous popular classics of the *Pilgrim's Progress* and the *Holy War* of John Bunyan. Moreover we can trace the direct influence of Catholic spiritual writers on Protestant ones, as notably in the case of the *Christian Directory* of the Jesuit Robert Parsons, itself derived from the *Spiritual Exercises*, which was adapted to the Protestant reader and became one of the most popular religious books in England (and even in Wales in a Welsh translation) in the 16th and 17th centuries.[2]

The Exercises existed before the Society and were being used during the formative years when the Society had not yet assumed its final form. Contarini, the leader of the humanist reformers, had already taken the Exercises, before he presented the first draft of the constitution of the new Society to the Pope in 1539, and they were being given to German bishops and princes at Ratisbon during the Diet of 1541. Here at last men found what they had been looking for—a new approach to the problem of reform, a reformation which started at the center and transformed the personality. As the Imperial ambassador at Rome said, in the forty days of the Exercises he learned a new philosophy which he had never learned during the years he had spent as a professor at the University of Paris, so that he appeared to himself to be a different man.

Thus the Exercises may be regarded as the starting point of the Counter-Reformation, and it is very interesting to compare this work—the Gospel according to St. Ignatius—with the Gospel according to Luther. Unfortunately there is no single work of Luther's that corresponds, and one has to use a number of different writings. What is clear apart from any difference in doctrine is the marked contrast of psychological types. Yet in spite of this there is a certain parallelism of situation and aims.

[2] There are seven Catholic editions and no fewer than twenty-nine of the Protestant adaptation.

The great strength of St. Ignatius and his Society was their single-mindedness. They were not distracted by the conflicting parties and vested interests that divided the Curia. They were unknown men with no interests to defend, who were uncommitted to the mistakes of the past.

Above all there could be no question of their orthodoxy—the stumbling block with the distinguished Catholic reformers of the older school such as Contarini and Pole and Morone, not to mention the Erasmians proper. Ignatius Loyola was definitely anti-Erasmian. He was not an intellectual, and he had no sympathy with the critical attitude in religious matters, as we see from the eighteen rules for thinking with the Church with which the Exercises conclude. Yet he was not precisely a reactionary or a traditionalist. He had no prejudice against new methods or new ideas. Indeed he was the first to break with the age-old tradition of the common singing or recitation of the office by religious communities, and similarly all external rules and practices were reduced by him to a minimum. Everything was designed to make the Society as flexible and as united as possible, so that it would be free to turn its energies in whatever direction they were needed.

Paul III was quick to appreciate the value of having such a body of dependable and disinterested men who were entirely devoted to the cause of the Church and the service of the Papacy. Even so, it is difficult to understand the rapidity with which the new Society developed and the many-sided activity in which the Jesuits became involved within a few years of their foundation. With Nadal at Ratisbon, Lainez and Salmeron at Trent, St. Francis Xavier in India and Japan, St. Peter Canisius in Germany, they were to be found everywhere in the front line. These were the decisive years when the tide turned in Europe and the coming of the Jesuits showed the nature of the new forces which were beginning to operate on the Catholic side.

The Society of Jesus would in fact exercise a far-reaching

influence on every aspect of culture and impress its character on the whole period. Each of the previous periods of Christian culture had been particularly associated with some form of monastic or religious life. Thus the age of the Fathers is associated with the origins of monasticism in the East and the Fathers of the Desert. The early Middle Ages and the Carolingian period was the great age of the monks of the West, when the Benedictine abbeys were the centers of culture and education. In the later Middle Ages it was the Friars, the Franciscans and the Dominicans, who represented the new spiritual tendencies of the period and who were the leaders of the great movement of speculative thought in the universities. And so now in the period from the Reformation to the middle of the 18th century it was the Jesuits who met the needs of the age with new forms of the religious life.

Of all the Orders the Jesuits were the most international, the most completely centralized and strictly disciplined. And they consequently provided a principle of unity amidst the divergent tendencies of the new national cultures. Their influence was particularly strong in the field of education. While the European universities were in a state of decline, the Jesuits succeeded in meeting the needs of the age in higher education, and their colleges provided a uniform type of classical and religious education from one end of Europe to another—from Vilna to Lisbon as well as overseas in America and elsewhere.

No less important was the missionary activity of the Jesuits, which was one of the outstanding achievements of the period. From the time of St. Francis Xavier onwards, the Jesuits were the chief pioneers and organizers of Christian missionary expansion in Asia and America, in India and Japan, in China and Siam, in Mexico, Brazil and Paraguay. Apart from its purely religious aspects, this activity produced important intellectual repercussions on European culture. Already in the 16th century the reports of the Jesuit missionaries had done more than the accounts of travellers and explorers to transform Western knowledge and understanding of the non-European world. The authors of the innumerable Jesuit *Relations* were the forerunners of the modern ethnologist and orientalist as well as of the modern missionary.

It is true that the Jesuits did not produce an intellectual genius who summed up the thought of the period in the way that St. Thomas or St. Bonaventure did in the case of the older Orders during the Middle Ages. On the other hand, no other Order has been so intellectually prolific in so many fields. They produced scholars, theologians, philosophers, men of letters, poets, historians and scientists. Their output ranges from enormous, long-range, cooperative works of learning, like the Bollandist *Acta Sanctorum*, to the books of elegant minor poets like Casimir Sarbievski, Rapin and Sanadon, whose works were printed alongside of the classical Latin poets in the Barbou classics. They did more than any other Order (except perhaps the Benedictines of St. Maur) to raise the standard of Catholic scholarship and to bring the Church into contact with all the living cultural forces of the time.

Above all, they established a standard of Christian humanism and Christian literary culture which had an extraordinarily wide range of influence, even in Protestant countries. For example, the prose writings of Henry Vaughan, the Anglican poet, are for the most part translations from Jesuit authors like Drexelius and Nieremberg.

It is difficult to exaggerate the importance of the fact that from the 16th century onwards a meeting of Eastern and Western culture took place at the highest level, owing to the presence of men like de Nobili, and Ricci, who represented the best elements of Western culture, at the capitals and courts of the great Asiatic monarchs, Akbar the Mogul, emperor of India, Nobunaga and Hideyoshi the founders of the Japanese Shogunate, and later of the founders of the Manchu dynasty in China. It was through these missionaries that Europe in turn acquired the knowledge of Chinese culture which was to have such an influence on Western thought in the 18th century.

During these middle decades of the 16th century, however, from 1540 to 1560, the balance of power between Catholic and Reformed was still undecided. Paul III's first attempts to convoke a council ended in frustration, owing chiefly to the rivalry of the two great powers, which caused France to obstruct any religious settlement which might strengthen Charles V. The latter, in the absence of a council, attempted to reach a direct settlement with the Protestants by way of conference and conciliation. This was the last attempt of the Erasmians to carry out the program of mutual concession which Erasmus himself had advocated in his last writing on restoring the concord of the Church (1533). At Ratisbon in 1541 this policy seemed on the verge of success when Cardinal Contarini, for the Catholics, and Bucer, for the Protestants, arrived at an agreed statement on the cardinal doctrine of justification, which had hitherto been regarded as the main obstacle that divided the Lutherans from the Church. Unfortunately, it soon became evident that there were other and more fundamental grounds of disagreement, and the conference of Ratisbon ended in failure. Contarini returned to Italy and spent the last months of his life working for the general council which was seen to be the only remaining alternative in view of the failure of the Emperor's policy of conciliation.

The bull which convoked the Council of Trent was actually issued in the summer of 1542, but more than three years were to pass before it met. This was due to yet another war between France and the Empire, and it was only with the Peace of Crépy that Charles V, by a secret clause in the treaty, induced the King of France to withdraw his opposition. At last in December, 1545, the Council actually assembled, but though it was held at Trent within the borders of the Empire, as the Protestants had always demanded, no Protestants attended, and the total attendance was pitiably small. It was twenty years too late, and Luther, now at the end of his life, had come to reject the very idea of a council. War between the Emperor and the Protestants actually broke out while the Council was in session.

Thus the Council of Trent could not be regarded as providing the answer to the German Reformation. That issue was now to be settled by force of arms, first in favor of the Emperor in 1547, and finally in favor of the princes in 1555. The Council, which was suspended from 1547 till its second meeting in 1551–1552, and again until a final convocation in 1562–1563, was important only for the Catholic Church.

But its importance for the Church cannot be overestimated. It provided the rallying ground for the scattered and disorganized forces of orthodoxy and a firm basis of dogma and discipline from which a new advance could be undertaken. Above all, it brought the full weight of authority to bear on the outstanding abuses which had caused the breakdown of ecclesiastical government—the non-residence of bishops and pastors, pluralism or the accumulation of benefices, the neglect of preaching, the neglect of clerical education and many others. Nevertheless the reform could not be applied without the consent and cooperation of the state, and in some cases this was not forthcoming. Thus the French courts stubbornly resisted the recognition of the Council, and therefore the glaring abuses that arose from the Concordat of 1516— above all the royal appointment of laymen to hold ecclesiastical benefices (*in commendam*, as it was called)—continued to prevail in France right down to the age of the Revolution. The Council of Trent was not blind to this problem. Indeed, in its last session, in 1563, draft proposals for the reform of the princes were introduced to follow the proposals for general reform.[3] But the proposals met with such violent opposition from the representatives of the princes that it was impossible to do more than pass a resolution framed in general terms

---

[3] See Pastor, *History of the Popes*, Vol. XV, pp. 340–50.

and expressing little more than a pious hope that the princes would try to do their best to protect the rights of the Church!

On the other hand, in matters of doctrine the decisions of Trent were accepted by the whole Catholic world. There was from the first no hope of their acceptance by the Protestants, since the distinctive Protestant doctrines were explicitly condemned. But at least they left no room for doubt as to what the Catholic Church actually believed and taught, so that the state of uncertainty which had favored the spread of the new doctrines in the first half of the century was no longer possible.

From this point Catholicism began to recover the ground it had lost. This was due not primarily to the policy of repression carried out by Spain and by the Catholic party in France—for as we have seen, this policy only produced an equally strong reaction on the part of the Protestants—but far more to the spiritual and intellectual revival which took place as soon as the Catholics were sure of their position.

In the first place, there was the religious revival—the renewal of preaching and catechetics and the cultivation of the spiritual life, carried out by the Jesuits above all, and by the other new Orders such as the reformed Franciscans, known as the Capuchins.

In the second place, there was the restoration of clerical education, according to the decrees of Trent regarding seminaries, and the new Catholic secondary education represented by the Jesuit colleges which exercised a wide and deep influence on lay society.

And thirdly, there was the revival of higher studies which showed itself alike in philosophy, in theology, and in history. In these fields, especially in the study of the Fathers and the history of Christian antiquity, the Catholics took up the Erasmian program and brought about a great revival of patristic studies which reached its climax in the 17th century.

And finally, on a still deeper spiritual level, there was the great mystical revival which had its origin in 16th-century Spain. This was particularly manifested in the life and writings of St. Teresa of Avila and St. John of the Cross, and in the Carmelite reform, which made its influence felt throughout the Catholic world and beyond it.

But nowhere is the renewed vitality of Catholicism more evident than outside Europe in the missions; in Mexico and South America, in India and Japan and China, and for a time even in Africa, from Abyssinia to the Congo. There was an extraordinary development of missionary activity so that it seemed as though the losses of the Church in Northern Europe would be recovered tenfold in the new Christendom that was being developed beyond the seas. Here the Catholics had no rivals, for though the Protestants took their share in the voyages and discoveries of their age, they had, as yet, no concern with missionary action. This is difficult to explain when one considers how strong the interest of the Protestant Churches in missions has been in modern times. It may have been due in part to the way in which the early Reformers depreciated good works, and to their emphasis on the doctrine of predestination and the small number of the elect. But whatever the cause, the monopoly that Catholics came to possess in this field was a considerable advantage to them, since it was a practical justification of their claim to a universal world mission.

But apart from this external expansion, the Counter-Reformation was followed by a movement of internal expansion which brought back Catholicism to many parts of Central and Northern Europe from which it had retreated in the 16th century. Some of the most strongly Catholic parts of Europe, like Flanders or Tyrol, Ireland or Poland, derive their religious character from this period rather than the Middle Ages. But this return to Catholic unity brought with it a serious rift in the unity of culture. Religion still divides Holland from Belgium and Savoy from Geneva, and in the past there were regions of Germany where religion changed almost from village to village, each remaining a closed world to the other. The Council of Trent is not responsible for this state of things—it is a result of the principle *cujus regio, illius religio*, which had its origin in the early years of the Reformation when the princes and cities began to organize separate territorial "church orders" in their dominions.

It was the acceptance of this principle in Germany as an early step in the Reformation—perhaps as early as 1526—that made it impossible to hold a really representative council and which caused the Council of Trent to be predominantly Italian and Spanish in membership. But the result was to accentuate the religious divisions of Europe, since the reformed and reorganized Catholicism which was based on the Council of Trent tended to be identified with Latin culture far more than medieval Catholicism had been, so that the peoples of Northern Europe became alienated from it culturally as well as theologically. This cultural opposition between the Protestant North and the Catholic South continued to develop in the following period, and, though it never became so exclusive as to destroy the unity of Western culture completely, it proved an almost insuperable barrier to any movement towards ecumenical unity. For three centuries the gulf between the Catholic and Protestant world remained and grew wider in the course of time. And it was this schism, which was cultural and political as well as religious and ecclesiastical, that was ultimately responsible for the secularization of Western culture.

IX

THE PURITANS AND THE FORMATION OF
THE NEW ENGLAND WAY

W E LEFT the history of the English Reformation as things stood in the earlier part of Queen Elizabeth's reign. The Queen herself, I think, would have been content to follow the path her father had laid down—a path which deviated as little as possible from the traditional Catholic pattern, except in the all-important question of the royal supremacy and the separation of the Church of England from the authority of the Papacy. Unfortunately this was no longer possible. The twelve years which had passed since Henry's death had entirely changed the situation by ending the artificial separation of England from the Continent which alone made Henry's Anglo-Catholicism possible. The supporters of his *via media* had been forced to declare themselves as Protestants, like Cranmer and Latimer who were burnt as heretics, or as Catholics, like Gardiner and the other Henrician bishops. These had made their submission to the Roman Church, which had now reasserted its doctrinal position at the Council of Trent.

Hence the coming of Elizabeth inevitably brought with it the triumph of Protestantism, since the assertion of the royal supremacy met with the resistance of the Marian bishops. These were deprived and imprisoned and their place was taken by Matthew Parker and a number of others, including the leaders of the exiles from the Continent like Grindal, Cox and Jewel.

Almost immediately there arose disputes between these exiles, who looked to Geneva or Zurich as the pattern of what a Church should be. In this, however, they were faced by the Queen's determined opposition. For she had no sympathy with Calvinist doctrine or practice. She saw from the beginning that her supremacy could not be maintained without a strict hierarchical discipline. As time went on a large and influential section of the Genevans became more determined and more outspoken in their attack upon the episcopacy to which Eliabeth had definitely committed herself.

"I affirm", declared Travers, "that Christ has left us so perfect a rule and discipline, which is common and general to all the Church and perpetual to all times, and so necessary that without it this whole society and company and Christian commonwealth cannot well be kept under the Prince and King Jesus Christ."

This was essentially the Presbyterian and Puritan contention. It was openly proclaimed at Cambridge in 1570 by Thomas Cartwright: it was opposed by Grindal, the future archbishop. Two years later the whole Puritan program was embodied in a manifesto entitled "An Admonition to the Parliament", which denounced the whole liturgy and order of the new State Church, and called for a further and more drastic reform. It marks the open breach between the bishops supported and prompted by the Queen, and the Puritans, who received considerable, if intermittent, support from the Commons. In 1572 the first Presbytery had been established at Wandsworth, and thenceforward there was a continuous movement for the introduction of presbyterian principles into the Church of England. Since these presbyterians believed that any episcopacy was anti-Christian, every congregation or "classis" was bound to choose its own minister, who submitted to the episcopal ordination afterwards as a purely civil requirement, but who regarded his calling by the *classis* as his true title to his ministry.

This system was not merely advocated as an ideal; it was actually introduced over a large part of England under the archbishopric of Grindal. But the coming of Whitgift put an end to this tolerance. Henceforward the episcopal order and the use of the Prayer Book were relentlessly enforced by the archbishop, with the support of the Court of High Commission, which was now, as in the days of Henry, the instrument by which royal authority was enforced in ecclesiastical matters. The Puritans appealed to the House of Commons, which often gave them its support; but here they were met with the outspoken opposition of the Queen, who was determined that Parliament should not interfere with her government of the Church.

The Puritans were not wholly united. Although there was a large body of opinion which accepted their ideal of Presbyterianism within the Church of England, there was an extremist minority who advocated "Reformation without Tarrying for Any", and who set themselves to create separate Churches which would be entirely independent of the State and the secular authority. These "Brownists", as they were called after Robert Browne of Cambridge, argued that the magistrate could have no authority over the Church, since he was himself subject to its authority; consequently it was absurd to postpone the Reformation of the Church until the magistrate was converted. The essential thing was the act of separation by which the chosen few set themselves apart from the assembly of the ungodly and undertook a covenant of agreement with Christ, their King, promising to be bound by His laws. Where this covenant existed, there was no need for any further authority than that of the single congregation, neither an episcopate nor the hierarchy of synods, classes, assemblies and councils which the Presbyterians advocated. This open defiance of the royal supremacy provoked the strongest measures of authority, and two of Browne's followers, Coppin and Thacher, were executed at Bury St. Edmunds in 1585. The rest of the Brownists took refuge at Middleburg in the Netherlands, where there was already a considerable body of Puritan refugees of a more orthodox type.

Thus the closing years of Queen Elizabeth's reign and the early years of King James's were a period of religious confusion. The Puritan refugees in Holland now included not only orthodox Presbyterians, but even more Separatists who maintained Congregationalist principles and a left wing of sectaries like John Smyth and Thomas Heloys who were the founders of the English Baptist tradition. More central was the position of John Robinson, the leader of the little band of exiles from Scrooby in Lincolnshire who settled first at Amsterdam and afterwards at Leyden, until their final migration to Plymouth and New England on board the *Mayflower*. But the strongest and most influential element in Holland was that represented by Henry Jacob and Robert Parker, and above all William Ames who was Professor of Theology at Franeker.

These men, together with Paul Baynes and William Bradshaw, maintained the theory of non-Separatist Congregationalism which was to become the official doctrine of the New England Churches from the date of the great migration to Boston in the year 1630. It is therefore insufficient to regard the several forms of Puritanism, and especially the Puritanism of the Independents in England and of the New England Churches in America, as local variants of a common Calvinist model.

A great change had passed over that theology in the century which had elapsed between the writing of the *Institutes* and the migration of the English Puritans to the New World —a change which had done much to restore the traditional view of the dispensation of sacramental grace and the order of a visible church as against the original Calvinist conception of an eternal order of divine reprobation and election which left little or no room for free human activity.

For the doctrine of the Covenant of Grace, as embodied in the Church Covenant, which was the foundation of the particular church's existence, brought the divine decrees of election and predestination out of the metaphysical order through the progressive unfolding of the federal or covenantal idea from the time of Abraham to the present. It was by the Church Covenant that the believing Christian became a member of the redeemed community, not merely in theory, but in actual fact—the "matter" of the Church being the collection of visible saints, and the "form" the covenant which unites the saints into one visible body.

"Some union or bond there must be among them," wrote Richard Mather, "whereby they come to stand in a new relation to God, and one towards the other, other than they were before; or else they are not a Church, though they be fit material for a Church; even as soul and body are not a man unless they be united, nor stones and timber a house till they be compacted and conjoyned."

The theology of the Covenant consequently involved a belief in the practical or pragmatic law of justification for the saints who participated in the Church Covenant. They could freely accept and work out all the graces which were presented to them in the Covenant, so that "the Spirit sanctifying draweth us into a holy confederacy to serve God in family, Church and commonwealth."

Thus they had in effect the same freedom of choice and the same power to cooperate with divine grace as the Arminians had secured by their anti-predestinarian theories, the only difference being in the historic circumstances which had brought about the predestination of the saints to accept the covenant which was offered to them by the congregational Church order.

It is true that there was an essential difference, since it involved the all-important issue of the foundation of the Church and the calling of its members. There was the historic mission to which the founders of the American Churches had been called—to carry out and complete the Reformation which could not be fulfilled in England, owing to the obstacles interposed by the prelates and the King's government.

Yet the emigrants had no idea of founding separate Churches (apart from the isolated experiments of the *Mayflower* pilgrims at Plymouth). As one of the original colonists is said to have explained in his farewell to England: "We do not go to New England as separatists from the Church of England; though we cannot but separate from the corruption in it: but we go to practise the positive part of Church Reformation, and propagate the Gospel in America." Similarly there was no idea of setting up any system of unrestricted liberty or general toleration, such as was advocated by Roger Williams, the founder of Providence in Rhode Island. Although the Churches of Massachusetts were congregationally independent of one another, they were all bound by the same law of ecclesiastical discipline—the power of the keys given by Christ to the people, that is to the covenanted fellowship, which they exercised by the ministers or elders they had appointed.

Thus the polity of the emigrants in New England differed not only from that of the Presbyterians, who subordinated the free Congregational Churches to a wider national order such as had been introduced into England by the Long Parliament and the Westminster Assembly, but also from that of the English Independents, who had been brought by their experiences during the Civil War to abandon the common platform of discipline of the Congregational Churches, and to accept a practical measure of toleration by which they admitted even Baptists and Quakers to an equality of citizenship in the Commonwealth.

But this acquiescence in toleration, which was the great result of the complex English experience of the Civil War and the Commonwealth, was ultimately an acceptance of defeat. It meant the abandonment of the Puritan ideal of the Reign of the Saints, and the admission of the principle of the Secular State. Although the full consequences were not realized until the next century, in the Age of the Enlightenment, the vital decisions were already taken by Cromwell and the Puritan leaders among the Independents and the Congregationalists in the middle years of the 17th century.

The American Churches, which had remained faithful to the earlier ideal of a Church Covenant binding the whole society under the rule of the chosen saints, now found themselves isolated. "We the people of New England", wrote Peter Bulkeley, "are as a City set upon a hill in the open view of all the earth, the eyes of the world are upon us because we profess ourselves to be a people in covenant with God."

There is abundant evidence to prove that this ideal of founding a covenant-bound community in America was a clearly defined purpose in the minds of the leaders of the great migrations of 1630, and that this purpose was rendered more explicit by the exceptional character of the intellectual leaders of the movement—ministers like John Cotton, Thomas Hooker, Peter Bulkeley, Richard Mather, John Norton and Thomas Shepherd. Many of them were well known in England as protagonists of the theology of the Church Covenant. Thus New England was from the beginning far more literate and theologically articulate than any other English colony or indeed than any colony whatever; and its colonists were trained by the constant propaganda of the Puritan pulpit to regard themselves as a people with a mission—a people "sent on an errand into the wilderness".

The nature of the compact entered into by the people was expounded by John Winthrop during the migration itself in the following terms:

"Thus stands the cause between God and us, we are entered into a Covenant with Him for this work, we have taken out a commission, the Lord has given us leave to draw our own Articles, we have professed to enterprise these Actions on these and these ends, we have hereupon besought Him of favour and blessing. Now if the Lord shall please to hear us, and bring us in peace to the place we desire, then hath he ratified this covenant and sealed our commission and will expect a strict performance of the Articles contained in it; but if we shall neglect the observation of these Articles which we therein have propounded, and dissembling with our God, shall fall to embrace this present world and prosecute our carnal intentions, seeking great things for ourselves and our posterity, the Lord will surely break out in wrath against us, be revenged on such a perjured people, and make us know the price of the breach of such a Covenant."

In the beginning, the Puritans in New England felt themselves to be in the forefront of the battle for Reformation, and when the Civil War in England broke out, they still remained conscious of the common interests which united them with the Saints in England. This seemed so evident that when the ministers of the Dutch Church at Middleburg wrote to the Independent minority in the Westminster Assembly, the preparation of an answer was entrusted to John Norton of Ipswich, Massachusetts. It was published in 1647 with a Preface from Thomas Goodwin, Philip Nye and Andrew Simpson, who were leaders of the Independent Party in the Assembly. These leaders were in agreement with the New England Churches in maintaining the standards of a non-Separatist Congregationalism. But their opposition to the conformist principles of the Presbyterian majority in the Assembly forced them more and more to become the champions of religious freedom and toleration, so that in the course of time they became the allies of the sects and the representatives of the great majority of opinions in the nation and the Army.

From this point, Congregationalism in America and in England followed two different paths. The former was strongly anti-tolerationist and firmly wedded to the Church Covenant and its dynamic presuppositions, whereas the latter went so far in its devotion to toleration that it came to deny the rights of the State to intervene in religious matters altogether. Moreover some of the leading Independents, like John Goodwin, even disputed the fundamental doctrine of Calvinism, teaching an almost unlimited doctrine of free and general redemption, and accepting the full philosophical consequences of Arminianism. In this Goodwin stands apart from the general judgment of Independency, which remained on the whole faithful to the ideas of the Westminster Confession. But in so far as Cromwell and the Army were Independents, they adopted the principles of religious toleration wholeheartedly, so that the English Independents came to stand (along with the Baptists who had acquired great influence in the Army) for that characteristic form of sectarian spirituality which became the final embodiment of the Puritan spirit in England during the 17th century.

There remained only the one further step to be taken which was in fact taken by George Fox and the Quaker community—the Society of Friends. They represented the furthest possible extension of spiritualist principles—the most complete renunciation of anything which could limit the freedom of the working of the Spirit. Consequently the coming of the Quakers to New England between 1656 and 1662 provoked the intolerance of the Congregationalist regime in the colonies. It was brought to an end by the intervention of the English crown. The theocracy of the ministers in New England was the most extreme example of the Calvinist attitude towards religious freedom, and the Quakers by whom they were defeated represented the opposite pole of English Puritanism.

X

THE NATIONAL DIVISIONS OF
DIVIDED CHRISTENDOM

WE have seen how the great schism of the 16th century was preceded by a long and gradual process of disintegration which transformed the international unity of the early Middle Ages into a society of independent sovereign states which were divided from one another ecclesiastically as well as politically. Thus the division of Christendom by the Reformation was closely related to the growth of the modern sovereign state. Indeed, as I pointed out, the beginnings of the Lutheran movement owed their immediate and revolutionary success to the direct appeal that it made to the spirit of nationalism, as we see in Luther's *Appeal to the Nobility of the German Nation*, which is his first propagandist work, dating, as it does, from August, 1520. This tendency to ecclesiastical nationalism is of course less obvious in Catholic Europe, which maintained its loyalty to the Papacy and to the principle of Catholic unity. Nevertheless, it was not absent there. Indeed, of all the factors common to both the Protestant and the Catholic world, the most important of all is this tendency to ecclesiastical nationalism: so that the union of Church and State is the most typical feature of European culture, both Protestant and Catholic, throughout the whole period from the Reformation to the French Revolution. America was in fact the first country to break with that tradition. Nevertheless we should remember that it was hardly less characteristic of New England than of old England, so that it was not until 1833 that the establishment by law of the Protestant Church in New England came to an end.

The basis of this ecclesiastical nationalism was laid in the later Middle Ages by the general tendency of the secular power to assert its control over the Church, a movement which finds expression in the anti-papal legislation of the English Parliament in the 14th century, in the Pragmatic Sanction of 1438 which asserted the rights of the Gallican Church against the Papacy, and by similar claims in Germany. Although these claims were regularized to a certain extent in a series of concordats, the State never really abandoned the gains it had made during this period. Even when the concordats conceded claims of the Papacy, they did so at the expense of the ecclesiastical, not the temporal, power. The king kept his gains and continued to control the Church in his dominions. He appointed the bishops, and exercised a wide control over the clergy and over ecclesiastical property. The autonomous rights of the local churches were lost and the supreme authority of the Papacy was limited and reduced. In these respects the first English Reformation only carried the Erastian or regalist tendencies of the later Middle Ages to their logical conclusion. For Henry VIII was no Protestant. He was an uncompromising regalist who was determined to be sole master in his own kingdom and was no longer content with the three-quarters share hitherto conceded.

But what was the situation in the kingdoms that remained Catholic? The King of France by the Concordat of 1516 had acquired a much greater control over the Church than the King of England possessed before the schism. He had the right to nominate not only bishops but also abbots and abbesses, and though the exercise of these powers was subject in principle to the papal right of confirmation, that confirmation could be taken for granted. Thus under the Concordat the King of France acquired an almost complete control over the Gallican Church, so far as personnel was concerned, though not of course in matters of doctrine. And the results were specially serious in the case of monasticism, since the great abbeys were used by the king as a sort of pension fund to reward his servants, without imposing any obligation of residence or even membership of the religious Order in question. This was the greatest of all the evils of the system since it made the reform of the old Orders almost impossible. It is true that similar evils had existed in the past owing to the ease with which important figures, such as Cardinal Wolsey in England, accumulated a plurality of benefices in their own hands, but the French system as laid down in the Concordat became the rule, instead of the exception, and permanently weakened the ideals and traditions of medieval monasticism.

From the Catholic point of view, however, the French Concordat had one important advantage. It enlisted the interests of the government on the side of the Church and gave the king a strong economic motive to maintain the existing order against any revolutionary change, whereas in Germany and in some degree in all the other Protestant lands, the princes obtained through the Reformation an important increase in their temporal power and their economic resources. But the Gallican Church was not only a great vested interest, it was an integral part of the national Constitution without which the monarchy as it had existed from the time of St. Louis and earlier could not have survived. And consequently when the long-drawn-out wars of religion were brought to an end by Henry IV's acceptance of Catholicism, his decision was due neither to a mere calculation of political expediency, nor to a purely spiritual change of religious conviction, but rather to a sense of the inherent contradiction between the official position of the king as "the eldest son of the Church", the protector of its liberties and the patron of its cause and his position as the leader of the Huguenot party which was devoted to the Church's destruction.

This bond between the Gallican Church and the nation embodied in the person of the Christian King continued to dominate French history and reached its climax in the reign of Louis XIV with the Revocation of the Edict of Nantes and the establishment of total religious unity. But it also worked in the other direction, against the international Catholic unity and the complete acceptance of Papal Supremacy. From before the Reformation down to the Revolution, the leaders of the Gallican Church like Cardinal Guise at the Council of Trent and Bossuet in the later 17th century, while asserting their loyalty to the Papacy as the head of the Universal Church, continued to maintain the conciliar theory—the doctrine of the Council of Constance as against that of the Council of Florence. And this ecclesiastical Gallicanism was linked, consciously or unconsciously, with a political nationalism which proved irreconcilable with the Counter-Reformation ideal of an international alliance of all the Catholic powers against Protestantism. This nationalism had already emerged in the Reformation period in the policy of Francis I, who allied himself with the German Protestants and even with the Turks against the Hapsburgs, and a similar policy was pursued by Henry IV after his conversion in his dealings with Spain, by Richelieu and Mazarin in their alliance with Sweden in the Thirty Years War, and finally by Louis XIV, whose long reign was devoted to a single-minded pursuit of national and personal aggrandizement at the expense of every other power, including the Papacy itself.

In comparison with Gallican France, Anglican England, and Lutheran Sweden, the power of the Hapsburgs always possessed a certain international character. This was especially clear at the time of the Reformation, when Charles V seemed to embody the international ideals of the Holy Roman Empire alike by the universality of his dominions and his independence of any single nationality. He was both a German and a Spaniard, but most of all a Burgundian, and Burgundy itself was an international unit, extending as it did from the frontiers of Savoy to the Zuider Zee. Moreover Charles was fully conscious of his universal responsibility, both as the defender of Christendom against the Turks and as the defender of the Church against heresy. His stubborn and conscientious effort to carry out this double mission provided the political basis on which the new order of the Counter-Reformation and the Baroque culture was built. Nevertheless his efforts would have been in vain had they not been backed by the resources and the national will of the Spanish peoples, and under his son and successor, Philip II, the alliance between the national power of Spain and the religious cause of the Counter-Reformation became the dominant factor in European history.

This Spanish Empire was hardly less international in its composition than the empire of Charles V, since it included the greater part of Italy and the Burgundian territories in Eastern France and the Netherlands, not to mention the greater part, and, after the annexation of Portugal, the whole, of the New World so far as it was yet known. But there was no longer any question as to the source of this power. It was the King of Spain in his palace monastery of the Escorial who was the center of the whole vast political and ecclesiastical organization. And though Philip II regarded himself, not without reason, as the international champion of the cause of the Church, there can be no doubt that this cause was also a national one, since the Spanish Church and people had become welded together in an indissoluble unity under the leadership of the Monarchy. The chief agent in this work of unification was the Spanish Inquisition, which had been created in the 15th century during the final phase of the reconquest to enforce a standard of total orthodoxy on the diverse religious and racial elements in Spain. It was not, like the Medieval Inquisition, an international organ of the universal spiritual society. It was a national institution, controlled by the national government for national, though strictly religious, ends. It therefore gave the Spanish Monarchy an ecclesiastical power and prestige which no other European government possessed.

Nor was this the only power which distinguished the Spanish Monarchy. The discovery and conquest of America was in intention, and in some degree in practice, a missionary enterprise. For it involved the establishment of the Christian Church in the New World, and the share of the government in the foundation and organization of the new Church gave the king a power of universal patronage and exclusive control which was far greater than any temporal power in Europe had hitherto possessed. In the Indies the King of Spain was in fact a kind of universal bishop—the overseer and superintendent of all the churches; and the expression that was commonly used in the Indies—the Service of both Majesties (meaning God and King)—well expresses the ideal of the Spanish Empire which united religion and politics in a uniform all-inclusive system of authority.

All this suggests that the Spanish and Spanish-American Church was totally dependent on the secular power, and that there was no room left for spiritual freedom. But actually this was not the case. The Spanish Hapsburgs, unlike the Bourbons, were still faithful to the medieval Catholic principle of the primacy of the spiritual. Although the king controlled the Church, he acted very consistently in the Church's interests, so that if either partner in the alliance of Church and State was sacrificed, it was the State rather than the Church. The Spanish Church had entered on the new age—the age that began with the conquest of Granada and the discovery of America—in a much more healthy and efficient condition than the Church in Germany, or France or England. For it was already undergoing a fairly drastic process of reform which had anticipated both the Protestant Reformation and the movement of Catholic reform inaugurated by the Council of Trent. The chief agent in this work was the Franciscan friar, Francis Ximenes Cisneros (1436-1517), who became successively confessor to Queen Isabella, Archbishop of Toledo and primate of Spain, Cardinal, Grand Inquisitor, and finally Regent of Castille. In addition to all this, he was also the reformer of the clergy and the religious Orders, the founder of the new humanist university of Alcala and a learned Greek and Hebrew and Syriac scholar who was responsible for the first great edition of the Bible in the original language—the famous Complutensian Polyglot.

It was Cardinal Ximenes (or Cisneros), supported by Queen Isabella until she died, who established the unitary theocratic reformist tradition of the new Spanish Monarchy, and it was this tradition that was handed down to Charles V and Philip II and applied to the new situation of the Spanish overseas empire. Thus it was due to the personal intervention of Ximenes himself that the Spanish government listened to the complaints of Las Casas against the oppression of the Indians and inaugurated the policy of control and protection which bore fruit ultimately in the famous Indian Code—the Laws of the Indies.

In spite of the nationalism of the Spanish Church and State, it never forgot its responsibility and especially its religious responsibilities towards the subject peoples. There was no attempt to hispanize them or to incorporate them as inferior members of a dominant colonial society. The government stood between the European settlers and the natives as their protectors and guardians. The regime of the missions of Paraguay as created by the Jesuits in the 17th century was a faithful expression of the nation's policy and the Spanish colonial empire. Thus in many respects the religious nationalism of Spain during the Counter-Reformation period is not a typical specimen of the new nationalistic development such as we find in France and England.

For one thing Spain was not a united nation, but rather a congeries of peoples and kingdoms which had only recently been united, so that it is really more correct to speak of Castilian nationalism rather than of Spanish. And in the second place the religious expansion of the Spanish peoples differed from that of the Northern peoples. The latter had been united in religion during the last eight hundred years and had now become divided, whereas the Spanish peoples had been divided during the whole of the Middle Ages between Christians and Muslims, and had now become united when the rest of the world was divided. The national mind (especially the Catholic mind) had been formed by the traditions of the Reconquest and the centuries of struggle with the infidel—a crusade which was also a civil war, since the Moors were also Spaniards. This explains to a considerable extent the intensely religious spirit of Spanish patriotism which found its characteristic expression not in a national state church in the Gallican or Anglican sense, but rather in a kind of Catholic caliphate with the king as the commander of the faithful. And this universal aspect of the Spanish conception of the monarchy was increased by the fact that the first real monarch of a united Spain, Charles I and V, was also the emperor, the temporal head of Christendom.

During the great age of the new monarchy in the 16th century under Charles V and Philip II, the universal aims and the crusading spirit of Spanish imperialism caused it to transcend the limits of the purely national policy and undertake an almost worldwide crusade for the Catholic cause. The enterprise was not altogether an impossible one—at least it did not appear so at the time. Spain was not only the greatest world power, it had also become united in 1580 with Portugal, the possessor of the other great colonial empire, and it was united by close dynastic ties with the Hapsburg empire in Central Europe. France was weakened by the religious wars and Paris was held for years by a Spanish garrison, and it was believed that the English Catholics and the partisans of Mary Stuart would welcome a Spanish invasion to be carried out by Alexander Farnese, the greatest general of the age, with the help of the Spanish fleet. But as in the case of Napoleon and Hitler, the failure of the invasion of England was followed by the gradual breakdown of the hegemony of Spain on the Continent, and Spain emerged from the conflict with the loss of her economic as well as her military supremacy.

Moreover the alliance of the Counter-Reformation with Spanish imperialism proved ultimately disastrous to the Catholic cause owing to the inevitable strengthening of national antipathies to Catholicism as a threat to national independence. This is to be seen even in the Far East where the great persecutions of the early 17th century which practically destroyed the flourishing Church of Japan were actuated by the suspicion that the missionaries were the agents of Spanish imperialism. It is also to be seen in the steadily increasing repression of Catholicism in England which accompanied the conflict with Spain during the second half of the reign of Queen Eliabeth: henceforward the fear of Spanish power became an essential part of the English anti-Catholic tradition, which still found an echo in the 19th century in the work of poets and novelists like Lord Tennyson and Charles Kingsley.

Nevertheless, even after her defeat in the West, Spain continued to play a leading part as the international champion of the Catholic cause, and it was owing to her support that the Austrian branch of the Hapsburgs were able to attempt the restoration of Catholicism in Germany and Central Europe during the Thirty Years War. Here, however, in contrast to the West, there was no clear relation between religion and nationality, since the religious divisions cut across national and linguistic frontiers. For Austria was never a nation prior to 1918, and the power of the Austrian Hapsburgs represented an amalgamation of a dynasty with a religion and a culture. Alike in Germany, in Bohemia, and in Hungary, the Protestants were the national party in so far as any sense of nationality can be said to have existed. It certainly did exist in Bohemia, and in Germany, as we have seen, the Reformation originally made a strong appeal to national feeling. As things developed, however, it was the local territorial state and not the nation that became the basis of the new ecclesiastical organization, and the principle—*cujus regio, illius religio*—which was favorable to nationalism in the kingdoms of the North and West had just the opposite effect in the jungle of regional jurisdictions which had grown up in Germany in the territories of the Holy Roman Empire. The Thirty Years War, which had begun as a simple Catholic–Protestant conflict over the crown of Bohemia, spread like an epidemic through the whole of Central Europe, dividing Germany from end to end and gradually involving all the neighboring European powers and some remote ones from Sweden to Spain and from France to Transylvania. It very soon ceased to be a German religious war and became an international power conflict fought out endlessly and inconclusively by mercenary armies at the expense of Germany. It left Germany weaker and more divided than ever, and from the religious point of view it decided nothing. It served as proof that war was no solution of religious differences, a conclusion which was sufficiently clear before the war had started.

Out of the chaos and destruction, however, one positive achievement emerged. This was the creation of Austria, which in these years began to acquire, if not nationality, at least a distinct social and cultural character. The Baroque culture of Austria did not achieve its full development until the beginning of the 18th century, after the reconquest of Hungary from the Turks; but already under Ferdinand II and III, Vienna had become the center of a cosmopolitan Catholic society, a meeting place of Spanish, Italian, and Germanic elements—the open gate through which Mediterranean culture reached Central Europe. Under these influences the century that followed the Peace of Westphalia (1648–1750) saw a remarkable revival of religious art throughout Catholic Germany and Austria. And though the great Baroque monasteries and pilgrimage churches of the Danube Valley and the Alpine lands owed much to the work of Italian architects and painters, they had a distinctive character of their own which shows the religious and cultural vitality of the new Austrian and South German Catholic culture. This culture had no literary expression—owing perhaps to the variety of peoples and languages in the Hapsburg Empire, the use of Latin as an official language, and the prevalence of Spanish and Italian influences at the Court. On the other hand it did possess a great musical tradition which was closely related to the spirit of the South German Baroque art. It was a tradition which had the support of the Hapsburgs themselves, for Ferdinand III was an accomplished musician, so that almost from the beginning Vienna was a center of musical culture.

But the chief historical significance of Austria in the centuries that followed the Thirty Years War is that it was the only great European power that was not identified with a particular nationality. It was the one exception to the general tendency of modern society towards the identification of nationalism and culture, and it still kept alive down to the 19th century the ideal of a common Christian society embracing different peoples and languages under one political authority while allowing room for considerable differences in institutions, manners and customs.

The contrast in these respects between the tendencies of Catholic and Protestant cultures comes out very clearly in the 18th century with the development of a great new Protestant power in North Germany—the Prussian monarchy. Prussia and Austria were not only political rivals, they were the embodiment of different social ideals, so that Berlin and Vienna became the two opposite poles of German culture. It is true that Prussia was originally no more a nation than Austria. It was a collection of scattered territories strung out from the east Baltic to the lower Rhine. But its policy of strict centralization and strong military discipline made it the center of unity round which the new forces of a German nationalism rallied in the 19th century. The Austro-Prussian conflict which began in 1740 and ended in 1866 was never a religious conflict, but it did involve strong forces of religious sympathy and prejudice, so that Austria's exclusion from Germany in 1866 was soon followed by Bismarck's attempt —the so-called *Kultur Kampf*—to destroy the cultural influence of Catholicism in the German Empire. But here again we have another example of the ineffectiveness of political repression to solve purely religious issues. For the *Kultur Kampf* was not only unsuccessful, it acted as a stimulus to the Catholic forces in Germany, so that the German Catholics acquired a new strength and self-reliance in the course of the struggle.

Remote on the frontier between Western and Eastern Christendom is Poland—Catholic and Latin Christianity was the creed of this Slavonic people. The Reformation produced an invasion of three distinct and mutually hostile forms of Protestantism—Lutheran, Calvinist and Unitarian. For an Italian anti-Trinitarian leader, Fausto Sozzini (Socinus), had made his way to Poland and won adherents. Many local magnates, petty kings within their own domains, adopted one of these warring professions and would even impose their choice on their subjects. In face of this situation, the Catholic monarchy adopted a policy of complete toleration, convinced—and, as the event would prove, correctly—that the mutual hostility of the Protestant confessions would make it impossible for them to substitute a Protestant religion for the official Catholicism, as the united French Calvinists were attempting to do in France. The Compact of Warsaw, January 28, 1573, granted entire liberty to all non-Catholic confessions. This policy of toleration was continued by two strong and successful monarchs, the Hungarian Stephen Bathory (1575–1586) and his successor, the Swedish Sigismund III when he was elected in 1587.

Thus it was that Unitarianism, elsewhere persecuted by all Protestant rulers, found a refuge in Poland, where it could even maintain a seminary for the training of its ministers. On the other hand these monarchs did their utmost to strengthen the Catholic Church in Poland by promoting moral reform and religious instruction. In particular the Jesuits were encouraged in their work of teaching and preaching.

In the following century, it is true, the Protestants were deprived of the full toleration they had so long enjoyed. But the Catholic victory had already been won and Protestantism decisively defeated without measures of persecution. Henceforward until its destruction by the combined power of Orthodox Russia, Protestant Prussia and (reluctantly) Catholic

Austria, the Polish kingdom would be Catholic. Indeed after its loss of political independence the Polish people was to remain a bastion of Catholicism in the East as the Irish people, also subject to foreign rule, has been in the West.

Finally we must consider the case of Italy, which is of exceptional importance for the study of Catholicism, since throughout the whole modern period the government and administration of the Church has been carried out by Italians and from Italy, to a greater extent than at any other age of the Church's history. But the case of Italy is very exceptional in other respects also. At the time of the Reformation Italy was the most culturally advanced country in Europe, and it possessed a very strong sense of cultural superiority. Yet no people in Western Europe was more completely deprived of national unity or the power of national self-determination. Italy was indeed almost a colonial territory. For two of the largest and richest Italian states—Naples and Sicily, and Milan—were under Spanish occupation or control down to the beginning of the 18th century and remained under Austrian rule thereafter.

But the most distinctive feature of Italian political life was the temporal power of the Popes, who ruled the greater part of Central Italy from Rome to Bologna. This stood in the way of the complete domination of Italy by the non-Italian great powers, but at the same time it was an obstacle to national unification, and consequently it was the object of the most bitter criticism on the part of political thinkers, like Machiavelli and Guicciardini, who cherished the ideal of national unity. This political anti-clericalism allied itself with the secularist tendencies in the thought of the Renaissance to produce a movement of opposition to Catholicism which was not very strong, but which never entirely disappeared; unlike Italian Protestantism, which won a few eminent converts in the early 16th century, such as Ochino and the Sozzinis, but which had little influence on Italian culture.

Italy, even in the age of foreign domination, remained

predominantly a land of city-states, and in the influence of the Church was so strong and its relations with the life of the people so close that there was no room for the development of any dissident movement. Thus the success of the Catholic revival in Italy owed far less to the influence of the State than it did in Austria or France or even Spain. It was due to the prestige and influence of particular individuals in particular cities—like St. Charles Borromeo at Milan and St. Philip Neri at Rome or, at an earlier date, of Bishop Giberti at Verona.

Certainly Italian Catholicism possessed its own distinctive national character—as much as that of any country in Europe—but this was not due to the unifying policy of a dynasty or a state church. It had roots deep in the past, in the medieval history of the Italian city state and in the distinctive Italian national culture, which had come to maturity at a time when the other European nationalities were still in the process of formation. It was no doubt a considerable advantage to the Catholic Church that this was so. Amid the intense national rivalries and power conflicts of the 16th and 17th centuries, the Papacy was able to stand outside the battle in a relatively stable and peaceful political world of its own. Throughout the whole period from the middle of the 16th century to the French Revolution, Italy was never engaged in a major war, and even though she was deprived of political influence, her cultural influence was all the greater. Throughout the whole period she attracted travellers from all over Europe—religious pilgrims from the Catholic lands and cultural pilgrims from the Protestant—and at Rome the two streams met and mingled: saints and scholars, artists and dilettantes: Crashaw and Queen Christina of Sweden, Goethe and St. Benedict Joseph Labre. And we may recall that it was owing to the impression produced by the death of this saint that the first Boston convert—the Rev. John Thayer—joined the Church in Rome in 1783.

Thus the national barriers which had grown up in the

centuries after the Reformation never produced a state of total segregation. Nevertheless it was not until they were broken down violently by the catastrophe of the French Revolution that the way was opened to a wider, more general contact between the two parts of divided Christendom. In this respect, above all, the 19th century marks the beginning of a new epoch in the history of the Church. National prejudices were still as powerful as ever, and each people remained strongly attached to its own divisive traditions, but the political obstacles to religious intercourse were gradually covered and eventually removed. Thus the Church recovered its universal super-national character at the same time that it lost the privileged position it had possessed in the Catholic states of the old regime.

XI

THE CATHOLIC REVIVAL
AND THE BAROQUE CULTURE

[1]

IN THE second half of the 16th century the age of the Reformation came to an end, leaving Christendom divided permanently. The point at which the process of change stopped differs, of course, in the different countries. In Germany it was the Religious Peace of Augsburg in 1555. In England it was the Elizabethan Settlement in 1559. In France it was the end of the Wars of Religion and the Edict of Nantes in 1598, while in the Netherlands the vital decisions were reached in the course of the forty-two-year-long struggle against Spain between 1567 and 1609.

For Catholic Europe as a whole, however, it is the Council of Trent which marks the turning point, and the Catholic revival was already far advanced by the time the Council came to an end in 1563–1564. This religious revival has a double importance—in the first place, it created the spiritual ideals and theological norms and ecclesiastical administration of modern Catholicism, and in the second place, it inspired the new forms of humanist or post-humanist culture, generally known as Baroque, which became dominant in the 17th century. In both these aspects it was an international movement and drew on all the different religious traditions which had already begun to make themselves felt in the earlier part of the century, especially in Spain and Italy.

First there was the movement of Christian Humanism, which was represented alike by the followers of Erasmus in the North and by the Christian Platonists in Italy. This tradition was the source, or one of the sources, of the revival of

Christian studies which renewed the study of theology and patristic and ecclesiastical history in the hundred years from 1560 to 1660, and which also had a profound influence on the vernacular literatures, for example in the work of Luis de León.

Secondly there was the tradition of Italian mysticism and pietism which had survived all through the age of the Renaissance. There was the tradition of St. Francis, continued or revived by St. Bernardine of Siena in the 15th century and by the Capuchins in the 16th. And there was its novel expression in the life of St. Philip Neri, who maintained in the age of the Counter-Reformation and in his new institute of the Roman Oratory the humanist elements of the Italian spiritual traditions.

Thirdly there was the tradition of Spanish mysticism which had made its appearance among the Spanish Franciscans in the first half of the 16th century. In the second half of the century it reached its highest development in the lives and writings of St. Teresa of Avila and St. John of the Cross and thus became one of the dominant elements in the Catholic revival.

Early in the 17th century it was introduced into France by St. Teresa's order of the Carmelite Reform and there contributed to the development of the French spiritual revival which was to produce such rich fruits in the course of the next two generations.

But this mystical movement was only one aspect of Spanish religious life. The 16th century was Spain's greatest age. It witnessed an extraordinary outburst of national energy in almost every field, both secular and religious. To a contemporary observer the Spanish genius must have appeared active rather than contemplative, and dynamic rather than mystical, and this seemed to be the case in religious as well as in secular matters. In fact, the greatest contribution that Spain made to the Catholic revival was the new moral dynamism which it introduced into the ecclesiastical world so long paralyzed by the conflicting forces of conservatism and reform, the vested interests of a clerical oligarchy and the predatory ambitions of the secular princes.

The classical examples of this moral dynamism were St. Ignatius and the Society of Jesus. As I have already pointed out, it finds a very clear expression in the book of the *Spiritual Exercises*.

In Catholic Europe this religious revival, alike in its ascetic and mystical forms, led to the intensive cultivation of the spiritual life of the individual among the laity as well as among the clergy, and this created a demand for individual guidance or spiritual direction which became one of the characteristic features of Post-Reformation Catholicism. Here also the Jesuits played an important part in the new development by the giving of retreats which, unlike those of the present day, were usually given to individuals rather than to groups, and by the special attention that was devoted to moral and pastoral theology in their training. But in addition to the Jesuits, St. Philip Neri from the beginning devoted himself to this task, so that in the course of his long life the Roman Oratory became one of the great centers of the revival of religious life among the laity. But perhaps the most famous of the spiritual directors of the age was St. Francis de Sales, the Catholic bishop of Geneva—at least those parts of the old diocese which were still part of Savoy. He was at once a humanist, a mystic and an active reformer who took the leading part in the restoration of Catholicism in Savoy, and his enormous correspondence thus reflects every aspect of the spiritual life of the Catholic revival.

This work of moral and spiritual reformation is in a sense the counterpart of the Northern Reformation, which was also concerned with the "interiorization" of religion and was inspired by a similar spirit of moral activism in the single-minded pursuit of the one end for which man was created.

But in almost every other respect the two movements were totally opposed to one another. For the Catholic accentuated just those elements in the Christian tradition which the Protestants rejected—the visible unity of the Church, the authority of the hierarchy, the grace of the sacraments, and the veneration of the saints. Whereas the Protestant Reformers destroyed the monasteries and abandoned the ideal of the monastic life, the Catholic Reformers found their center of action in the new religious orders that they created. Consequently, as soon as the Catholic Reform was strong enough to exert its influence on culture, it was able to continue the old medieval tradition of popular religion and once more to embody the old Catholic imagery and ideas in the new artistic forms which had been developed by the Renaissance. Thus there arose the new forms of the Baroque culture which rapidly transcended the limits of the Mediterranean countries and extended its influence over the whole Catholic world.

Despite its great historical importance, Baroque culture has not received much understanding or appreciation from modern historians, largely owing to their religious or national prejudices or limitations. The very word Baroque had a pejorative sense both to the strict classicists and to the men of the Gothic revival. Indeed, to call it "Counter-Reformation" inevitably suggests that it was a negative, retrograde movement opposed to the current of progress. Nevertheless, Baroque culture was enormously productive—in art, in literature, in music.

Looked at from a Northern and Protestant angle, the Baroque culture appears as a secularized version of medieval Catholicism; from its own standpoint, however, it represents rather the desecularization of the Renaissance and the reassertion of the power of religion and the authority of the Church over social life. All the resources of art, architecture, painting, sculpture, literature and music were enlisted in the service of Catholicism, and if to the Northerner the result appears theatrical and meretricious, this was due to no lack of spirituality. It was, however, a different spirituality. It was a passionate, ecstatic, mystical spirituality that has little in common with the sober pietism of the Protestant North, but it was intensely vital, as we see from the lives and writings of the Spanish saints and mystics of the 16th century who initiated the great movement of Baroque mysticism which swept Catholic Europe in the first half of the 17th century.

[11]

The Baroque culture represents the alliance of two traditions—the humanist tradition of the Renaissance and the tradition of medieval Catholicism as revived or restored by the Counter-Reformation. These traditions are often regarded as contradictory, but they came together in the Baroque culture, to which each made an important contribution.

During the previous period the efforts of the humanists had been devoted to the recovery of classical literature and learning, and the restoration of the old liberal arts education on a higher plane of scholarship. Similarly in art there had been a corresponding movement to return to classical models and to revive classical forms. In both cases there was a strong emphasis on imitation of the classical past and an equally strong revolt against the tradition of the later Middle Ages.

In the second half of the 16th century, both these causes were won, at least in Southern Europe, and the main problem was how to apply the new education and the new forms of art to the needs of contemporary society, and above all of the contemporary Church, which then, no less than in the Middle Ages, was the great educator and the chief patron of the arts.

Nevertheless, in spite of this reaction against the Middle Ages, it is impossible not to recognize that Baroque art is more akin to the art of the Middle Ages than to the rational idealism of the classical Renaissance. It expressed in fact the Gothic spirit through classical forms. It is not merely that Baroque art served the same religio-social functions and employed the same religious symbolism as that of the Middle

Ages. It resembles Gothic architecture—especially the Flamboyant Gothic of the later Middle Ages—in its attempt to transcend the limits of matter and space by mobility of line, and a restless striving after infinity. This attempt produced a break with the fixed lines and strict rationality of classical architecture by a bold use of sweeping curves, vast proportions and sharp contrasts of light and shade. In the same way it is characterized by an extraordinary luxuriance of imagery and ornament which utilizes every available space and makes every church a treasury of religious symbolism. So too in painting, after the serenity of Raphael and the exuberant paganism of Corregio we find the dark fire and ascetic ecstasy of the Spanish masters El Greco, Ribera and Zurbaran.

[III]

Thus the 17th century saw the rise of a new religious art which, in so far as it became the current artistic language of the Church, represented a popularization of the more aristocratic Renaissance tradition and moulded the popular taste of the Catholic world from Mexico and Peru to Hungary and Poland. Its predominance is especially marked in Southern Germany and Austria, where there was a great revival of ecclesiastical architecture after the Thirty Years War, so that the Baroque style is as universal and typical of the churches and monasteries of central Europe as was the Gothic style in England and France during the later Middle Ages.

Hence the Baroque age created a new cultural unity, based like that of the Middle Ages on a religious foundation, but it was no longer all-inclusive; it proceeded from a Mediterranean focus instead of the medieval center in Northern France. There was no similar movement in Protestant Europe, owing to the divorce of art from religion, and in so far as the Renaissance style penetrated into Northern Europe, it preserved the more classical tradition of the earlier Renaissance.

Nevertheless in literature and painting the Baroque culture had an almost European range, and diffused itself even in Northern Europe through the influence of the courts, which were now, except in Holland, the great patrons of art and culture. This court culture could not, of course, affect the life of the whole nation as had the popular and religious art of the Middle Ages. It was the privilege of the select few. But within this narrow circle there was an intense appreciation for artistic achievement, and the individual genius had a greater chance of recognition than either before or since. Men like Rubens and Velasquez had no need to struggle for a bare livelihood, and their whole life was spent in the triumphant exercise of their art; Bernini, above all, held throughout his life a position which could now only be reached by a film star or a newspaper magnate.

At one point, however, the influence of the court met with that of the general public to create a great popular art—the Renaissance drama; and alike in London and Paris and Madrid the age produced a flowering of dramatic genius such as can only be paralleled in the great age of the Attic drama. Shakespeare himself was a Baroque genius, and however much he seems to transcend the limitations of his generation, he can only be fully understood as an offspring of the same age and culture which produced Campanella, Galileo, Lope de Vega and Cervantes—the age that expressed itself in stone in Bernini's great colonnade in the Piaza of St. Peter's.

Hardly less important than the drama was the development of the European national literatures in poetry and prose. It was the age of the great essayists, the popular philosophies of the educated world, Montaigne and Bacon and Quevedo, of the founder of the modern novel, Cervantes, who perhaps comes nearest in genius to Shakespeare of all the men of his time. In poetry there are not only the great names like Tasso and Spenser, Milton and Vondel, but a host of lyrical poets. Of these some of the most famous, like Marini and Gongora, were Baroque in the bad sense of the word, disfigured by meretricious ornament and fantastic verbal conceits, but in the majority of them, poets such as Donne and Crashaw, Luis de León and John of the Cross, Scheffler and von Spee, it is the deeper spirit of the age, its profound thought and mystical emotion, which finds expression.

Nor does all this exhaust the creativeness of the age. It also saw the beginnings of modern music. For the Baroque culture created not only a new religious art, but also a new church music, which found its great exponent in Palestrina. This new art grew up in particularly close contact with the Counter-Reformation, and it was St. Philip Neri, the friend of Palestrina, to whom was due the institution of the oratorio, which was the ultimate ancestor of Italian opera.

Nowhere are the vitality and fecundity of the Baroque culture better displayed than in Mexico and South America, where there was a rich flowering of regional types of art and architecture, some of which show considerable indigenous Indian influence. This power of Baroque culture to assimilate alien influences is one of its characteristic features, and distinguishes it sharply from the culture and artistic style of the Anglo-American area.

The sheer volume of material achievement of the Spanish Baroque culture in America is extraordinary: dozens of cathedrals, hundreds of monasteries, thousands of parish churches, many of them richly adorned with sculpture, painting and metal work. All this artistic activity is the expression of a great cultural effort which also had its intellectual and religious aspects, as for example, in the foundation of universities and the lives of the great missionaries and saints.[1]

None of this has received adequate attention from the historians of culture and art, and it is only in our own days that any attempt has been made to protect or record the monuments that survive.

[1] For a view of Baroque art in Central and Southern America, Pal Kelemen's richly illustrated study, *Baroque and Rococo in Latin America* (New York: Macmillan, 1951), is indispensable.

The cause of this neglect is partly the general lack of appreciation of Baroque culture and all its works in the 19th century, but still more the catastrophic break in cultural development which followed the Wars of Independence and the separation of Latin America from Spain. For the Baroque culture of Latin America was not only a colonial culture, it was a highly centralized and hierarchical culture, which derived its whole impetus from two centers, Church and State. The whole cultural edifice was sustained by an intense effort of will on the part of a very small ruling class, and when this effort was broken by historical circumstances, the whole edifice was shattered from top to bottom. The Creoles (the American-born Spaniards) were not in a position to carry on the work because they were essentially intermediaries between the rulers and the subject population. The great viceroyalties of Mexico and Peru were really Indian states under a paternal authoritarian European government.

Nevertheless it does not follow that American Baroque culture was an artificial mechanical reproduction of an alien original. Christianity entered very deeply into its new American environment, and there was a real collaboration between European and Indian elements: far more indeed than in the architecture and art of independent Latin America in the 19th century. Moreover, the predominance of the Church and the influence of the religious Orders led to the immigration to America of exceptional individuals—missionaries, saints and scholars—like Las Casas, St. Peter Claver, Bl. Alvarez de Paz, St. Toribio Alfonso Mogrovejo, who was Archbishop of Lima, Archbishop Zumarraga of Mexico, the lay mystic Gregory Lopez, Bernardino de Sahagun, the historian of the Aztecs, and many more. The stimulus of this spiritual elite had a profound influence on America, and accounts for the sudden and almost miraculous expansion of Baroque culture from the 16th to the 18th centuries. The revolt of Latin America put an end to this transfusion of cultural energy, and equally disastrous was the dissolution of the religious Orders, especially the Jesuits. Moreover this culture was still living and productive on the eve of its downfall. Alike in Mexico and Portuguese Brazil some of the most original art and architecture belongs to the closing decades of the colonial epoch. And it was the latest Baroque, some of it as late as the 19th century, which Spanish missionaries brought northwards into Florida, Texas, New Mexico and California.

In spite of this premature collapse of the Baroque development of Christian culture in America, it retains its historic importance. Even in the United States, all over the West and the extreme Southeast the traces of this culture underlie the origins of contemporary American civilization, from Florida through Texas and New Mexico to the Pacific and extending northwards till it meets the parallel French Catholic missionary movement which expanded south and west from Canada. And when one considers how extremely sparse the settlement was and how small the population, it is remarkable how much was achieved by a few remarkable men like Kino and Junipero Serra on the Spanish borderlands and by the Jesuit missionaries and martyrs from Canada.

In Canada the effort to create an American Christian culture which would include the Indian population was no less intense than in Spanish America, but the material conditions were far more difficult and the environment even harder and more unfavorable than that of the Puritan colonies in New England. The heroism of the Jesuit missionaries and martyrs like St. Isaac Jogues and Jean de Brebeuf was unable to overcome the ferocious resistance of the Iroquois, who destroyed the work again and again. The economic basis of the colony was the fur trade, which penetrated far into the West and led to the discovery of the interior of the continent. But it was an economy which provided no basis for the creation of a settled culture. Yet the quality of the human material was exceptionally high.

All that was best in the great age of French spirituality—

the friends of Cardinal de Bérulle, St. Vincent de Paul, M. Olier, and M. de Bernieres—cooperated in the work. One of the greatest of the French mystics, Mme. Martin, usually known as Marie de l'Incarnation, whom Bossuet called the St. Teresa of the New World, spent her life in the Ursuline Convent at Quebec, where she wrote those remarkable letters to her son, Dom Martin, O.S.B., which are among the most interesting documents of 17th-century America.

At first sight it seems a waste that such remarkable human material should have been spent on such a sterile soil—that great mystics should educate little Hurons or that Fénelon's elder brother should live on hominy in Indian wigwams. But at least the foundations were laid more firmly than anywhere else in America, so that French Canada, unlike Spanish America, has always remained firmly attached to the religious tradition that was established in the 17th century.

XII

THE CULTURE OF DIVIDED CHRISTENDOM

[I]

THROUGHOUT most of the colonial period there is no comparison between the Catholic and Protestant achievements in the New World. The whole of South and Central America was Catholic, and their missions were spreading across the plains of the Southwest and up the Pacific Coast; it must have seemed merely a question of time before the whole of North America west of the Mississippi and North of the Ohio would be either Spanish or French in speech and Catholic in religion. No one would have supposed that the English colonies, which had barely succeeded in establishing themselves along the Atlantic coast, were destined to swallow up the Spanish development and impose a single English-speaking civilization on the whole continent from the Atlantic to the Pacific and from the Gulf of Mexico to the Great Lakes.

The causes of this revolutionary change are certainly not religious, for both the Spanish and the French Catholic cultures showed a much stronger missionary spirit and a greater understanding of the native peoples than either the English or the Dutch colonists of the East. Nor was it due to lack of enterprise, for the Spaniards and the French took the lead in the exploration of the Continent. The decisive factor is, I believe, to be found almost entirely in the sphere of political and social organization. In Catholic America the movement of expansion came from outside and from the Old World. The great missionary Orders, like the Jesuits and the Franciscans, had their center in Europe and recruited their missionaries from the home countries. And similarly the work of conquest and exploration was controlled from above and out-side, so that the native white population—the Creoles—always held a very subordinate position. But the English Protestant colonies almost from the first tended to form independent centers of English-speaking culture on American soil which, in spite of the remote control of the English government, were free to create their own society and social institutions. This is especially clear in New England, where the desire for independence, above all for spiritual independence from English ecclesiastical control, was the main motive that inspired the settlement.

Nevertheless the English Protestant colonists were in their way no less concerned with the problem of planting a Christian civilization in the New World than were their Catholic contemporaries. But it was a very different kind of civilization just as it was a different kind of Christianity. Indeed nowhere is the social contrast between Catholic and Protestant culture more sharply defined than in America during the colonial period. In Latin America the conditions of conquest and settlement only strengthened the unitary authoritarian aspects of Catholicism, whereas in the English colonies the separatist and individualistic tendencies of Protestantism were exaggerated in the new environment.

To some extent this may have been due to the fact that the English government deliberately used the colonies as a safety valve for opposition elements and encouraged the emigration of religious minorities not only to New England but also to Maryland and Pennsylvania and later on to Georgia. But the progress of separation continued on American soil and has remained a characteristic feature of American Protestantism down to our own days. In this Protestant society, it was the sect or Church, and in many cases the individual congregation, that was the real cultural unit. It was the source of education and the creator of public opinion, usually exerting a very close supervision on the behavior of the individual, either by moral pressure or, as in New England, by direct legal enactment. In and above the Church the only standard of belief and conduct was the Bible, and above all the Old Testament. Indeed in many respects the Puritan movement, most of all in New England, represents a Christian reversion to Judaism in which the Mosaic law replaced the canon law of the Catholic Church, and the characters of the Old Testament replaced the Catholic saints as the archetypes of spiritual perfection.

A religious culture of this kind was undoubtedly narrow and restricted, but it was well adapted to the needs of society. The moral asceticism of the Puritan ethos was in harmony with the strict utilitarianism of the colonial economy. For by retrenching all that was superfluous, by restricting the opportunities for enjoyment and display, it tended to concentrate men's energies on the necessary economic tasks on which the welfare of the community rested. It may seem paradoxical that a religion which depreciated good works and denied human merit should have produced a race of hard workers and keen men of business. But that is the paradox of Calvinism, and wherever Calvinist ideals and discipline triumphed, whether among the French Huguenots, the Scotch Presbyterians or the English and American Puritans, we find a similar spirit of moral energy and social activity which everywhere produced important results in the political and economic fields. Thus the social pattern of Puritan culture is extraordinarily different from that of Baroque Catholicism, and nowhere are the differences more sharply contrasted than in the New World, above all between New England and New Spain.

Meanwhile in Protestant Europe, especially in Calvinist countries, the Reformation had swept away the accumulated treasures of medieval art and religious symbolism and had destroyed the liturgical character of popular culture—its annual cycle of feasts and fasts, and its religious drama. Not that the Reformers had any deliberate intention of secularizing culture. On the contrary they wished to raise the standard of religious knowledge and practice. But they did this by exclusively intellectual and rational means. The sermon took the place of the liturgy. Bible reading took the place of religious imagery and symbolism, the communal character of the medieval festivals and pilgrimages was replaced by an individualistic type of piety which was, however, very different from that of the medieval hermit or ascetic, since it inculcated the strict performance of a man's social and economic duties.

Calvinism found its true sphere of activity not in the courts and among the nobles, but among the new commercial and industrial classes that were coming into existence in the towns of Holland and England. There was a natural affinity between the Puritan spirit and the spirit of the bourgeois. The strict asceticism of the Puritan ideal, which severely repressed man's natural tendency to ease and enjoyment and condemned all outward display as worldly vanity, inculcated industry and frugality as the first Christian duties, and this gave a supernatural sanction to virtues that were naturally dear to the bourgeois heart.

Thus Calvinism gave the middle classes a spiritual and moral background which enabled them to assert their social independence and to build up a new order that depended on individual industry and enterprise rather than on corporate responsibility and hereditary social sanction. Already in the 17th century we can trace the emergence of a new type—the hard-working, honest, respectable man of business who was destined to take the place of the noble and the courtier and the priest as the leading force in society.

Thus the contrast between the mature Baroque culture of Southern and Central Europe and the nascent bourgeois culture of Calvinist society was at once a contrast between opposing spiritual ideals and opposite social tendencies. The Baroque culture of Spain and Austria was that of a society of princes and monasteries—even palace-monasteries such as the Escorial—and left a comparatively small place to the tradesman and the manufacturer. It was an *uneconomic* culture which spent its capital lavishly, recklessly and splendidly, both to the glory of God and the adornment of human life.

The Puritan culture of Holland and England, on the other hand, was the culture of a society of tradesmen, yeomen and artisans whose life centered in the meeting house, the counting house, the farm and the workshop. They had neither time nor money to expend on artistic creation or external display. All their energies were concentrated on the task of saving their souls and earning their livings, and they reckoned every moment of time and every penny of expenditure as something for which they must render an exact account to the great Taskmaster in the day of final reckoning. And so while the Baroque culture was spending its wealth on pilgrimage churches and palaces and monasteries, the Puritans were laying the foundations on which the capitalist order of the future was to be built.

The ideal of the bourgeois culture is to maintain a high average standard. Its maxims are "Honesty is the best policy", "Do as you would be done by", "God helps those who help themselves." But the Baroque spirit lives in and for the triumphant moment of creative ecstasy. It will have all or nothing. Its maxims are: "All for love and the world well lost." "*Nada, nada, nada.*" "What dost thou seek for, O my soul? All is thine, all is for thee, do not take less, nor rest content with the crumbs that fall from the table of thy Father. Go forth, and exult in thy glory, hide thyself in it and rejoice, and thou shalt obtain all the desires of thy heart."

This mystical idea inspired Baroque culture in Spain and Italy in the later 16th and 17th centuries. It was not entirely absent from Germany and Holland and England in the 17th century, where it found literary expression in the work of the convert poets, like Scheffler ("Angelus Silesius") in Silesia, Vondel in Holland and Richard Crashaw in England. But it was in France during the early and middle decades of the 17th century that it produced the most direct results on the progress of Catholic reform. Here the application of the Tridentine reforms had been delayed by the religious wars and the obstacles created by the concordat and the commendatory system.

But in the 17th century a number of remarkable men devoted themselves to the reform of the clergy. First there was the work of Cardinal de Bérulle (1575–1629) and his successor Charles de Condren (1588–1641) in the foundation of the French Oratory, secondly there was St. Vincent de Paul (1576–1660), who was the founder of the Society of the Mission and of the Sisters of Charity. And thirdly, there was M. Olier (1608–1657), the founder of the famous Seminary of St. Sulpice in Paris, whose members had so much to do with the beginnings of Catholicism in the United States and in Canada.

These men, especially the cardinals de Bérulle and Olier, are of great importance in the history of French religious thought, for they created a new school of mysticism, which was based on the theology of the Incarnation and on the Pauline doctrine of man's incorporation with the Divine Humanity. This doctrine, which is first set forth in Berulle's book *Des Grandeurs de Jésus*, published in 1623, had an enormous influence on the whole movement of French Spirituality during the 17th century down to time of Bossuet and beyond. It might well have provided a point of contact with the contemporary spirituality of the English Puritans, which was also Pauline, though in a less mystical way, but so far as I know, none of the characteristic writings of this school were translated into English at this time.

It is, however, worthy of note that this movement had a direct influence on the Catholicism of North America, just as English Puritanism had a direct influence on the foundation of New England. M. Olier, in collaboration with a devout layman, M. D'Auversière, founded the Society of Our Lady of Montreal, which established the first settlement at Montreal as a missionary center in 1642 and, as we have seen, a few years earlier one of the greatest woman mystics of the age, Marie de l'Incarnation, founded the famous convent of the Ursulines at Quebec which played such an important part in the development of Catholic culture in Canada.

But in France itself this intense religious movement did not survive the 17th century. The reign of Louis XIV was accompanied by religious and cultural changes which proved fatal both to the Catholic spiritual revival and to the Baroque culture itself, and this change gradually spread to the rest of Europe. It was not, however, peculiar to France or to the Catholic world, for we find a similar process at work in England which led to the downfall of English Puritanism in the last half of the 17th century.

The secularization of Western culture, which some historians have regarded as implicit in the Renaissance, but which was in any case postponed by the Protestant Reformation and the restoration of Catholic culture in the Baroque period, was clearly manifest during the last years of the 17th century in that movement which Paul Hazard has described so fully in his book *The Crisis of the European Consciousness.*

[11]

Common to both halves of divided Christendom is the development of modern science, which was the work of this period. For as A. N. Whitehead wrote, "A brief and sufficiently accurate description of the intellectual life of the European races during the succeeding two centuries and a quarter, up to our own times, is that they have been living upon the accumulated capital of ideas provided for them by the genius of the seventeenth century." [1]

Catholic and Protestant Europe contributed almost equally to this work, and there was a close collaboration of scholars in spite of their religious differences. But this was not due to the

[1] Alfred North Whitehead, *Science and the Modern World* (New York: Macmillan), pp. 57–58.

progress of secularization, for some were extremely religious men. There is indeed a certain affinity between the religious and scientific thought and ideology of the period. In both there was an emphasis on the *via experimentalis*—in religion this meant the inner way of spiritual experience, in science it involved the empirical study of nature. And here it was not so much a matter of inductive versus deductive reasoning as it was a cult of direct intuitive contemplation of nature, as opposed to a merely literary and theoretical knowledge derived at second hand from the thinkers of the past.

There is no question of the importance of the new science and the new scientific method, since it has had a revolutionary effect on every aspect of our civilization. And there is no doubt that it is the original achievement of Western culture at this period. But the reasons for its emergence at this time and place are less clear. It is strange that so little study has been devoted to this subject.[2]

Personally I believe that modern science is not merely the creation of Western culture, but of Western Christian culture, although the influence of the Greek and Humanist tradition is also of key importance. But it is very difficult to see what were the decisive factors in the early stages of the development. One thing that stands out clearly is that the movement was an international one, not confined to a single country or to Catholic or Protestant Europe. Italy, England, France, Germany, Holland and Poland all made important contributions.

This internationalism of science followed the path that had already been opened by classical scholarship, which was the great bond of unity between the divided provinces of Western Christendom. Throughout this period, Latin remained the common language of scholarship, and there was

---

[2] Apart from the early chapters of Whitehead's volume cited above, Herbert Butterfield's *The Origins of Modern Science* (New York: Macmillan), A. R. Hall's *The Scientific Revolution* (Beacon, 1956), and A. C. Crombie's *Medieval and Early Modern Science* (Anchor, 1958) are useful studies.

a relatively free communication between classical scholars in different countries.[3]

The common world of classical scholarship was the background for the smaller and more esoteric common world of the scientists, and both of them had their centers in the academies rather than in the universities, although of course the universities still played a considerable part. Of particular importance was the University of Padua for the origins of science in Italy and indeed in Europe, Oxford for English science (especially the group which founded the Royal Society) and the University of Leyden for classical scholarship. But the development of the academies was one of the most characteristic features of this age, and beyond, from the 16th to the 18th centuries. And this is an aspect of European culture which has been rather neglected by the historians. The change from the university to the academy corresponds with a considerable change in intellectual attitudes and techniques: a change from the *ex cathedra* teaching of the professor to the free discussion of a group of equals together with greater opportunities for individual research.

Related to the rise of modern science is the immense widening in the intellectual horizon of Baroque culture by the movement of geographical discovery, trade and colonization. The progress of discovery was dependent on scientific knowledge, and in its turn the progress of science was dependent on the growth of geographical knowledge. It is also intimately associated with the missionary expansion which was one of the main religious activities of the Baroque culture, and the Jesuit missionaries in particular were among the most active agents for the diffusion of the knowledge of the non-European world. This is very evident in the writings of

[3] This lost world of classical scholarship is surveyed briefly and ably in Sandy's *History of Classical Scholarship* (New York: Hafner). But the relation of classical scholarship to medieval culture and to vernacular literature has been dealt with recently at some length by E. M. Curtius in his *European Literature and the Latin Middle Ages* (New York: Pantheon).

G. Botero, one of the greatest popularizers of the Baroque period. In reading his works, one is immediately struck by the complete change in the world view due to his new resources of knowledge, and he makes it clear that his main source of information, especially for the Far East, was the reports and books of the Jesuit missionaries.

But all of this new knowledge, even in the 16th and 17th centuries, involved a great challenge and problem for Christian culture. In the past, for example, in the early Middle Ages, when Christendom was small and weak and poor, there was no problem, because the average Christian was ignorant of the situation, and believed that Christendom was the center of the world. But now when Christendom had become powerful and was beginning a triumphant career of world expansion, Christians suddenly realized how large the world was and how small a place Christendom occupied. The Catholic and Protestant reactions were somewhat different, since the Calvinist view of the Elect had accustomed men's minds to the idea that the Church must form an infinitesimal portion of mankind. But, with the Catholics, and especially the more civilized and sophisticated ones, such as the Italians, the new knowledge often produced a certain reaction against the old ethnocentricity of the Christian world, as we see in the case of Botero. In his tract on *The Greatness of Cities*, he is inclined to stress the superiority of the cultures of the non-European world. Similarly, with secularizing writers like Montaigne the new knowledge led to cultural relativity and scepticism.

[111]

While Western Europe was advancing in power and wealth during the Baroque age, the whole of this period was a time of decline for the Christian cultures of the East. With the exception of the little kingdom of Georgia in the Caucasus, the Christian East was divided between the two empires of Turkey and Russia. The Christian peoples of the Balkans had practically lost their cultural independence, and had become the peasant serfs of their Muslim masters. The Greeks alone had a more privileged position, but only because they provided the official personnel of the Ottoman civil service. They maintained the traditions of the Byzantine culture, but it was no longer living or creative. Russia, on the other hand, gained a new prestige as the only surviving Orthodox power. But it was exposed to the cultural as well as the political pressure of the West, and the cultural revolution which was to transform Russian society in the 18th century was already beginning to make its influence felt in this period. It is important to remember that the great Schism, which represents the traditionalist and nativist reaction to foreign influence, belongs not to the age of Peter the Great but to the time of his father, Alexis.

There were two main sources of occidentalization at this period: (1) Western Europe, through the German, Dutch and British merchants and mercenaries; and (2) Central Europe, through Poland and the Ukraine, which at this time was the scene of an intense conflict between Orthodoxy and Catholicism. The first of these became predominant in the Petrine period, but in the 17th century, the influence of Kiev and of Ukrainian and Polish culture was very strong. Indeed the revival of learning which began at Moscow in the middle of the 17th century would have been impossible without the importation of Kievan scholars who knew Latin and Polish.

Similarly White Russia, which had enjoyed its greatest prosperity under Lithuanian rule, had also become a channel for the diffusion of Western culture in an Orthodox Slav society, and the recovery of Smolensk by Alexis, though of less cultural importance than the annexation of Kiev, provided further opportunities for contact between Muscovy and the West. No doubt the spirit of Russia remained intensely anti-Western in the 17th century, as we see in the Old Believers (above all in their great leader, Avvakum), and in the Cossacks of the Dnieper and the Don, who preserved an independent subculture of their own. But the central fact in Russian history is the beginning of the process of acculturation, which brought Russia step by step into the orbit of Western culture.

XIII

THE AGE OF LOUIS XIV AND
THE FORMATION OF
CLASSICAL FRENCH CULTURE

B Y THE second half of the 17th century Europe seemed
to have recovered from the disturbances that followed
the Reformation and the age of religious war and to have
returned once more to stability and order. The close of the
Thirty Years War left the exhausted lands of Central Europe
craving only for peace and utterly submitting to the will of
their princes. In England the Great Rebellion had ended in
the restoration of the monarchy and the triumph of the royal-
ist sentiment, while in Scandinavia the royal power had rendered itself absolute, both in Denmark and Sweden. But it
was in the France of Louis XIV that the triumph of authority
and order was most complete.

By 1655 the forces of disorder had been finally vanquished
and all the material and spiritual resources of the nation were
united in the vast and imposing structure of the absolute
monarchical state. The absolutism of Louis XIV was at once
more completely centralized and more efficiently organized
than that of Philip II or the empire of Austria. The success of
French arms and diplomacy, the splendor of the court of
Versailles, the national organization of economic life, the
brilliant development of French literature and art under royal
patronage all contributed to raise national prestige and establish the political and intellectual hegemony of France in
Europe.

The leadership of Catholic Europe had passed from Spain
to France and from the Hapsburgs to the Bourbons, and as
the Baroque culture of the Empire had dominated Europe in
the early part of the 17th century, so French culture formed

the standards of European taste and public opinion during the Grand Siècle.

The two cultures were so closely akin that the French culture of the age of Louis XIV may be regarded as a specialized form of the Baroque. But it was also a rationalization of the Baroque culture which subjected the vitality of the Baroque spirit to the rules and formulas of classical order, in the same way that in the religious sphere it subordinated the spiritual passion of Counter-Reformation mysticism to the moral discipline of the patristic tradition.

But although the French classical culture possessed a logical cohesion and order which Baroque culture itself lacked, it was a more conscious and artificial order which tended to produce a feeling of tension and constraint. Even the splendor of court life became wearisome when a noble could not absent himself from Versailles without incurring the royal displeasure. Even the grandeur of the classical style became oppressive when it left no freedom of expression to individual tastes and feelings. There was no longer any room for the unbridled fantasy and spiritual ecstasy of the Baroque genius. The watchwords of the new culture were order and regularity, good taste and good sense, reason and clear ideas. The age of Henry IV and Richelieu had indeed witnessed a great movement of Catholic revival which, like the Spanish revival in the previous century, produced a galaxy of saints and mystics. But unlike the latter it was not a universal movement which embraced and inspired the whole culture, but a minority movement which, like the Puritan movement in England, was a protest against the secularizing tendencies of the national culture. The analogies with Puritanism are especially visible in the left wing of the French Catholic revival which is represented by the Jansenist movement.

Jansenism owes it name and its doctrine to Jansenius (1585–1638), a Louvain theologian who became Bishop of Ypres. But his famous book *Augustinus* was not published—by his friend and disciple, the Abbé de Saint-Cyran (1581–1643)—until two years after his death. It was Saint-Cyran who was the real founder of the movement, since he brought the ideas of Jansenius into contact with the French Catholic revival, as represented by the newly reformed Cistercian Abbey of Port Royal, and with the Arnauld family who controlled it through the Abbess, Angélique Arnauld. Port Royal was already a center of the Catholic revival, and we must distinguish Jansenism as a theological movement from Port Royal as a spiritual center; though the two came together and influenced each other, they were never identical. Jansenism can be seen as an archaizing movement of Augustinian revival or as a kind of Catholic Puritanism. Jansenius and Saint-Cyran conceived it as a movement of moral and spiritual reform based on strict Augustinian principles, but they particularly emphasized the need for the revival of the ancient discipline of penance which involved what the Presbyterians call "Fencing the Tables", or the exclusion from communion of grave sinners even after repentance and confession. This brought them into conflict with the Jesuits, who were the chief theological supporters of the doctrine of free will, and also strong advocates of the practice of frequent communion.

Jansenism was predominantly an upper-middle-class movement, which drew its main support from the highly educated and serious-minded families of officials and parliamentarians like the Arnaulds, the Du Fossés and the Pascals. The most important belonged to the enormous Arnauld family, which peopled Port Royal—from the Abbess, Mère Angelique (1591–1661), who became abbess at the age of nine, to her sisters like Mère Agnès (1593–1671) and her brother Arnauld d'Andilly (1588–1674), and her nephews, Antoine Lemaître (1605–1658) and Isaac Lemaître, who founded the eremitical community of Solitaires. These lived at the gates of the abbey and devoted themselves to the production and the translation of works of piety which did so much to spread Jansenist opinions. But the most important of all was the youngest, the twentieth child of the family, Antoine, "Le Grand Arnauld" (1612–1694), the author of the famous work *De La Fréquente Communion* (1643), an indefatigable controversialist. He was forced to take refuge in the Netherlands, whence he carried on an unceasing warfare with the opponents of Jansenist opinion. Under the leadership of Arnauld and his younger companions in exile like Quesnel, the Jansenist movement exerted a powerful influence on the religious thought of the Grand Siècle, especially on its literature, notably in the case of Pascal, Racine and Boileau.

Eventually, in the course of the 18th century, Jansenism became both a sect and a political party, which concentrated the middle-class opposition to the policy of Louis XIV, the Jesuits, and the Ultramontanes. Its influence was particularly strong among the lawyers of the Parlement of Paris; and the attack on the Jesuits by the Parlement in the second half of the 18th century—which was the immediate cause of the dissolution of the Society of Jesus in 1765—was inspired and supported by them. In the 17th century, however, above all at Port Royal, it still formed part of the Catholic revival, and exerted a far-reaching influence on French society through its schools and its writings. In spite of its ultimate defeat, it made a profound impression on French religion and French culture, which has never been altogether effaced. It stood in conscious opposition to the dominant spirit of the age which expressed itself in Louis XIV's policy of national self-assertion and military aggrandizement, and in the pomp and magnificence of the court of Versailles. This Court set the pattern that was imitated and repeated in the courts and palaces of Europe for the next hundred years and more.

We must return, however, to the culture and polity against which Catholic mysticism and Jansenist austerity protested in vain. As we have already pointed out, the French culture of the Grand Siècle represents a national adaptation of the Baroque Counter-Reformation, as represented by the two Hapsburg monarchies, by the classical ideals of a national

Gallican monarchy and French vernacular culture. The foundation of this culture was laid in the Age of Richelieu by his creation of the Académie Française, which established the strict standards of French classicism. But French classical culture owed its European diffusion to the triumphant expansion of the power of France. This surrounded the monarchy of Louis XIV with a halo of glory, which was increased by the achievements of French literature and by the splendor of the Court.

No less important than this policy of military aggrandizement was the policy of economic expansion which accompanied it and made it possible. This was the work of Louis' great minister, Colbert, who devoted himself to increasing France's national wealth by an almost totalitarian system of state protection of industry and commerce, and by the development of French colonial and naval power. At the same time, by his construction of roads and canals, notably the great canal which linked the Atlantic and the Mediterranean, and by the reduction of internal tariff barriers, he increased the nation's trade and prosperity.

It was Colbert's aim to make France a great industrial and commercial power which would rival and replace the power of Holland, which had by its economic policy raised itself to a position of economic hegemony. It was his belief that the amount of European commerce was an almost constant quantity, amounting to about twenty thousand ships, of which ten to fifteen thousand were Dutch, three or four thousand English and only five or six hundred French. Since the total amount could not be increased, he concluded that France must carry on a commercial war, a "war of money", with her rivals. To wage this war successfully, France must concentrate all her energies on the activities which would subserve this central purpose. "It is necessary", he wrote to Louis XIV, "to reduce the professions of your subjects, as far as possible, to those which can be useful to these great designs. These are agriculture, commerce, the army and the navy. If Your Majesty can reduce all your people to these four professions, . . . he can become master of the world."

But although Louis XIV in the early part of his reign supported Colbert's efforts to establish and maintain the economic power of France at the expense of her rivals, and above all by the destruction of the power of Holland, he never fully understood or accepted his utilitarian ideal of concentration on economic production. His personal ideals were those of the Baroque culture: they centered upon glory embodied in his military conquests and the splendor of his court, and upon religious orthodoxy. In the later years of his reign, after his marriage to Mme. de Maintenon and his religious conversion (1683), he became increasingly absorbed in religious questions. Indeed in these years the whole spirit of his reign changed. It was as though the Spanish side of his inheritance from his mother, Anne of Austria, and her grandfather, Philip II, became dominant. He undertook the formidable task of establishing religious uniformity in his kingdom: to suppress French Protestantism, he revoked the Edict of Nantes in 1685.

Nothing could have been more opposed to Colbert's policy of encouraging the economically productive classes in the nation than this decision, for it resulted in the emigration of a minority which had always been distinguished for its industry and economic enterprise, and the enrichment of France's enemies—Holland, England and Brandenburg—who gained proportionately from the influx of Huguenot exiles. At the same time it provided foreign powers with a strong Fifth Column of secret or open sympathizers with the enemies of the French government. This was of great importance in the War of the Spanish Succession which mobilized against Louis XIV the Grand Alliance of Holland, England and Austria, while the Huguenot minority in the Cevennes cooperated with the enemy in a bitter partisan war for eight years.

At the beginning of the 18th century, however, nothing of

this was obvious. The splendor of the Court of Versailles was at its height and the monarchy of Louis XIV was without a rival in military power and cultural leadership. When, on the death of Charles II of Spain, Louis XIV accepted his bequest of his undivided dominions to Louis' grandson, Philip Duke of Anjou, in November 1700, he destroyed the traditional balance of power in Europe, which had rested on the rivalry of the Hapsburg and Bourbon dynasties, and raised France to a position of world hegemony which Louis' great-grand-father, Philip II of Spain, had been unable to achieve. Yet Louis, no less than Philip, failed to realize his ambitions. His moment of triumph united the other European powers in the grand coalition which initiated the last, greatest, and most disastrous of his wars—the War of the Spanish Succession—which occupied all the later years of his reign.

Nevertheless throughout these disastrous years Louis' indomitable character triumphed over both external and internal difficulties. He had always had a very high idea of his royal vocation and devoted all his energies to its fulfillment. For over fifty years he had been the most indefatigable Servant of the State. After the deaths of Colbert (1683) and Louvois (1691) he was his own first minister and personally carried on the work of government. Under the influence of Mme. de Maintenon and his successive Jesuit confessors, Pères de la Chaise and Le Tellier, he strove unceasingly from 1683 to realize his ideal of religious unity. In his suppression of Protestantism and Jansenism, he was supported by the fervent Catholicism of his ministers and courtiers, as well as by the religious devotion of his heir, the Duke of Burgundy, and the latter's confidant, Fénelon.

But the Jansenists continued to sow dissension in the Catholic ranks, and in the last years of the reign they united with the Gallicans to constitute a party of opposition to both the King and the Pope, an opposition embodied in the resistance to the bull *Unigenitus*, in which Pope Clement XI had condemned 101 propositions from the writings of Quesnel. Thus although Louis had escaped almost miraculously from the disasters of an unsuccessful war—after defeats between 1704 and 1707 at Blenheim, Ramillies, Oudenarde and Malplaquet—by the dissolution of the Grand Alliance and by the unexpectedly favorable terms of the Treaty of Utrecht, he was powerless, even with the help of the Papacy, to crush the religious opposition of this obstinate minority. This opposition continued long after his death and became the center of the parliamentary opposition through the 18th century.

The religious controversies of Louis' later years bequeathed a disastrous legacy to Europe and the Church. The classical French culture of the Grand Siècle was vitiated by the spirit of controversy which divided and weakened its spiritual forces. We see this most clearly in the case of Arnauld, who lived for controversy and contributed greatly to the controversial temper of the age. But it was true also of Bossuet, who gave expression to all that was deepest in the religious life of his age, yet was at the same time carried away again and again—as in his famous controversy with Fénelon on Mysticism and with Richard Simon on Biblical Criticism—into extremes of theological intolerance and personal injustice.

Consequently the remarkable outburst of Catholic thought and literature which characterized the later years of the Grand Siècle failed to provide the religious synthesis which the age required. No doubt the victory of Cartesian ideas contributed largely to this result by its advocacy of "*les idées claires*" and the procedure of "methodic doubt". This created an atmosphere of rationalist criticism, which spread rapidly in intellectual circles. Even the coordination of Cartesianism and Augustinianism which characterized the leading philosopher of that age, Nicholas Malebranche (1638-1715), in spite of its profound religious inspiration, failed to conciliate the suspicion of such typical Augustinians as Arnauld and Bossuet, who saw his philosophy as preparing the way for the influx of Socinian rationalism or for the pantheism of Spinoza.

Hence it came about that the strict orthodoxy of the later years of Louis XIV failed to realize itself in a general revival of Catholic culture. In spite of all the repressive action directed against them by King and Church, subterranean forms of religious opposition remained too strong to be suppressed. And the moment that the great king was dead—smallpox having left, of all his heirs, only his infant great-grandson to succeed him—there was an outburst of free thinking and free living which had its center in the court of the Regent, the Duke of Orleans (1675–1723), who represented the extreme opposite of his uncle in both character and ideas.

It was in this atmosphere of moral relaxation and intellectual reaction against the orthodoxy of the Grand Siècle that the French Enlightenment had its origins. The short-lived Entente with England promoted by the Regent and Cardinal Dubois brought about an intellectual rapprochement with English culture at the moment when the latter was profoundly influenced by Deism and by the action of the Huguenot exiles like Bayle and Le Clerc who had created an international center of anti-Catholic thought and propaganda in Holland. But the effect upon religion was very different on the Continent from its effect in England, still more in America.

XIV

THE WESLEYAN MOVEMENT
IN AMERICA

THE 18th century created the patterns of American
ecclesiastical and religious life. It was a creative and
original age both in England and America, in contrast to the
development on the European continent. No doubt the 17th
century was also very creative, and the Puritans who founded
the Churches of New England were the Founding Fathers of
American Protestantism. But the decline of Puritanism in
England after the Revolution was accompanied and followed
by a similar weakening of Puritanism in America. Its last great
representative, Jonathan Edwards, was already an anachro-
nism, and his successors, like Samuel Hopkins, were conscious that the spiritual forces of New England Puritanism
were becoming sterile and losing their hold on the mind of
society, so that by the beginning of the 19th century, religion
had ceased to be a living issue in the traditional strongholds of
New England culture. In spite of Jonathan Edwards and the
Great Awakening, the history of the native religious tradition
in New England follows a very similar course to that of
English Presbyterianism, by way of the Enlightenment, to
Unitarianism and Liberalism.

The religion of 19th-century America, in spite of its patri-
otic insistence on its inheritance from the Pilgrim Fathers,
really owed far more to the new religious forces which had
entered America from the Old World, and especially from the
British Isles, in the 18th century. It is impossible to discuss all
these different streams of influence, and I shall confine myself
mainly to the English contribution as represented above all by
the Episcopalians and the Methodists (as distinct from the
Scottish and Irish contribution).

The Episcopalians inevitably suffered a tremendous setback in the Revolutionary period, owing to the association of the Church with the English State, and the loyalty of its most active elements to the crown. The surprising thing is that it managed to survive at all; and the fact of its survival is, I believe, almost entirely due to the new forces which were developed in the 18th century. If the Episcopal Church had merely represented the 17th-century establishment, as it did in Virginia and the South, it is very questionable whether indeed it would have survived. But thanks to the efforts of Thomas Bray and the Church Societies, especially the Society for the Propagation of the Gospel (SPG), the 18th century saw a continuous expansion of Episcopalianism throughout the colonies, especially in New York and Connecticut.

The clergy whom the SPG sent out were men of a different type to the indifferent and incompetent clergy of Virginia and Maryland, who for the most part had come to the colonies because they were unable to get a living in England. The new missionaries were zealous and well-instructed men who were convinced and often aggressive exponents of High Church Episcopalian doctrine and who were not afraid to maintain their principles in the strongholds of the old Puritan tradition. They maintained their contact with the parent society by a regular system of bi-annual reports.

This extremely active movement of Episcopalian propaganda gained its first and most striking successes at Yale in 1722 when Dr. Cutler, the rector of the college, and six other members of the faculty announced their conviction of the invalidity of Presbyterian Ordination and their conversion to the Episcopal Church. This, as Josiah Quincy says, "was an event which shook Congregationalism throughout New England like an earthquake and filled all its friends with terror and apprehension". It may be compared in its effect on public opinion with the secession of Newman and many of his disciples to Rome in 1845, especially as one of the converts, Samuel Johnson, who was afterwards to found King's College at New York (now Columbia University) became one of the foremost representatives of colonial culture.

Thus in the 18th century American Episcopalianism began to develop on new lines, sharply differentiated not only from the Calvinist tradition of New England but also from the older type of the Established Church of Virginia. It was intellectually active, since it was kept in touch with contemporary English culture by the action of the SPG in establishing libraries and encouraging their missionaries to study by providing them with current English literature, as well as by the influence of men like Samuel Johnson and Bishop Berkeley, who spent three years in Rhode Island while attempting to establish his college at Bermuda and who was a generous patron of colonial culture.

By the time of the Revolution the Episcopal Church had come to number upwards of 480 parishes and missions, and would no doubt have been much stronger, had it been possible to provide a sufficient supply of American ministers. But this was impossible so long as there was no one in America who was able to ordain them. It was no light matter to cross the Atlantic in the 18th century! Dr. Samuel Johnson states that of all the candidates who went to England for ordination, no less than one fifth died before their return. His own experience was typical, for of the three Yale men who went to England in 1722, two went down with small-pox and one died. The mortality of the missionaries who came to America from England was even heavier, especially at the beginning of the century.[1]

Thus the question of an American episcopate was literally a matter of life or death for the Episcopal Church. Every Episcopalian in America or in England who had the welfare of his Church at heart was united on this issue. But they were never able to overcome the opposition of the Established Congregational Church in New England or the indifference

---

[1] John Wesley states in 1738 that nine-tenths of the SPG missionaries had died during their first four years in America.

of the English government and of the laymen—the vestry-men and lawyers—who controlled the Established Church in the South. The fear of an American episcopate was, as John Adams noted, one of the first causes of the agitation which prepared the way, in New England at least, for the American Revolution.

But at this moment a new movement made its appearance in America which was strong enough to find its own solution to the problem of Church government and thus was able to take over the missionary activities of the SPG when these were ended by the American Revolution and extend them to new fields.

This was the Methodist movement, which was closely linked in its origin with the SPG and derived its inspiration in some degree from the same sources. Its founder, John Wesley, was himself an Episcopalian and a High Churchman who never intended to found a new denomination, and saw his societies not as rivals but as auxiliaries to the Church of England, after the pattern of the older Church societies which played such an important part in the Church of England at the beginning of the 18th century and which had been strongly supported by his own father.

These societies had originated in the age of Charles II, possibly in imitation of the *collegia pietatis* which were characteristic of the Pietist movement in Germany and Holland. But at the time of the Revolution they increased greatly in numbers and fervor, under the influence of the High Church movement and often under the leadership of the Nonjurors. One of the most popular of all Anglican works of devotion— Nelson's *Festivals and Fasts*—was written in 1703 by a Non-juror and a layman for the use of members of these societies.

At the beginning of the 18th century there were more than forty societies in London, and they had begun to spread throughout the kingdom. So far as I know, there has been little study of their development in the reign of George I, but it is evident that they provided the milieu out of which the religious revival of the 18th century proceeded. Thus it was among the religious societies in South Wales that Howell Harris, the first lay evangelist, began his work about 1735; and similar societies were also strong in Bristol and the North of England before the coming of Methodism.

Above all it was a religious society of this type over which John Wesley, then a young Fellow of Lincoln College, Oxford, presided in 1730 and which was soon to be known as the "Methodist Club" owing to the strictness with which it adhered to a systematic "method" of spiritual exercises and good works. But Wesley's Oxford group represents an extreme development of the type. For he followed the guidance of Nonjurors like William Law and Thomas Deacon, who was the close associate of his friend, John Clayton. Deacon was one of the leaders of the most advanced wing of the Nonjurors, who were attempting at this time to bring about a counter-reformation of the Anglican Church by restoring the rites and doctrines of the primitive Church as represented by the Apostolic Constitutions. The revised Prayer Book based on these principles, which Deacon published in 1734, was much studied by John Wesley.

If Methodism had developed on these lines, it could hardly have avoided a break with the Establishment, and John Wesley might have gone down to history as the founder of an obscure Anglo-Catholic sect. But an old friend, Dr. John Burton of Corpus Christi College, who was probably aware of the danger, proposed that Wesley and his companions should offer their services to the SPG for missionary work in the newly founded colony of Georgia.

Accordingly, Wesley and his Oxford associate, Benjamin Ingham, went to America in 1735 as missionaries of the SPG, while his brother Charles went with them as secretary to the Governor-General, Oglethorpe, and another member of the Oxford Society, George Whitefield, followed in 1737. During his stay there Wesley maintained a scrupulous conformity to the regulations of the Society and the extreme High

Church doctrines that were characteristic of it. But while he was in America—indeed during his voyage there—he came into contact with German Moravians from Herrnhut, and this influence had a transforming effect on his life and teaching. Thus America was already acting as a melting pot.

When he returned to England in 1738 he became the close associate of the Moravian missionary, Peter Bohler, and later in the same year made a journey to Germany with his old Oxford friend, Charles Ingham, to visit Herrnhut and meet Count Zinzendorf himself. But even before this time he had taken part in the creation of the first Methodist Society in London at the house of the Huttons. The older Hutton, a High Churchman and a Nonjuror, had been very active in the work of the Religious Societies, and the new society— known as the Fetter Lane Society—represents an adaptation of the old Anglican model to Moravian ideas by James Hutton under the influence of Wesley himself.

The spirit of the new society was very different from that of the original Oxford Methodism. Wesley had gone to America a strict High Churchman or, as we should say, an Anglo-Catholic. He returned an evangelical Protestant who had become convinced by the Moravians that the essence of Christianity was the experience of conversion and the immediate personal conviction of saving faith.

This change of direction was reinforced by the influence of the youngest member of the Oxford Society, George Whitefield, who returned from America at this juncture and set about preaching to the religious societies at London and Bristol and to crowded audiences in the churches. Whitefield was to be the second great leader of the Evangelical Revival, above all in America, where he became one of the chief agents in the Great Revival which was about to sweep through the colonial churches.

Although he was far inferior to Wesley in originality of mind and strength of character, he never possessed Wesley's intense and scrupulous attachment to the authority and practice of the Church of England, and consequently when he found the churches of Bristol closed against him by the Anglican clergy, he took the law into his own hands and began to preach in the open air to the colliers at Kingswood in February, 1739.

Before he left for his second visit to America in the same year, he had persuaded Wesley to come to Bristol and take over his work, both in the religious society and in the practice of field preaching which Wesley began, with considerable misgiving (in April, 1739). Almost immediately this became the characteristic instrument of the Methodist apostolate. Thenceforward for more than fifty years Wesley preached daily (often several times daily) in fields and barns, private houses and churches through the length and breadth of the British Isles. No doubt Whitefield did the same over a much wider area from New England to Georgia, as well as in England and Ireland. But Wesley did much more than preach. In the course of his long life he built up an elaborate and highly centralized organization of Methodist societies, which were united not only by their common faith and religious experience but by an extremely strict system of discipline and inspection through which Wesley exercised his personal authority and control.

It was an amazing achievement which can only be compared with the most centralized religious Orders such as the Jesuits. Indeed Wesley's authority was at once more universal and more personal than that of any head of a religious Order. It is true that the members of his societies were not trained and disciplined like monks. They were gathered almost at random from the highways and hedges—half-savage miners from Cornwall and Northumberland, solid yeomen from Yorkshire and Derbyshire, artisans and shopkeepers from the cities, clergymen, schoolmasters, soldiers, eccentrics and visionaries—all were recruits for Wesley's motley army and marched together in their societies and classes and bands at his word of command.

And his achievement was the more remarkable in that he never professed to teach a new doctrine or to form a new Church. Down to the end of his life he remained a priest of the Church of England, and until the last years he stiffly resisted all attempts at separation. For nearly fifty years he kept the whole of his great organization suspended between the Established Church and the sects by a sheer act of autocratic will.

But this *tour de force* executed with unflinching determination for half a century involved Wesley in a series of conflicts with ecclesiastical authority on the one hand and with the other leaders of the religious revival on the other. At the very beginning of his evangelical career he found himself in conflict with the bishops whose authority he acknowledged in all things lawful, and the particular bishop with whom he had to deal was no Hanoverian court prelate but the great bishop Butler whom Wesley revered as a writer and a thinker. It was during this interview at Bristol on August 18, 1739, that Butler uttered his famous remark, "Sir, this pretending to extraordinary revelations and gifts of the Holy Ghost is a horrid thing—a very horrid thing." And he concluded the interview by saying, "Well, sir, since you ask my advice, I will give it to you freely. You have no business here; you are not commissioned to preach in this diocese. Therefore I advise you to go hence." With any other man this would have meant either submission or separation. But Wesley merely asserted his right as an ordained priest and a Fellow of Lincoln College to "an indeterminate commission to preach the Word of God in any part of the Church of England."

This collision with authority was immediately followed by a conflict with the Moravians to whom Wesley owed his conversion and with whom he was associated in the Fetter Lane Society. In spite of his new evangelical convictions, Wesley still remained a High Churchman, and he refused to accept the Moravian attitude towards the sacraments and religious ordinances. His mind revolted against the introverted

Pietism of the Moravian teaching, which seemed to him to encourage antinomianism and Quietism. In consequence he broke with the Fetter Lane Society in which Moravian influences predominated; and with the minority that followed him he founded a new society at the Foundry in Moorfields, London, in December 1739, which was the first true Methodist society of the Wesleyan connection. Unfortunately this breach with the Moravians involved a breach with the members of the old Oxford group who had been closest to him, Benjamin Ingham and John Gambold, who was to become a Moravian bishop, as well as his old London friend, James Hutton.

Almost at the same time Wesley became separated from George Whitefield by the Calvinist issue. Nowhere is the Catholic element in Wesley's thought more apparent than in his teaching on grace and free will and in the vehemence with which he always opposed what he called the "Horrible Decree" of reprobation. Whitefield, on the other hand, during his second visit to America, had come under the influence of Jonathan Edwards and the Tennents, and had become an enthusiastic supporter of strict Calvinist principles. On his return to England in 1741 he did not hesitate to denounce Wesley's Arminian teaching; and his followers separated themselves from the Methodists of Wesley's connection by a schism which was marked by considerable bitterness and *odium theologicum*. The leaders themselves retained their respect and affection for one another, and even to the end Wesley met Whitefield and Howell Harris on friendly terms. But this was not the case with Whitefield's disciples like Toplady and Roland Hill and Romaine, who attacked Wesley and his brother with extraordinary virulence and scurrility down to the end of their lives.

Thus Wesley was isolated between the Moravians and the Evangelical Calvinists, on the one hand, and on the other, their extreme opposites, the typical Whig Latitudinarian Anglicans, like Bishop Lavington, Warburton and Dr. Trapp.

These were the sworn enemies of Enthusiasm, who did not attempt to distinguish between Wesley and Whitefield, or even distinguish Wesley from the extreme Antinomian fanatics who hung onto the skirts of these movements. But Wesley went his own way with matchless vigor and resolution.

In what did his originality consist? To his contemporaries he appeared primarily a great revivalist, an itinerant field preacher whose meetings were accompanied by all those manifestations of mass hysteria which have always characterized religious revivals.

But here Wesley has no claim to originality. Field preaching and mass hysteria appeared in South Wales (with Howell Harris) before they reached England, and they were introduced into England by Whitefield rather than Wesley. Moreover Revivalism had already appeared in America with the Dutch Calvinists in New Jersey, with the Presbyterians at New Brunswick, New Jersey, and with Jonathan Edwards at Northampton, Massachusetts. It was in America that Whitefield had found his spiritual home, and he was far more in sympathy with the Presbyterianism of the Tennents and the Puritanism of New England than with the Church of England to which he nominally belonged. But he was no organizer, nor were the other leaders of the Great Awakening. They were essentially Revivalists, and they left the fruits of the revival to be gathered or scattered by the local churches.

Wesley, on the other hand, was essentially an organizer. It was his special office to follow up the revival with a methodical work of social organization, in which the faith of his converts should be tested by their works. There is an extraordinary contrast between the excitement and emotionalism that accompanied the revivals and the experience of personal conversion, and the hard practical common sense with which Wesley judged the spirit of his converts and by which he governed his preachers and his societies. And this was the secret of his success.

Revivalism, enthusiasm, asceticism, mysticism were all anti-pathetic to the 18th-century mind, to such a degree that the natural tendency of 18th-century culture was towards a purely rational religion like Deism, or an irreligious rationalism like that of the French Enlightenment. But John Wesley, in spite of the intensity of his religious convictions, was a typical 18th-century Englishman who possessed the virtues and limitations of his age, nationality and class. In many of his traits and idiosyncrasies, as well as in his physique, he has a curious resemblance to his cousin, the great Duke of Wellington, and like him he was, as Leslie Stephen remarks, above all a great captain of men.

He was a man of authority and order who held that "the Gospel of Christ knows no religion but social, no holiness but social holiness." In the *Plain Account of the People Called Methodists* which he wrote for Perronet in 1748, he says hardly anything about revivalism or the experience of conversion. He traces the whole development of Methodism from the principle of Christian fellowship and from his realization that "this is the very thing which was from the beginning of Christianity" but which had been destroyed by the secularization of the Church so that in the majority of parishes membership of the Church had become "a mere rope of sand". The aim of Methodism was to bring Christian fellowship out of the clouds into immediate relation with the lives of the common people of 18th-century England.

Thus Methodism in Wesley's idea was a return to primitive Christianity or a new Reformation, in so far as this means a revival of the spirit of Christian fellowship in moral life and social action. On the other hand, he expressly disavowed all doctrinal innovations, as well as theological dogmatism and ecclesiastical schism or sectarianism. On these points he became more and more critical of the Reformation itself, and he concludes *A Farther Appeal to Men of Reason and Religion* with a remarkable passage in which he contrasts his attitude to the Church of England with that of the Reformers towards

Catholicism. Whereas he was determined to remain a member of the Anglican Church, "the grand stumbling block" of the 16th-century Reformers "was their open, avowed separation from the Church . . . and their continual invectives against the Church they separated from". And this was true also of the Reformation in England. "The main stumbling block remained, namely, open separation from the Church."

Wesley's conception of what the relation of Methodism to the Church of England should be is perhaps best seen in the definite proposals which his friend and designated successor, Fletcher of Madely, drafted in 1775. It is easy to see that any such formula of union between the amorphous Erastianism of the Hanoverian establishment and the highly centralized organization of the United Methodist societies was entirely impracticable. Nevertheless the final breach was delayed year after year, and when at last it came in 1784, it was in direct response to the desperate situation that had arisen not in England but in America, after the winning of Independence, when the Church of England found itself left derelict without a bishop or any system of ecclesiastical jurisdiction.

At this time the American Methodists were still a small and uninfluential body. For it was not until 1769 that Wesley had sent his first preachers to the colonies, and their work was only beginning when the outbreak of the war with Britain interfered with its progress.

At first sight it is difficult to explain this delay of thirty years in extending the work of the Methodist societies to America, seeing that Wesley himself had spent some years in America and the work of his friend Whitefield had shown how great was the opportunity for evangelization. But it must be remembered how widely Whitefield differed from Wesley both in doctrine and method and how much of Whitefield's success was due to his close cooperation with the most extreme school of Presbyterian revivalists, whose work had aroused the intense hostility of the conservative Congregationalists and Anglicans in the East. In his early years Wesley had been on very friendly terms with Dr. Cutler, the ex-President of Yale, who had become a convert to Anglicanism. Now as Rector of Christ Church, Boston, Cutler was the leader of the opposition to the revival and denounced both Whitefield and Tennent in violent language.

"Whitefield", he wrote in 1744, "has plagued us with a witness. It would be an endless attempt to describe the scene of disturbance and confusion occasioned by him; the division of families, neighborhoods and towns; the contrariety of husbands and wives, the undutifulness of children and servants; the quarrels among the teachers; the disorders of the night; the neglect of husbandry and the gathering of the harvest. . . .

"When Whitefield first arrived here the whole town was alarmed. . . .

"The fellow treated the most venerable with an air of superiority, but he for ever lashed and anathematized the Church of England, and that was enough. After him came one Tennent—a monster! impudent and noisy—and told them they were all damned! damned! damned! This charmed them, and in the most dreadful winter I ever saw, people wallowed in snow night and day, for the benefit of his beastly brayings; and many ended their days under these fatigues." [2]

Wesley's personal sympathy with Whitefield and the practice of field preaching was counterbalanced by his Arminianism and his loyalty to the Church of England, so it is not surprising that he delayed embarking on a mission in which he would inevitably have come into conflict with both parties.

By the end of the '60's, however, the situation was changed. Whitefield had renewed his friendly relations with Wesley. His mission to America was drawing to an end (with his death at Newburyport in 1770) so that when, in 1768, Dr. Wrangel, the King of Sweden's representative among the Swedish Americans, appealed to him to send preachers to

[2] L. Tyerman, *Life of Whitefield*, Vol. II, pp. 124–25.

help the American Christians, "multitudes of whom are as sheep without a shepherd", he was ready to take action to help the group of Methodists who were already established at New York.

Wesley's missionaries had not the resounding success which attended Whitefield's preaching. Their ministry was most successful among the Anglicans or ex-Anglicans of Maryland and Virginia. Moreover, as I have mentioned, their progress was interrupted by the Revolution. Wesley himself was an outspoken supporter of George III, his preachers were Englishmen and their American followers were largely loyalist, so that it is surprising that they were able to survive.

Their success was largely due to Francis Asbury, the only one of Wesley's preachers who was able to hold his ground throughout the Revolution. Though an uneducated man, the son of a Staffordshire gardener, he resembled Wesley himself in his love of discipline and order as well as in his tirelessness as a traveller and a preacher. (He is said to have travelled 250,000 miles and made 300,000 converts.) His voluminous journals which recount these travels in minute detail are not, of course, to be compared with Wesley's journals in psychological and literary interest. Nevertheless, they remain a primary source for the history of religious and social conditions in the revolutionary and post-revolutionary age and one which I think has not been sufficiently utilized by historians.

Asbury was an independent and stubborn character who not infrequently had sharp differences of opinion with Wesley himself. But he was fundamentally loyal to his leader and to Wesley's idea of Methodist principles and organization. So that when finally in 1784 Wesley began to ordain ministers and to create an autonomous Methodist church in America, the task of implementing his decision fell on Asbury, who was appointed joint superintendent with the Welshman, Dr. Coke, of all the Methodists in America (about fifteen thousand in number).

This assumption of episcopal authority met with bitter opposition from Charles Wesley and from many other Methodists. But John Wesley himself still protested that he was faithful to the Church of England and that he only took this step from necessity since the bishops refused to do anything to help this scattered flock in America.

His dilemma is shown in the letter which he wrote to Bishop Lowth in 1780 when the latter had refused to ordain one of the preachers that Wesley was sending to America on the ground of his ignorance of Latin and Greek. "I mourn for poor America, for the sheep scattered up and down therein. Part of them have no shepherds at all, particularly in the Northern colonies, and the case of the rest is so little better, for their own shepherds pity them not. They cannot; for they have no pity on themselves. They take no thought or care about their own souls. Your Lordship did see good to ordain and send into America other persons who (unlike the Methodists) knew something of Latin and Greek, but who knew no more of saving souls than of catching whales" (Letter of August 10, 1780).

Now Wesley had long been convinced (by Lord Chancellor King's arguments) that the primitive church order made no distinction between priests and bishops and that the power of ordination was common to both of them. But he was not consistent in the matter. For when the new superintendents of the Methodists in America began to take the official title of Bishop (in which they were perfectly justified on Wesley's own theory), he upbraided Asbury most bitterly for the assumption of the title and declared, "Men may call me knave or fool and I am content, but they shall never by my consent call me Bishop." Yet he wrote this in 1788—the very year in which he had commenced ordaining ministers for the Methodists in England.

In reality the authority which Wesley exercised over the Methodist societies was far wider than that of any bishop, and he was so convinced of his apostolic mission to raise up a new

Christian people that he was not willing to let any ecclesiastical order or tradition stand in the way of it. That is why he insisted in his last letter to America, written in 1791, that come what may there must be no separation between the American Methodists and their brethren in Europe. "Lose no opportunity of declaring to all men that the Methodists are one people in all the world; and that it is their full determination so to continue

> though mountains rise and oceans roll
> to sever us in vain" (Letter of February 1, 1791).

This aim was in fact secured by the centralizing force of Wesley's life-work which was continued in America by the similar tendency of Asbury's dominating personality. It is true that the other bishop, Dr. Coke, was still desirous of maintaining the old relation to the Anglican Church, and in the years 1791–1792, he entered into negotiations with the new Episcopal bishop in Philadelphia (who had been consecrated in England in 1789) in order to bring about a union.

I think there is little doubt that such a union would have been of immense benefit to the Episcopal Church, especially in Virginia and the South, where its whole organization had been wrecked by the Revolution. The confiscation of Church property in Virginia which followed disestablishment was the final blow which brought the Church to the brink of dissolution.

The Methodists, on the other hand, were exceptionally strong in Virginia. Nor would it have been without advantage to the Methodists; since it might have supplied the cultural and intellectual element that they lacked, especially after the death of the two Wesleys.

At the same time the whole temper of Virginian Episcopalianism, apart from a very few exceptional characters like Devereux Jarrett, was so utterly different from that of popular Methodism that it is difficult to imagine how such a union could have ever succeeded. Bishop Madison of Virginia and

Bishop Asbury, the Methodist, belonged to two different worlds, and their denominations followed opposite paths—Methodism with its circuit riders, like Peter Cartwright, following the moving frontier to the West, and Episcopalianism keeping its hold on the most conservative social elements in the East.

Yet in spite of this there is a certain parallelism between the two cases. In both, the severance of relations with England had shaken the bases of ecclesiastical order and seemed to open the way to a religious revolution. At the Fluvanna Conference in 1779 the Methodists proposed to solve their problems by ordaining themselves to administer the sacraments, while in Virginia and the South the Episcopalians proposed to reorganize the Church on a democratic basis which would ensure the control of the laity.

But in both cases these plans were defeated and the principles of order and unity were maintained by the transmission of hierarchical authority, from Wesley in 1784 to Coke and Asbury, from the Scottish bishops to Samuel Seabury of Connecticut in 1784, and from the English bishops to Bishops White and Provoost in 1787. Thus at the very moment when the political link between America and England was broken, a new religious link was established both with the Methodists and the Episcopalians through which these two religious societies were able to create the first national American organization.

XV

THE SECULARIZATION OF
MODERN CULTURE

THE whole situation in Western Europe was transformed in the 18th century by the advent of the new scientific and technological culture which was common to both Catholic and Protestant Europe. But this was far from being the only factor that made for the growing secularization of Western culture. We must also study the more general social factors of the process. Obviously we cannot understand the present situation of Christianity in Western Culture unless we have studied the causes that have led to the weakening or occultation of Christian Culture during the last two centuries. And it is not sufficient to do this in the abstract: we must trace the process historically in Protestant and Catholic Europe, and above all in England and France, where the processes of change were parallel to one another, but very widely different in their modes of operation.

The immediate cause of the secularization of European culture was the frustration and discouragement resulting from a century of religious wars, and above all from the inconclusiveness of their end. After the Peace of Westphalia in 1648, the necessity for the coexistence of Catholics and Protestants in Europe became generally recognized, and since men still valued their common culture they were forced to emphasize those elements which were common to Catholics and Protestants, i.e., its secular aspects. This had already been recognized in the United Netherlands since their foundation by William the Silent, and to a somewhat lesser degree in France during the period of the Edict of Nantes (1598–1685), and after 1648 it became the international law of the Empire as between states (though not between individuals). In England also the experience of the Civil Wars and of the mutual intolerance of the sectarian extremists produced an important movement towards mutual toleration supported by Cromwell himself, though the Restoration brought back a State Church and a regime of conformity. But it is noteworthy that the really successful weapon against Puritan extremism was not the persecution of Church and State, but the ridicule of men of letters like Samuel Butler in his *Hudibras* and Dryden in his *Absalom and Achitophel*.

One of the chief factors in the changed climate of opinion was the growth of a lay intelligentsia, and the creation of a class of journalists and professional men of letters in France, England and the Netherlands. On the higher social level this new intelligentsia was represented by the academies, which played a very important part in the development of scientific studies. On the lower level it covered a wide range down to the penniless scribblers who were ridiculed by Pope in the *Dunciad*.

In France, especially, this class tended to favor free thought and lax morals. They were the "libertines", the forerunners of the "*philosophes*" of the following century, and the inheritors of the tradition of Rabelais and Montaigne. Their most distinguished representative was Saint-Évremond, who spent the last forty years of his long life in England (and Holland) and is buried in Westminster Abbey.

These influences were growing beneath the surface throughout the 17th century with thinkers like Gassendi and Hobbes, and writers like Cyrano de Bergerac, Molière, Samuel Butler, and La Fontaine, until in the 18th century they came to the surface and dominated Western culture. This growth of a lay intelligentsia was only one aspect of the rise of the middle classes which was already far advanced in Holland by the 17th century and in England and France by the 18th. The merchant class in Holland and England and the lawyers and officials in France gradually took the place of the nobility as the real leaders of culture. Unlike the men of letters, the new middle classes were by no means hostile to religion, and they maintained much stricter standards of moral behavior than the old aristocratic classes. But on the other hand, they were apt to be critical of authority and naturally tended to adopt a sectarian type of religion—Puritans and Nonconformists in England, and Huguenots in France. Theirs was among the strongest influences making for the secularization of culture, as so many writers have argued (like Max Weber, Ernest Troeltsch, Tawney, and Groethuysen). They regarded religion as a private matter which concerned the conscience of the individual only, whereas public life was essentially business life; a sphere in which the profit motive was supreme and a man's moral and religious duties were best fulfilled by the punctual and industrious performance of his professional activities. As it was the ideal of the nobleman to win honor on the field of battle, so it was the ideal of the bourgeois to win profit in the field of business, and the latter often required as much courage and daring as the former.

We fortunately possess a remarkable type-specimen of the new bourgeois psychology and ethics at the moment when the great transition to secular culture was taking place, namely the life and work of one of the greatest English writers of the Augustan Age—Daniel Defoe (1661–1731). He was a professional author and journalist, who wrote, and wrote well, on every subject of public interest—history, geography, economics, politics, ethics, religion and fiction. In fact his output was so enormous and covers so many different fields, that no one can hope to read it all. Fortunately, however, his most famous and popular work, *The Life and Adventures of Robinson Crusoe*, in its three parts (most readers confine themselves to the first only) reflects almost every aspect of Defoe's many-sided genius. It is the epic of Protestant individualism, which is not merely a story of adventure but a moral allegory or parable, which shows how the Nonconformist conscience can survive when it is uprooted from its sociological background and forced to come to terms with the realities of a wider alien world.

For in spite of Defoe's secular temperament, he is fully aware of the importance of the religious element in culture, and the greater part of the third part of the book is devoted to a discussion of the religious state of the world, the failure of Christianity to become a worldwide religion, and the possibility of a union of Christian states to extend the boundaries of Christendom. Throughout this part of the work, it is the absurdity and evil resulting from the divisions between Christians that are most insisted on, and though he maintains the traditional medieval concept of a union of Christian princes for a crusade against the infidels, he finally admits that such projects are entirely outside the range of practical politics. But strangely enough, the concluding passage of the book in which he arrives at this pessimistic conclusion is the only one that seems to show religious feeling. "For I doubt", he says, "no zeal for the Christian religion will be found in our days or perhaps in any age of the world, till Heaven beats the drums itself, and the glorious legions from above come down on purpose to propagate the work and to reduce the whole world to the obedience of King Jesus—a thing which some tell is not far off, but of which I heard nothing in all my travels and illuminations, no, not one word."

This is a strange conclusion to a book which is justly praised as the most realistic story of adventure ever written, and few readers even know that this is Crusoe's last word! For the third part of *Robinson Crusoe* is generally dismissed as a piece of hackwork to attract the religious public. But however that may be, it throws a very interesting light on Defoe's mind, which reflects the whole world of his time—physical, cultural, and religious—with extraordinary fidelity. And in the passage I have just quoted, we see the new world of bourgeois individualism looking back with a pang of nostalgia towards the disappearing shores of the religious world that it had left behind it.

Defoe, in spite of his doubts and hesitations, was still loyal in his own way to the tradition of Christian culture. But already during his lifetime, and increasingly after 1685, a new type of culture was arising which was in conscious revolt against Christianity, and which aimed at the creation of a new rational and philosophical basis for a united Western culture. This was the Enlightenment, which found expression first in the English Deists at the close of the 17th century and secondly in the French philosophers and Encyclopaedists who gave the movement a worldwide diffusion in the second half of the 18th century.

There was moreover one influence which lies behind both of these movements, and was of great historical importance in many different directions. This was the influence of the Protestant refugees who left France after the Revocation of the Edict of Nantes in 1685 for Holland, England and Prussia; indeed for every Protestant country. These refugees represented the most active and independent elements in the French bourgeoisie, and they acted as a two-way channel of cultural influence between France and the rest of Europe, especially England. For half a century they were the leading journalists and translators who made English culture, especially the thought of Locke and Newton and Shaftesbury, known in France. The refugees were thoroughly French in mentality, but were the sworn enemies of Louis XIV and of French Catholicism; so that the result of the Revocation was to create a most powerful and well-organized underground movement against Catholicism. The headquarters of this campaign was in Holland, and its chief organ was the free press, edited by brilliant scholars like Bayle and Le Clerc, which reached a European public.

The strength of these writers was their critical spirit. They did not try to defend Protestantism—indeed they no longer believed in it—but to attack at all points the intolerance and credulity of the orthodox—all the orthodox, everywhere and in all ages. In this way the exiled intelligentsia were the forerunners of the French Encyclopaedists. Their greatest writer, in fact, Pierre Bayle (1647–1706), was himself an encyclopaedist in the literal sense of the word, and his *Diction-naire Historique et Critique* (Rotterdam 1697, English translation 1730), was the indispensable *vade mecum* of every rationalist and sceptic from the beginning of the century to the days of Gibbon. The influence of the Huguenot exiles is perhaps shown most clearly in the case of Gibbon. His thought and learning were nourished not by the English deists, nor the French philosophers, but by the older tradition of critical scholarship that owes its origins to the Protestant exiles in Holland and Switerland—Bayle and Le Clerc, Basnage and Beausobre and Barbeyrac. It was not long before their influence united with that of the non-Protestant French intelligentsia to form the new culture of the Enlightenment. In this connection it is highly significant that Bayle's disciple, biographer and editor, the Huguenot Des Maiseaux, was also the disciple, biographer and editor of Saint-Évremond, the aristocratic free-thinker whose voluntary exile in England had nothing to do with Protestantism.

The effect of the Revocation of the Edict of Nantes was, however, not confined to the formation of the Huguenot *diaspora* in Protestant Europe. It also produced profound changes in French culture. Defoe (in the third part of *Robinson Crusoe*) quotes a French Protestant as saying that the Huguenots who left France had left their religion behind them, and those who stayed had done so by the sacrifice of their principles: so that a new type of Protestant-Catholic had been created, men who practised a religion that they did not believe and "went to Mass with Protestant hearts". They created a center of religious disaffection and resentment in France, and especially among the bourgeoisie which remained in fairly close contact with the Huguenot refugees in Holland and England. Though this disaffected minority were unable to profess or defend their old religion for fear of reprisals, there was nothing to prevent them from criticizing Catholicism on purely rational grounds, and thus their influence combined with that of the secular rationalists to create the atmosphere of criticism, scepticism and hostility to authority which permeated French 18th-century culture.

In England the influence of the Deists, which was at its height during the reign of George I, was checked by three factors. In the first place the strongest force in the English Enlightenment was not consciously anti-religious. The founders of the Royal Society, Wilkins, Newton, Boyle, Wallis, and Wren, were all professing Christians, and some of them pious. For example, Thomas Sprat (1635–1713), the historian of the Royal Society and one of the leading champions of religious toleration, was an Anglican bishop, and Boyle, the author of *The Sceptical Chemist*, devoted part of his property to the foundation of a lectureship in apologetics which still survives. In fact the Baconian philosophy which inspired the Royal Society in its early days—the idea of an experimental science combined with mathematics and applied to the conquest of nature and the service of man—had its roots in English medieval philosophy and was easily reconcilable with a religious view of the world and the acceptance of revelation.

In the second place the differences between the Deist advocates of a purely rational religion and the Latitudinarian divines of the established Church or the Nonconformists who tended towards Socinianism and Unitarianism were so small that it is often difficult to detect shades of opinion. Indeed the title of one of the ablest of the Deist works, *Christianity as Old as Creation* or *The Gospel a Republication of the Religion of Nature* by Tindal (1655–1733) is borrowed from one of Bishop Sherlock's sermons.

In the third place the defenders of orthodoxy proved to be better writers and abler controversialists than their critics. Thus the tables were turned. The English rationalists had no Voltaire, whereas the Christians produced a remarkably able set of apologists and pamphleteers of all shades of opinion from Latitudinarian Whigs like Warburton, through Moderates like Bishops Butler and Berkeley, to High Tories like

Swift and Nonjurors like William Law and Charles Leslie. Thus it came about that at the moment when the French Enlightenment was launching its triumphant attack on Christianity, Deism was in a state of decline and English Protestantism was undergoing the remarkable revival associated with the names of John Wesley and George Whitefield. Consequently (and independently of Wesley's influence), the second half of the 18th century tended to be more religious than the first, and some of the greatest figures in the literary world (such as Dr. Johnson and Cowper) were exceptionally religious men.

Thus the English Enlightenment did not lead to the defeat of Christianity by the forces of rationalism. English opinion rallied from the Deist attack and found a satisfactory compromise in the moderate and tolerant Liberal Protestantism which finds its classical expression in Addison's *Spectator*. On the other hand, there is no doubt that this period did see a general secularization of English social and political life. The Revolution of 1688 was followed by the triumph of the middle classes and the enthronement of private property, with the man of property as the foundation of the new social order. After the death of Queen Anne and the establishment of the Hanoverian dynasty, the crown lost its traditional halo of Divine Right and became an organ of the new secular regime. Even the religious revival of the Wesleyan movement helped to increase the secularization of public life by emphasizing the importance of individual conversion and the private character of religion. But already in the first decades of the century the world so vividly depicted by Defoe, not only in his novels but in his *Tour through Great Britain* and his *Complete English Tradesman*, is a wholly secularized world in which individualism and the profit motive rule supreme.

Hence it was that England became regarded on the Continent, especially in France, as a political model for the New Age. The writers of the Enlightenment, headed by Voltaire and Montesquieu, saw England as an embodiment of liberal ideals: political freedom, religious toleration, free trade, and personal independence. In the eyes of the French philosophers, England had shown that these things were not only possible, but were the secret of the phenomenal prosperity and power she had achieved since the Revolution.

XVI

THE AGE OF THE ENLIGHTENMENT

NOTWITHSTANDING the contribution made by England to the European Enlightenment and the profound influence it exerted on French thought, it was in France itself that the Enlightenment achieved its fullest expression and from France that it was diffused throughout the rest of Europe.

This was no doubt largely due to the international prestige that French culture had already acquired during the reign of Louis XIV, when Versailles had become not only the pattern of European monarchy, but also the arbiter of European manners and taste. Moreover this classical culture was extremely rational in spirit, though not yet rationalist. It consisted indeed of two diverse and actually contradictory elements. There was the Gallican Catholic culture which flowered in Bossuet and the great preachers, in Mabillon and the Benedictine scholars, and in the spiritual culture of the mystical and spiritual writers like St. Vincent de Paul. But on the other hand there was a strong movement of scientific rationalism deriving from the thought of the later Italian Renaissance—the work of such men as Gassendi and Campanella, above all of the outstanding genius who embodied this movement, René Descartes (1596–1650).

It was Descartes' aim to reorganize the world of thought on abstract mathematical principles. He was a revolutionary genius who made a clean sweep of the principles of authority and tradition, and built a new intellectual world on the basis of scientific and geometrical reason. Yet there was a profound affinity and even a spiritual identity between the rationalism of this most independent of thinkers (who spent his life in voluntary exile in Holland) and the spirit of the new classical

French culture. In spite of the opposition of all the vested interests in the Church and the universities, the Cartesian movement won the support not only of the scientific world but of all the leaders of French culture, including metaphysicians and theologians like Malebranche and Thomassin, as well as the teachers of Port Royal, like Lancelot and Nicole. So that the philosophy of the classical culture was Cartesianism based on methodic doubt and rigid mathematical reasoning, and valuing clarity above all things. Its literary ideal, as expressed by Boileau, was also a purely rational one. "Le Bon Sens" was his supreme principle, and he counsels the poet,

> Aimez donc la Raison et que tous vos écrits
> Empruntent d'elle seule et leur lustre et leur prix.

Boileau understood "bon sens" and the rule of reason in a strictly orthodox form, though his orthodoxy made room for the Gallicanism of Bossuet and the Jansenism of Arnauld.

But as soon as the death of Louis XIV replaced the rigid authoritarianism of the Grand Siècle by the liberty and license of the Regency, Reason became Rationalism and "le bon sens" the kind of "common sense" which regards mystery and miracle as absurd, and defines faith as belief in what is irrational. At this stage of the French Enlightenment, the most representative figure was Fontenelle, whose long life covers the century from 1657 to 1757. Fontenelle was a Cartesian with wide scientific interests and a gift of exposition which made him the inaugurator of the new science and philosophy of the Salon, which was henceforward to be characteristic of the French Enlightenment.

The powerful movement of scientific and philosophical ideas which influenced the course of English culture during the 17th century owed little to Descartes or his school. It was a parallel movement which had similar roots in the scientific culture of the later Renaissance, but differed widely from the French development, though to some extent it shared a common social and political background. In the culture of the

Enlightenment the two elements met. There was indeed more of Locke than of Descartes in the philosophy of Voltaire and the Encyclopaedists.

The acceptance of English empiricism and experimentalism, however, did nothing to change the spirit of Rationalism which had been impressed so strongly on French thought by Descartes and Fontenelle. Consequently the influence of Locke in France was very different from what it was in England.

The spirit of the English Locke was readily assimilated by English Protestantism and became a bridge between science and religion, but the French Locke was made the standard-bearer of a party far more revolutionary and destructive than were even the English Deists in England. The French philosophers were not merely anti-clerical, but openly anti-Christian.

Yet the movement was not purely negative. The Enlightenment had a positive ideal which finds its best expression in the great Encyclopaedia, above all in D'Alembert's *Discours Préliminaire* (1751). Nevertheless it was the negative and destructive genius of Voltaire that remained the dominant spirit of the movement. He was perhaps the most brilliant pamphleteer that has ever existed, and certainly the most long lived, for his literary productions never flagged for sixty years, and throughout the most of that time he ruled literary Europe with the scourge of his ridicule and the sword of his wit.

This destructive and negative aspect of the French Enlightenment contributed very materially to the French Revolution and the destruction of the Gallican Church. When the war against authority which the *philosophes* had carried on for fifty years was transferred from the sphere of culture and religion to that of politics, it was inevitable that it should carry with it the ideology which had inspired it in its pre-political phase. Indeed the relation between the two phases of the movement is to a very great extent one of cause and effect, since you cannot have a cultural and spiritual revolution without ultimately producing a political revolution also. By this I do not mean that the *philosophes* were political revolutionaries. On the contrary their political ideal was in general that of enlightened despotism, and the most representative figures like Voltaire and D'Alembert and Baron Grimm did their best to ingratiate themselves with the courts of Russia, Prussia and Austria.

But even if this alliance with the autocrats had been wider and more thorough than it was, it is highly doubtful if the revolutionary effects of the new ideas could have been permanently excluded from politics. "The destructive criticisms of the philosophers", as I have written elsewhere, "had undermined the order of Christian culture more completely than they realized, and it only needed the coming of a dynamic emotional impulse which appealed to the masses for the revolution to become a social and political reality. This element was supplied by Rousseau and his disciples, who found in the democratic ideology of the rights of man and the general will a new faith strong enough to transform the rationalist and aristocratic spirit of the Enlightenment into the passionate and democratic spirit of the Revolution. The theories of Rousseau had the same relation to the ideology of the Jacobin party as the theories of Karl Marx to the ideology of communism. Indeed there is a genetic relation between Rousseauist Jacobinism and Marxist Communism. For the history of the modern European revolutionary movement has been a continuous development, so that democracy, nationalism, socialism and communism are all of them successive or simultaneous aspects of the same process. Thus there is a socialist element in the thought of a typical nationalist like Fichte, a democratic element in Marx, and a nationalist element in Stalin."

Jean-Jacques Rousseau spent his life in close relation with the French Enlightenment, but in bitter hostility to its great leader, Voltaire. At first sight the forces were unevenly matched—on the one side, the friend of princes and the master mind of a brilliant intellectual society, on the other a lonely persecuted neurotic, who lived an underground existence in hiding from his real and imaginary enemies. And yet this outsider and natural Ishmaelite succeeded in gaining the enthusiastic support of the French intelligentsia, and unleashed the new emotional forces that found expression more than ten years after his death in the world-shaking upheaval of the French Revolution. Rousseau, in contrast to the Encyclopaedists, had a genuinely religious temperament, and the cult of nature and humanity, to which the Deists in England and France had offered their sincere but cerebral allegiance, acquired from him a religious fervor and an emotional conviction which proved contagious and irresistible.

For a generation—during the last third of the 18th century—the Religion of Nature became a real religion and no mere ideological fantasy, a faith in which men believed with their whole souls and for which they were prepared to die. In spite of the vagueness of its belief—its faith in progress, its hope in the coming of an age of social perfection and universal happiness, its optimistic faith in a providential order of nature, its belief in Democracy and the doctrine of political freedom, social equality and spiritual fraternity—it would be a mistake to underestimate its religious character, since it continued to be the dominant creed of a great part of Western civilization down to the beginning of the 20th century. Indeed the present spiritual crisis of our culture is due not so much to the loss of the traditional faith in Christianity, which had already occurred by the time of the French Revolution, as to the collapse of this new religion which has occurred in the present century, especially after the two world wars.

Thus in France and the countries under the direct influence of the Revolution, it is perhaps more accurate to speak of the de-Christianization of culture than of its secularization, while in England the course of development was the reverse.

However, as in all periods of religious revolt, more people were detached from the old religion than were converted to the new. A very large part of the population was left in a state of moral confusion, acquiescing in the destruction of the old order without giving any profound adhesion to the religious ideals of the new. The French Revolution created a bourgeois society and a secular culture, and yet the average French bourgeois remained a lukewarm Catholic, and his wife a pious and practising one. It was the intelligentsia and the urban working class which remained faithful to the revolutionary tradition. It was from these two classes that 19th-century socialism originated, and its earlier "utopian" forms were still inspired by the same ideals of the Religion of Nature and Humanity which had inspired the French Revolution.

The American Revolution owed a great deal to the influence of Locke and the culture of the English Enlightenment, and it made in turn an important contribution to the French Revolution. But it also possessed its own intrinsic importance and made its independent contribution to the culture of the modern world. The classical figure of the American Enlightenment is Benjamin Franklin, who stands in an analogous position to Locke in England and Voltaire in France, and in the following generation we have Thomas Paine, an American by adoption, who is equally important as a politician and a religious (or anti-religious) propagandist, and, a little later, Jefferson, who represents the culture of the American Enlightenment in its most mature form. All three men were Deists, and it is difficult to distinguish any clear theological differences between them, but they differed remarkably in personality and social attitude. This difference was in part due to the differences in the several colonial cultures, and in the case of Paine, to the fact that he was thirty-seven when he first came to America. Nevertheless, the American Revolution itself exerted a formative influence on American culture to a much greater degree than the English Revolution in England, or the French in France. This was partly owing to the fact that the established Church of Virginia and the other Southern colonies was almost destroyed, and there was for a time nothing to take its place, so that the organized forces of religion were weaker during the years that followed the Revolution than at any period in American History.[1]

But, apart from this, American culture had been already secularized by the influence of the frontiers where settlements had been made beyond the control of the Churches. The Quakers at least were aware of this, and took disciplinary measures against migration into regions beyond the reach of the regular meetings. In this matter there is a sharp contrast with the tradition of Spanish and French America, where the Church accompanied the pioneers from the beginning. The responsibility lay of course largely with the Church of England, which failed to create any American bishops. But New England was founded by men who wished to get away from bishops anyhow, and there the Revolution produced less secularization than elsewhere, since the Congregational Churches kept their hold on their people.

Yet in spite of the growing secularization of culture from above through the Enlightenment which primarily affected the intelligentsia, the European masses remained faithful to Christianity throughout the 18th century; and in England where the movement of secularization had begun first, and had been least affected by political repression, the 18th century actually saw a spontaneous religious revival on a very large scale. This revival had its center in the unprivileged classes, often the poorest and the most uneducated, such as the miners of Cornwall. It did not attempt to influence Church or State directly, and it was not until the end of the century that the related evangelical movement as represented by William Wilberforce and the so-called "Clapham Sect" began to have a direct influence on public life, first by its

[1] Cf. G. A. Koch, *Republican Religion: The American Revolution and the Cult of Reason* (New York: Holt, 1938), on this point.

propaganda against the slave trade and later on by an alliance with the humanitarians of the Enlightenment.

In particular Wesley and his well-organized followers powerfully affected the history of American culture. For it was largely through his influence and that of his ally Whitefield that the secularizing efforts of the Revolutionary epoch were overcome. No other non-American has ever had such a strong and lasting effect on America, and it is hardly an exaggeration to say that he was one of the Founding Fathers of the 19th-century American culture. This is all the more remarkable since he was himself a strong Tory and an outspoken opponent of the Revolution.

One of the most important effects of this religious revival was the rise of Protestant missions. Hitherto, Protestantism had been notably lacking in missionary enterprise. But in the 18th century the Moravians, the German pietist sect which had had a great influence on Wesley and the first stages of the Methodist movement, were the first to turn their attention in this direction in 1731. It was not until the close of the century, with the foundation of the Protestant missionary societies and Carey's mission to India, that the movement became widespread. Thenceforward throughout the 19th century it increased steadily, decade by decade, and had a considerable influence on world culture by its promotion of cultural contacts and the spread of Western Christian education in the East. The 19th century was in fact a great missionary age for Protestants and Catholics alike, and the secondary effects that these missions produced on culture deserve more study from secular historians than they have hitherto received.

In Catholic Europe the impact of the Enlightenment on the tradition of Christian culture was more destructive, though there also it was slow to affect the peasantry and the masses. As we have seen, the tendency to sectarian division that is the characteristic note of this period in Protestant Europe also affected the Catholics, at least in France and the Netherlands. But where the Baroque culture was strongest—

in the Mediterranean lands, in Central and Eastern Europe, and in Latin America—this was not so. There the unity of religion and culture was almost complete, and it is very doubtful if it would ever have been dissolved had it been left to itself. But the change in the balance of power in the second half of the 17th century produced far-reaching changes in the sphere of culture as well as that of politics which ultimately extended to religion as well.

For the age of Louis XIV was an age not only of French political predominance, but also of French cultural prestige. The new models of classical taste and style evolved at the French court and in the salons and academies outside the old Baroque patterns, and though Louis XIV prided himself on his orthodoxy, the spirit of French classical authors was deeply influenced by Gallicanism, Jansenism, and Cartesian rationalism. From the moment that this spirit triumphed, the retreat of the mystics (as Henri Bremond calls it) begins, and from the end of the 17th century classical culture led on without a break to the culture of the Enlightenment and the great rationalist attack on revealed religion.

Moreover, since Louis XIV had succeeded in obtaining the Hapsburg inheritance of the Spanish Empire for his grandson, Spain had passed into the Bourbon orbit and had ceased to exercise an independent leadership in Catholic culture. The result was a breach in the continuity of Spanish culture which led to the divorce of Spain from her old connections with Austria and Baroque Europe and incorporated her artificially and externally in the new international society of French culture with which she had no organic historical relation.

But in parts of Europe the Baroque culture lasted far into the 18th century, especially in the Hapsburg empire, which extended from the Turkish frontier to the Rhine at Freiburg im Breisgau. Here the reigns of Charles VI and Maria Teresa witness its last great achievements in architecture, sculpture and music, though not in literature and thought. When the Enlightenment did reach this part of Europe, it did so through the Enlightened Despotism of Joseph II and encountered considerable popular resistance.

In Latin Europe, on the other hand, the Enlightenment advanced more rapidly and was more overtly anti-Christian. Though the Bourbon monarchies were everywhere officially devoted to the defence of the Christian order, their defence was half-hearted and ill-directed and the enemies of religion had powerful friends at court, especially at the court of Louis XV in the time of Choiseul (1759–1770), when the Bourbon courts, after the expulsion of the Jesuits from their respective countries, took joint measures to force the Papacy to abolish the Order, which it finally did in 1773. This was the most disastrous blow ever inflicted on the Counter-Reformation culture. It weakened and disorganized Catholic higher education throughout Europe, wrecked the work of the missions in the East and in America, and destroyed the only force capable of meeting the anti-Christian propaganda of the Encyclopaedists.

INDEX

Index

Index